מכתב ברכה מאת מו"ר הרב חיים מינץ שליט"א

אדר הראשון תשע"ד

על החובב כל אחד מישראל, ספר זה נתון ממוסד עזרה קירוב רחוקים לאות של הכרת הטוב של ההשתתפות שלך עם מוסדנו, ללמד עם ישראל תורה ומצוות.

מוסד זה נתקן מתחלה כדי לתקן ההתבוללות והשפעת הרע על עמנו מגויי האמות.

ובודאי הדרך והתכלית לתקן מצב זה הוא לימוד התורה שמסר לבני זמנו.

וראינו בעינינו, ושמענו באזנינו, שלימוד זה הועיל לקרב הרבה, במדה גדושה, אחינו בני ישראל לתורה ומצוות.

ואתה זכית שנשתתף לבך לנדב כח וזמן לענין קדוש זה.

ובודאי בשביל זה, ה' יברך אותך בכל הברכות בגשמיות וברוחניות, באריכת ימים, בבריאות ונחת.

בחביבות והוקרה

חיים מינץ

ArtScroll® Series

Rabbi Nosson Scherman / Rabbi Gedaliah Zlotowitz
General Editors
Rabbi Meir Zlotowitz ז״ל, *Founder*

Published by

ARTSCROLL®

Mesorah Publications, ltd

Ask *the* Rabbi 2

Honest answers to candid questions

From live Q&A sessions with

RABBI CHAIM MINTZ

FIRST EDITION
First Impression ... March 2024

Published and Distributed by
MESORAH PUBLICATIONS, LTD.
313 Regina Avenue / Rahway, New Jersey 07065

Distributed in Europe by
LEHMANNS
Unit E, Viking Business Park
Rolling Mill Road
Jarow, Tyne & Wear, NE32 3DP
England

Distributed in Australia and New Zealand by
GOLDS WORLDS OF JUDAICA
3-13 William Street
Balaclava, Melbourne 3183
Victoria, Australia

Distributed in Israel by
SIFRIATI / A. GITLER — BOOKS
POB 2351
Bnei Brak 51122

Distributed in South Africa by
KOLLEL BOOKSHOP
Northfield Centre, 17 Northfield Avenue
Glenhazel 2192, Johannesburg, South Africa

ARTSCROLL® SERIES
ASK THE RABBI
VOLUME 2

Readers are invited to submit their own questions to asktherabbi@oorah.org. You can also search the video archive of previous sessions and join the interactive discussion every Tuesday night at 9pm EST at oorah.org/asktherabbi.

ITEM CODE: ASK2H
ISBN 10: 1-4226-4034-5 / ISBN 13: 978-1-4226-4034-0

Typography by CompuScribe at ArtScroll Studios, Ltd.

Printed in the United States of America
Bound by Sefercraft, Quality Bookbinders, Ltd., Rahway, N.J. 07065

Contents

Section 1

Connection to Hashem

Section 2

Understanding Suffering and Tragedy

Section 3

Religion

Section 4

Bechirah — Free Will

Section 5

Middos — Character Traits

Section 6

Greatness of Mankind

Section 7

Torah Study

Section 8

Prayer

Section 9

Mitzvos

Mitzvos Bein Adam LaMakom

Section 12

General Life

Daily Life

Dress and Looks

Life and Death

Animal Life

Section 13

Shabbos

Section 14

Yamim Tovim — Jewish Holidays

Pesach

Chol HaMoed

Sefiras HaOmer

Shavuos

Rosh Hashanah

Succos

Chanukah

Purim

Asarah B'Teves

Section 15

Jewish Heritage and History

Section 16

Kiruv Questions

Author's Introduction

With Hashem's help, I have the privilege of presenting to you the second volume of *Ask the Rabbi*. Since the release of the first volume some three years ago, the world has seen great change, and through it all, I have had the opportunity to continue to respond to questions at Oorah's "Ask the Rabbi" sessions. Many additional fundamental points in Torah *hashkafah* (worldview) have been raised and clarified, *b'siyata d'Shmaya*.

As mentioned in the introduction to the previous volume, these sessions began at Oorah events as an opportunity for those less learned or observant to pose their questions on Judaism. But it quickly became evident that this was really a forum to address queries from Jews of all backgrounds, at all levels of observance. Even those frum from birth and yeshivah-educated began acquiring a greater understanding of many concepts, customs, and mitzvos, and were excited to gain a fresh perspective on many topics and ideas. And as modern technology has progressed, these sessions have become accessible to an ever-increasing number and a wider demographic of Jews thirsty for increased understanding of the fundamentals of the Torah, and a community of devoted weekly adherents from across the globe has formed. Fielding questions from such an array of angles and perspectives has shed new light on concepts that were thought to be simple, and all of us have gained a fresh appreciation for so many aspects of Jewish life.

So why questions, you ask. Why not just a book of Torah-based concepts of Judaism, without the question and answer format? Well, questions have been an integral part of Jewish learning forever. Much of the Talmud is in question and answer format, and Torah has been studied throughout the ages by capitalizing on the give-and-take of questions and answers. When we hear or read a question, we feel challenged in a way that a straightforward presentation of information cannot achieve, leading us to a much deeper insight into the concept. Additionally, puzzling and engaging questions make an indelible imprint on the mind, helping us remember the answer in the future.

It is important to note that the ideas presented in this work are not intended to be *the only* response. There can be many answers to a single question, and the answers given can also inspire us to raise other approaches to the topic, as long as they are based on reliable, classic Torah sources. If you would like to share your own response to any of the questions, or would like to question or discuss my response, I would be happy to hear from you. You can do so by emailing: AskTheRabbi@oorah.org.

I wish to express my deep appreciation and praise to Hakadosh Baruch Hu for the kindness He has done for me, giving me the privilege and honor to devote my days to teaching His holy Torah, and the opportunity to clarify fundamentals of *emunah* and *hashkafah* to fellow Jews, His holy nation. This is the greatest mitzvah that a Jew can perform in this world.

It is my fervent hope that the ideas expressed in this book find favor in the eyes of Hashem, and bring to light some of the greatness, depth, and beauty of His Torah. I also hope that you find it educational and inspiring, and that it arouses increased excitement in serving Hashem, which will surely bring great *nachas ruach* to our Father in Heaven.

Many individuals had a hand in the preparation and publication of this *sefer*, and I am grateful to them all. I would especially like to express my feelings of appreciation and *hakaras hatov* to **Rabbi Shmuel Zitter, Rabbi Nechemia Levi,** and **Rabbi Chaim Asher Reichman of Oorah**, for all they have done in the writing of this book. A special thank you to my dear friend **Rabbi Pinchos Lipschutz** of the ***Yated Ne'eman*** for graciously publishing a weekly "Ask the Rabbi" column in his newspaper, which has served as a preview for much of the content of this book.

I also would like to thank **ArtScroll/Mesorah**, and especially my dear friend, **Rabbi Avrohom Biderman**, who has been actively involved in "Ask the Rabbi" and has served as our devoted moderator from its very beginning, as well as for his invaluable guidance as senior editor at ArtScroll/Mesorah.

It is my hope and prayer that they be blessed with all the special blessings of those who spread Torah in the world.

Chaim Mintz
Adar I 5784

Oorah's Introduction

Be'ezras Hashem, the first volume of ***Ask the Rabbi*** was very well received by Jews of all backgrounds. Readers on all levels of religious observance from across the globe gained newfound knowledge and appreciation for Torah and Jewish concepts, and were clamoring for more. With much gratitude to Hashem, we have been privileged to answer the call, presenting you with ***Ask the Rabbi* Volume 2.**

We'd like to share some background on how this series came to be: Every thinking person — those on their way to becoming religious, as well as someone frum from birth — has questions about Hashem, Torah, and mitzvos, as well as life in general. However, many people mistakenly assume that faith and questions cannot coexist, and that being Torah observant means never asking why, sweeping any questions they have under the rug.

HaRav Chaim Mintz, *shlit"a,* Mashgiach (spiritual mentor) of Yeshiva of Staten Island and the founder and spiritual leader of Oorah, has taught us that this is not the Torah-true approach. In fact, the Torah actually encourages questions, as our Rabbis tell us (*Avos* 2:6): "A shy person cannot learn." The shy person will be embarrassed to ask for clarification, and without asking, it is impossible to acquire clear knowledge and understanding. Indeed, the entire Talmud is composed of questions, answers, arguments, discussions, and multiple perspectives in all areas of Torah.

It was with this perspective that **"Ask the Rabbi"** was introduced at Oorah's weekly Torah Spot in Staten Island and at every Oorah Yom Tov event, Shabbazone, and "TheZone" summer program. "Ask the Rabbi" provides a forum for people to raise any issues they may be struggling with, explore concepts they have taken for granted, discuss any aspect of Judaism or Jewish practice they find confusing, or learn about any Jewish topic they are simply curious about. More than that, it places an emphasis on questions and encourages people to delve more deeply into Judaism, and this program indeed has become an exciting highlight of every Oorah event.

What should I tell an atheist on his deathbed? Can I attend a funeral in a church? Does the role of women in Judaism need an update? How do we part with our beloved pet? What's so special about fish? What's so bad about public school? These are some of the common questions and issues that were raised by people from the secular world exploring Torah life.

But once "Ask the Rabbi" launched, we discovered something surprising: even men and women from Torah-observant backgrounds found these discussions enlightening! They were hearing answers to questions they had been uncomfortable asking, or simply never thought about. Additionally, light was being shed on many concepts found in the Torah that appear outdated and unacceptable in today's modern, democratic society, such as monarchy and eradicating Amalek, which even many Torah-observant Jews have trouble understanding and appreciating.

For both newcomers to Torah observance and those from yeshivah backgrounds, "Ask the Rabbi" has become a tremendous tool for enhancing and building their belief in Hashem and gaining a deeper understanding of Torah and Judaism.

In addition, living as Jews in today's confusing world, we need clarity and guidance in how to act according to Torah values. Can I study Kabbalah? What should I do on my birthday or vacation? Can I pray from a smartphone? Is Pesach cleaning overdone? And the list goes on.

While many people are offering advice, how much of what they say is rooted in authentic Torah sources, and how much is apologetic to Torah values or, even worse, coming from sources antithetical to the Torah? To navigate our journey through these turbulent times, it is crucial to turn to our Torah leaders for guidance.

HaRav Chaim Mintz, *shlit"a,* merited sharing a close relationship with many Torah sages of the previous generation — including **HaRav Moshe Feinstein *zt"l,* HaRav Yaakov Yitzchak Ruderman**

zt"l, and **HaRav Dovid Kronglas *zt"l.*** He draws upon the guidance he received, as well as his own wellsprings of Torah wisdom, to offer us a Torah-true outlook on life.

With the diverse audience it attracts, every week's "Ask the Rabbi" session brings one unexpected question after another, eliciting insightful answers and fascinating discussions. And now, with the publishing of this second volume of *Ask the Rabbi*, readers everywhere can continue to experience the best of "Ask the Rabbi."

In this work, we share with you a sampling of the questions Rabbi Mintz fields on these various topics, from the most basic to the most esoteric. With his *daas Torah* (Torah-true outlook), common sense, decades of experience, and clarity, he responds with clear and concise answers, distilling the point to its essence and bringing deep concepts within reach. For the beginner, it's digestible. For a long-time observant Jew, it illuminates ideas and practices that they never properly understood, making them crystal clear.

This book can be used in many ways. It can be read as a book of *hashkafah* (worldview). Easy-to-read and in "bite-size" format, it is a great option for when a person has a few minutes to sit and relax. It can also be a helpful tool for initiating discussion at the Shabbos table. You can choose an appropriate question based on the audience, and go around the table, giving each person a chance to offer their perspective, thereby enhancing the Shabbos table with intriguing Torah discussion.

Of course, this book is not meant to take the place of a teacher or mentor. As mentioned numerous times in the book, HaRav Mintz strongly encourages every person to have a personal Torah mentor, who knows them and can guide them in their specific situation. In addition, we have tried to the best of our ability to present HaRav Mintz's outlook properly — **indeed, he reviewed the entire book and spent much time clarifying, adding, and making changes.** But if, for whatever reason, a mistake is found, it should be attributed to the writers.

We invite you to enjoy these fascinating questions and illuminating answers, and we hope that, just as many participants in our programs have improved their lives, your life will be enriched and changed for the better.

Of course, **you can submit your very own questions by emailing AskTheRabbi@oorah.org. You can also search the video archives of previous sessions on TorahAnytime.com and on our Ask the Rabbi channel, and we invite you to join the live interactive discussion every Tuesday night at 9 p.m. EST at oorah.org/asktherabbi.**

We express our deepest feelings of gratitude first and foremost to Hashem, for giving us the opportunity to present this book to the public. We would also like to thank the individuals who invested countless hours and tireless effort into this undertaking. **Rabbi Shmuel Zitter** sifted through many years of recordings to identify the most appropriate questions and answers, and present them in a clear, elegant, easy-to-read fashion. **Rabbi Nechemia Levi** had much input in clarifying and polishing the content.

We also express our heartfelt thanks to the members of ArtScroll/Mesorah's team of professionals, including senior editor **Rabbi Avrohom Biderman,** who edited the entire manuscript and offered us general guidance, **Reb Mendy Herzberg** who managed the editing and production process, **Reb Eli Kroen** for the gorgeous, eye-catching cover design, **Mrs. Esther Feierstein** for the meticulous proofreading, and **Miss Chanie Ziegler,** who designed and laid out the pages.

With tremendous gratitude to Hashem for giving us the *zechus* and opportunity to share with the reading public these timeless questions and answers from our esteemed Rebbi, and with our fervent hope and prayer that this book will help bring Jews of all backgrounds closer to Hashem and His Torah,

Chaim Asher Reichman   Yehoshua B. Weinstein
Oorah Inc.
Adar I 5784/March 2024

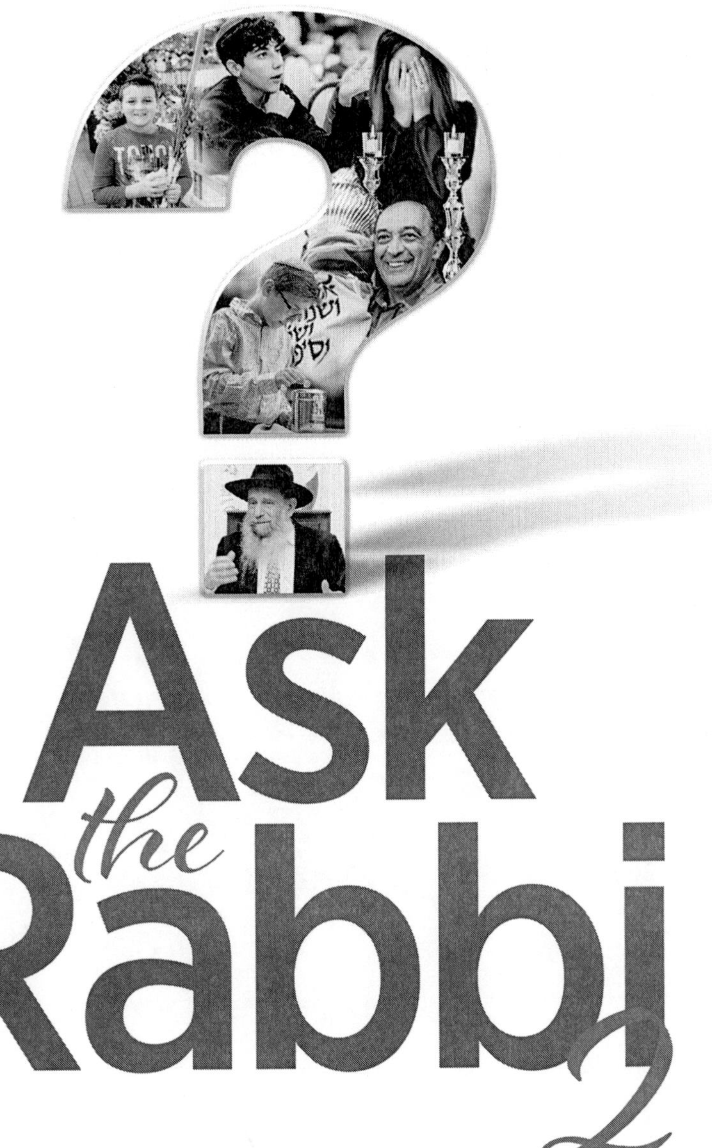

Ask the Rabbi 2

Section 1

Connection to Hashem

1

Purpose of Creation for Hashem's Honor?

Q ***The last Mishnah in Avos states that everything in the world was created for Hashem's honor. We also know that our entire purpose in this world is to serve Hashem. Isn't it selfish of G-d to create the world entirely for His own benefit?***

A This question is based on a fundamental misunderstanding. Hashem is the epitome of perfection and completely self-sufficient. He doesn't need anything from anyone, and He doesn't gain anything from our service and honor. Everything we do in this world to serve and honor Him is purely for our benefit.

As the *Mesillas Yesharim* writes at the very beginning of his classic work, Hashem created us so we can be close to Him. He is the Source of all enjoyment, and closeness to Him is the greatest pleasure attainable. The ultimate place to connect to Hashem and experience this pleasure is in the World to Come, but it is in this world that we can work to earn this great reward. By perfecting our character and performing mitzvos here, we become worthy of reaping the fruits of our labor and meriting eternal reward in the World to Come.

In his *sefer Derech Hashem*, Ramchal adds that the reason Hashem didn't just place us directly in the World to Come is because we would have felt the shame of someone receiving a handout. It is only through earning this closeness that we can experience the optimum pleasure of the World to Come.

Thus, when we honor and serve Hashem, it is we who gain. The more we recognize Him and draw close to Him, the more we can connect to Him for eternity.

This is the correct way to understand why we were created to serve Hashem, and why everything in this world was created to bring Him honor. The better we serve Hashem and the more we bring honor to His Name, the more we are able to recognize His greatness. This makes us worthy of enjoying the great pleasure that is in store for us.

So it's not for Him, but for us.

Furthermore, every mitzvah we perform infuses us with holiness. By taking the physical world and using it for Hashem's honor, we channel Hashem's light and holiness into the world, and connect with Him on a deeper level. For example, by using delicacies to enhance a Shabbos meal, we are infusing the material world with spirituality, bringing ourselves and all of creation even closer to Hashem.

In short: Serving Hashem and bringing Him honor is for our benefit. The more we recognize Him and are able to get close to Him, the more we connect to Him, and become worthy of enjoying the great pleasure that is in store for us in the World to Come.

2

How Do I Make G-d a Priority?

Q ***I find myself so busy juggling my many responsibilities, such as raising a family and making a living, that I don't seem to have a moment of free time. With so much going on, how can I remember to think about G-d?***

A If you would only realize how much G-d is part of your life, you would never be able to forget Him! The only reason you can function — breathe, hear, see, walk, talk, etc. — is because Hashem is giving you all these abilities on a "silver platter," every second of your life!

In *Pesukei D'Zimrah* each day, we recite the final chapter of *Tehillim*, which ends with the words, "*Kol ha'neshamah tehaleil Kah* — Every soul shall praise Hashem." The Midrash (*Bereishis Rabbah* 14:9) tells us that this can also be read as, "*kol ha'neshimah tehaleil Kah*," which means that with every breath one shall praise Hashem. In other words, with every breath we take, we should be grateful to Hashem for giving us the ability to breathe.

And the same is true for every aspect of our bodily functions. Hashem is giving us all these abilities on a "silver platter," every moment of our life. With every beat of our hearts, we should feel Him pumping blood through our bodies, and with every morsel of food that enters our mouths, we should feel like we are being "spoon-fed" by Him.

Of course, the same is true for every aspect of our lives: our homes, our families, our jobs, and all the other blessings we have. Since without Him we wouldn't be alive, Hashem is everything in our life, and we must feel indebted to Him at every moment. And just in case we might forget about how much Hashem does for us, we recite 100 blessings daily, reinforcing the fact that Hashem is our only source of sustenance.

But even greater than life in this world, Hashem has given us the greatest gift of all: the opportunity to come close to Him — through Torah and mitzvos — thereby achieving eternal bliss, both in this world and the next. Just thinking about this ultimate kindness should make us eternally grateful to Him.

So yes, we live in a world full of distractions that make us forget about our innate connection to Hashem. But by actively thinking about these ideas, you will start to feel His presence more and more.

In short: If you realize how much G-d does for you every second of your life, you will feel indebted to Him, and you will never be able to forget about Him.

3

Seeing Is Believing

Q ***Rabbi, you claim that G-d created the world, but I follow science and subscribe to the motto "seeing is believing." So do you really expect me just to accept your philosophy without any evidence?***

A You don't have to accept it without evidence, because evidence of a Creator is everywhere! All you need to do is open your eyes and look at the world around you — the trees, the grass, the sky, and even your own body — and you will see His "fingerprints" everywhere! Do you think these creations developed on their own? Imagine if someone would tell you that the book you are reading is just the product of some spilled ink. It wouldn't pass the laughing test! Certainly, a magnificent and complex world like ours couldn't have just developed on its own.

Just analyze a "simple flower," with its multitude of wondrous components, or a "little seed," which contains a tiny factory with all the tools and information needed to reproduce a towering tree, and you will be left speechless. And the complexity of every bird flying in the sky and every animal running around is awe-inspiring. All these wonders that surround us are the clearest proof of a masterful Creator.

Getting closer to home, let's take a look at our own bodies. As *Iyov* (19:26) declared: "From my flesh, I see G-d." Simply contemplate the wondrous and complex functions of the body's multiple systems — digestive, nervous, respiratory, and so many more — and how they work in tandem, complementing each other, and G-d is clearly evident.

In reality, the very same scientists that you mention see so much more than we do, and they should actually be the ones to recognize the Creator on a much deeper level. Studying a drop of blood for its DNA — which contains all the information about the functions of a human being — should render them much greater believers. A person just has to be willing to see things clearly, without any preconceived notions or agendas.

Truth be told, it is those who subscribe to absurd theories such as evolution and the like who are believing in things they don't see. They make claims about events that transpired "millions of years ago," based totally on speculation and hypothesis. On the other hand, any sane person who seeks the truth will agree that the existence of the Creator of our world is patently obvious.

In short: Since such a wonderful and complex world could not have just developed on its own, evidence of our Creator is quite obvious.

4

Bumper Stickers and Singing "I Love You, Hashem"

Q ***I have recently seen people "promoting" love of Hashem by singing "I love You, Hashem!" or displaying it on bumper stickers and sweatshirts. Are these good techniques for acquiring ahavas Hashem — love of Hashem?***

A Songs and emblems may help a person who is working on acquiring love of Hashem, but externalities alone are not really going to get you anywhere!

Achieving true *ahavas Hashem* — loving Hashem in our minds and feeling it in our hearts — is an art, something that needs to be developed with hard work and diligence, no different from any character trait. Although a full analysis of the steps needed to reach this lofty level is beyond the scope of these few lines, here are some of the main methods and pointers discussed in the classic *sefarim*:

Rambam writes that by studying the wonders of the world and the vastness of creation, a person will begin to recognize some of Hashem's greatness, arousing him to love Hashem and seek to come close to Him. Additionally, recognizing the insignificance of man in comparison to the infinite greatness of Hashem will fill a person with *yiras Shamayim*, awe of Hashem. Besides for *yiras Shamayim* being a mitzvah unto itself, true *ahavas Hashem* cannot be attained without it.

The *Mesillas Yesharim* discusses another method that can bring a person to love Hashem: reflecting on the abundance of blessing Hashem showers upon us. When a person recognizes that he is the recipient of Hashem's boundless kindness every moment of his life

— with every breath and every step he takes — his feelings of love toward Him will intensify.

In addition, love of Hashem is like a reflection. Since Hashem loves us more than a parent loves a child, the more a person feels His tremendous love, the more he will love Hashem. Indeed, in the very last words of the *berachah* recited before *Shema* — both in the morning and at night — we declare that Hashem loves the Jewish nation. This, in turn, arouses our feelings of love for Him, enabling us to then recite the words "*Ve'ahavta es Hashem* — You shall love Hashem," at the very beginning of *Shema*, with true feeling.

Songs and emblems alone, without internalizing these concepts, are not truly meaningful. Some may even argue that they minimize the seriousness of the wonderful mitzvah to love Hashem. This is similar to some everyday expressions, such as "*baruch Hashem* — blessed be G-d," or "*im yirtzeh Hashem* — if G-d wills," which people just throw around, without really thinking about what they are saying.

However, these practices may be better than nothing. Firstly, they can serve as a reminder to those who have worked on this *middah*. Additionally, they can help bring a person who thinks about the message to some superficial level of loving Hashem. But one should not falsely assume that this will suffice.

When the going gets rough, and when faced with real-life challenges, only someone who has worked to develop true love of Hashem will be able to rise above, and it is highly doubtful that these externalities alone will help very much.

In short: True love of Hashem takes work. Songs and emblems alone without internalizing their message are generally shallow.

5

Is Fear of G-d Healthy?

When the Torah was given, the event was accompanied by awesome fire and booming thunder, instilling fear in the hearts of the Jews. Additionally, fear of Hashem is a mitzvah mentioned in the Torah time and again.

But isn't it unhealthy to live with anxiety and fright? Wouldn't it be more appropriate for the mitzvah to be to "respect G-d"?

A Fear can be a positive and healthy feeling, and when used correctly, fear helps a person lead a productive life. It is only modern-day "thinkers" who have turned it into something negative and unhealthy.

While it is true that misused or misplaced fear is unhealthy, that is true for all character traits, every one of which can be used for good or for bad. For example, love is an important component in relationships, but also must be properly channeled.

The word *yirah* has two meanings: fear and awe, and the mitzvah of *yiras Hashem* involves both of these dimensions. One component of the mitzvah is *yiras ha'onesh* — fear of punishment. Of course, the reason one should never sin is simply because Hashem forbade it, but it is often the fear of punishment that keeps a person from sinning.

In general, fear keeps people in line. Without law and order, chaos reigns, as the Mishnah in *Avos* (3:2) observes, "If not for fear [of the government], one man would swallow the other alive." This unfortunate reality has been proven throughout history — when governments are being overthrown, there is chaos and disorder, and all types of immoral and criminal behaviors are rampant. Indeed, in today's society, although the dangers of reckless driving are obvious, many people refrain from speeding only out of fear of being ticketed.

It is also important to remember that Hashem's punishments are for our benefit, not because He is taking revenge. When a loving parent warns the child, "If you run into the street, you will get a slap," the stern warning helps keep the child from doing something dangerous — and if the child does run into the street, suffering the consequences serves as a reminder not to do it again. Similarly, Hashem — our loving Father — punishes us out of love, to help us stay on track.

The second aspect of the mitzvah is *yiras haromemus* — awe of Hashem. When one feels Hashem's presence, he will stand in awe before Him, but at the same time he is also thrilled to be close to our great Creator, Master of the entire universe. This is similar to someone given the opportunity to spend time with a great Torah leader; although he will have awe and respect, these are not negative emotions. On the contrary, he will be exhilarated at the opportunity to be in close proximity to greatness, and will try to hold onto this singular experience for as long as possible.

Indeed, King David proclaimed (*Tehillim* 16:8): "*Shivisi Hashem lenegdi samid* — I place Hashem before me at all times." Similarly, Rambam (in *Moreh Nevuchim*) highlights that the greatness of our forefathers — Avraham, Yitzchak, and Yaakov — was that they lived every moment thinking about Hashem. These great people were by no means full of anxiety; on the contrary, they were exhilarated to be close to Him at all times. It is this wonderful feeling that will inspire a person to feel close to Hashem 24/7, emulating Him and His remarkable ways.

In short: There are two parts to yiras Hashem: fear and awe. Fear of punishment keeps a person from sinning. Standing in awe before Hashem is feeling His presence, an exciting feeling, and not a negative one.

6

Is Bitachon a Guarantee?

Q ***I have heard that having bitachon, trust in Hashem is a great mitzvah, and if a person has bitachon, he will definitely get whatever he wants. How does this work, and is it really a guarantee?***

A The topic of *bitachon* is discussed at great length by many wonderful *sefarim*. According to *Chovos HaLevavos*, *bitachon* means relying on Hashem to provide whatever we need, but at the same time understanding that whatever He does is for our best. There are many levels of *bitachon*, and the more one relies on Hashem, the more deserving he becomes, and the more Hashem will feel "obligated" to supply him with his needs.

My rebbi, Rav Dovid Kronglas, compared this to a person who fell on hard times and turned to his well-to-do friend, crying bitterly. "You are the only one who can help me," he tells his friend, "and if you won't help me, all is lost!" If the friend sees that this is truly the case, he will certainly feel obligated to help. However, if he knows that the petitioner has others to turn to for help, he will not feel as compelled to help him out.

Similarly, if one turns to Hashem for help with the clear recognition that He is the only true source of his salvation, He will definitely want to help. On the other hand, if one asks Hashem for help as one of the many avenues he has available, Hashem will not feel the "need" to grant the request. In fact, the *Chovos HaLevavos* adds that if someone puts his trust in other things — his skills, his job, his rich uncle, etc. — Hashem will respond in kind, leaving him — to some extent — "in their hands."

True *bitachon* also results in a true and deep inner tranquility brought about by complete trust in Hashem. A person with true *bita-*

chon is relaxed and serene no matter the circumstances, secure in the knowledge that he is in "Good Hands."

Unfortunately, there are people who convince themselves that they have true *bitachon*, and they may even preach about the greatness of having *bitachon*, but they do not truly rely on Hashem. Some may be relying on their financial resources or some assurance that everything will go well. Others who claim to have *bitachon* in Hashem say so simply because they have no other means of helping themselves. Having never internalized these profound feelings of total reliance on Hashem, when they lose their resources or face a difficult challenge, they may panic and even question the ways of Hashem.

But even when a person places his full trust in Hashem, only Hashem is in charge, and there is no guarantee that his requests will be granted. There can be many reasons for this. Hashem may know that this is not for the person's good, or one may be deemed unworthy due to his sins. Even after Hashem Himself promised our forefather Yaakov that He would take care of him, Yaakov was afraid that his sins might cause him to become unworthy of being protected from Eisav.

But one who has *bitachon* also doesn't get flustered when things don't turn out the way he had hoped they would. On the contrary, even if because of his limited perception he cannot see how it is for his good, he will rest assured that whatever Hashem did is for his best.

In short: The stronger one's trust in Hashem, the more Hashem will feel "obligated" to provide for his needs. But only He is in charge, and there is never a guarantee that one will get what he wants.

7

Maintaining Spiritual Momentum in the Workplace

Q ***When I was in yeshivah, I felt like I was really growing in Torah and my service of Hashem. Now that I am married and busy with my family and making a living, I don't have much time to study and daven, and I feel like I'm losing my connection to Hashem. Is there anything I can do to keep up the momentum from my yeshivah years?***

A First of all, no matter what a person does for a living, he must have a set time for serious Torah study, and maintain it at all costs. One of the first questions posed to a person in the Next World is, "*Kavata itim laTorah* — Did you set aside fixed times for Torah study?" Torah is the very life and essence of a Jew, and besides making a living, you must find time to *actually live.*

Additionally, Torah keeps a person connected to Hashem, thereby enabling him to transcend the materialistic world and corrupt society we live in. Ideally, you should study first thing in the morning, starting off your day with a strong dose of spirituality. But if that doesn't work, find a time that works for your situation, such as during a lunch break or in the evening.

You should also be sure to give your prayers the proper focus they deserve. Coming on time — or even early — to davening will give you time to make the most of this sacred opportunity, reinforcing the fact that Hashem is the True Source of our sustenance. Prayer is essential for everyone, all the more so as life becomes hectic and more complicated. Our prayers keep us constantly connected to Hashem, and help us rise above the immoral world and its relentless pressures, which pull us away from Hashem.

It is also crucial to have a rebbi who can guide you and help you grow. With today's technology, it has become easier than ever to keep in touch with a rebbi, even when living in a different country from him. Perhaps you can even set up a time to learn together and discuss how you can continue serving Hashem to the best of your abilities. If possible, it is worthwhile to meet in person from time to time, keeping your relationship personal, and helping you grow even more.

It is also important to realize that this new stage of life can also help you grow spiritually. When a person is forced to leave the yeshivah environment and is confronted with challenges and distractions he has never before faced, it becomes necessary for him to find within himself the ability to rise to the occasion. Indeed, when Hashem finished creating the world, He saw that it was "*tov me'od* — very good," which the Midrash says is a reference to the evil inclination. This is because a person is able to realize his full potential and become great only by overcoming the challenges that come his way.

In short: You must have a set time for Torah study, daven properly, and also have a rebbi to guide you. This will help you overcome the adversity and hurdles that come your way, and thereby realize your full potential.

8

Changing My Religious Path

Q ***Rabbi, you've discussed many times the importance of being faithful to tradition. Does that also apply to choosing a path in serving Hashem? For example, if someone grew up in a yeshivah environment, with its focus on intense Torah study and intellectual study of mussar (ethics), but now feels that the passion and fire of Chassidus works better for him, or vice versa. Or someone whose rabbis had trained him in the tradition of Novardok mussar, with its focus on self-negation — but feels that he would serve Hashem better by adopting the Slabodka approach, with its focus on every person's innate greatness. Is it appropriate for him to switch?***

A While one's customs and traditions must be steadfastly adhered to, choosing the correct approach to serve Hashem is different. A path in serving Hashem is not considered a custom, and there are many acceptable paths that were designed and practiced by some of the greatest Torah personalities throughout the generations.

As long as a specific path is within the parameters of accepted Torah law and thought, a person can and should choose the approach that works for him, the one that will help him come closest to Hashem and serve Him as best as he can.

However, the correct path for each person varies based on each individual situation, and there is no one-size-fits-all answer to your question.

But it is vital to keep in mind that although there are definitely people who would gain from a change of pace, that is not always the correct decision. Sometimes, what appears to be a loftier way of serving Hashem is not really so. Other times, the true — perhaps even subconscious — reason that one is enthralled by that method of serving Hashem is because that way of life seems more pleasant or less demanding. Such motives are obviously not valid reasons to embrace that approach in serving Hashem. And there is frequently a combination of motivations — some good and some bad — behind a person's newfound interest, making it extremely difficult to assess his true motive.

Because of all these factors, it is almost impossible for a person to be objective and properly assess whether he is choosing a new path for the sake of serving Hashem better or for ulterior motives. Therefore, it is imperative that he discuss the pros and cons with a mentor or someone else who is familiar with his situation and personality — someone who can objectively help him make the right decision.

But once a person is certain that this other Torah-true path is indeed one that is better for him, he should definitely adopt the approach that will help him reach greater heights in his service of Hashem.

In short: If it is clear that a person will be able to serve Hashem better with a different valid approach, one can and should take that approach, but it would be strongly advisable to first discuss this with a qualified Torah scholar.

9

What Should I Tell an Atheist on His Deathbed?

Q ***I have a relative who is a non-believer and is now on his deathbed. I would like to visit and talk to him about G-d, but since he has always been antagonistic to religion, is there any point?***

A Yes! The best thing you can do for this unfortunate soul is give him a chance to accomplish something eternal with his life, and save it from having been a totally wasted opportunity.

Discuss having faith in Hashem and how He orchestrates everything in this world for our good. You might also remark, "Listen, your grandfathers all the way back to Sinai believed in G-d, were they all crazy?" Even if he claims to be an avowed non-believer who doesn't want to hear about this "old-fashioned stuff," deep down — as he sees his end approaching — he may appreciate what you're telling him. As the saying goes, "There's no atheist in a foxhole."

Even a moment of realizing the truth and repenting in this world turns a spiritually empty life — a waste for the soul — into one of accomplishment. You can explain that it is never too late to change, and nothing stands in the way of *teshuvah* (repentance) and sincere remorse. As the Talmud (*Kiddushin* 40b) says, "Even if one was wicked his entire life but repents sincerely at the last moment, he will not be punished for his sins!"

You may never know if you had any impact, because even if he appears to have disregarded your words, he may actually take your words to heart and start to believe. And even if he does not fully accept what you are telling him, he may at least consider the possibility of the truth. The mere fact that thoughts of Hashem's existence pass through his mind before he leaves the world will be a great merit for his soul.

We see the importance of having such a thought when the Torah tells us about the destruction of the wicked people of Sodom. The Torah mentions that the city's destruction took place as the sun was beginning to rise. Rashi explains the importance of this timing: Some of the Sodomites worshiped the sun while others worshiped the moon. Had the destruction taken place while it was either day or night, these idolaters may have believed that had this occurred at the time their own god was shining, he would have certainly come to their rescue.

Hashem therefore chose precisely the time of day when both the sun and the moon are visible in the sky, so that the Sodomites would recognize that their gods were completely powerless, and Hashem is the only power.

Although these people had always worshiped idols, Hashem orchestrated the events in this way to give them a chance to end their lives recognizing and acknowledging Him. Surely, then, helping this person attain a moment of belief in Hashem is priceless.

In short: You should talk to him about Hashem, as it is never too late to do teshuvah, and your words may have some influence. Even a moment of repentance in this world changes a spiritually empty life into a life of accomplishment.

Section 2

Understanding Suffering and Tragedy

10

Physical Suffering Cleansing the Soul

Q ***I have been suffering a lot, and I was told that suffering is necessary to attain full atonement for certain sins. But how does physical suffering cleanse the spiritual soul? Additionally, I don't think I've been such a bad person, so why am I suffering so terribly? Is it because my soul was wicked in a previous lifetime, or is there some other way to understand my distress?***

A Sin taints the soul, and the greater the sin, the deeper the blemish and the more purification needed. While *teshuvah* (repentance) and Yom Kippur have the power to wipe away most spiritual impurities, there are certain grave sins that require an even stronger purification process. To be purified from these sins, the sinner must uproot the very cause of his misdeeds. This is where suffering comes in.

A person is comprised of a body and a soul. The body craves physical pleasures, such as tasty food, vacations, and fun, while the soul seeks spiritual bliss and closeness to Hashem, so there is an ongoing conflict between the two. A person generally follows his bodily desires, which pull him toward an animalistic and materialistic lifestyle. The pursuit of physical desires and worldly pleasures is the root of all sin, and lures a person away from Hashem and His mitzvos.

A person undergoing suffering is preoccupied with his pain and has less interest in good food, designer clothes, or fancy cars. By disconnecting from physical desires, he becomes a more spiritual being, thus uprooting the root cause of sin. Since the body and soul are connected, when the body is uplifted, the soul is also elevated and strengthens its connection with Hashem, thereby achieving atonement for sin.

As far as why you deserve all this suffering, there can be many reasons. Firstly, it is possible for a person to commit severe sins without even realizing it. For example, the *Mishnah Berurah* writes in his preface to the laws of Shabbos that one who is not well-versed in the laws of Shabbos will inevitably desecrate Shabbos. Similarly, a casual remark that inadvertently embarrasses someone is considered to be akin to murder.

Furthermore, the greater the person, the more Hashem expects of him, so a righteous person is held accountable for actions that may not be considered sins for an average person.

It is also true that Hashem sends souls back to this world, and at times suffering is an atonement for sins committed in a previous lifetime.

However, there are reasons aside from atoning for sins that Hashem, in His infinite wisdom, causes a righteous person to suffer. Sometimes it spares others, who are not so righteous, from punishment until they repent. The righteous person is then richly rewarded for facilitating their repentance. At other times, Hashem makes a pious person suffer to further negate his physicality and elevate him to an even higher level of spirituality. So instead of your suffering indicating that you have sinned, it may actually be a sign of your piety, a gift from Hashem to help you become even greater.

In short: Suffering enables a person to become more spiritual. A person can transgress severe sins without realizing it, and the suffering helps purify him. Suffering can also serve as an atonement for others, earning the sufferer great spiritual reward, or as an opportunity to become greater.

11

Why Did Pious People Suffer in the Holocaust?

Rabbi, you often say that the Holocaust was foretold in the Torah, as it states clearly that if we don't keep the Torah properly we will be punished severely. But so many pious Jews also suffered in the Holocaust. Why did they deserve all that terrible pain and suffering?

A Why the righteous suffer is an age-old question. Even Moshe Rabbeinu asked this question to Hashem, and much has been written on this topic, but we will try to touch on some of the basic points:

Ramchal (in *Derech Hashem*) explains that because the souls of all the Jewish people are connected to each other, the suffering of the righteous can atone for their entire generation, saving them from suffering in this world and the next. At the time of the Holocaust, Hashem was obviously very, very displeased with us, and these great people may have suffered in place of many others, calming Hashem's anger, and giving those others a chance to improve themselves.

Ramchal adds that because the suffering of the righteous helps the entire nation, their souls reach much greater heights, both in this world and the next. Undoubtedly, many of the miracles people experienced during the Holocaust were in the merit of these pious people, and if not for them, it is quite possible that the Germans would have inflicted much more harm. This makes those who perished true heroes of the Holocaust, and for this, their souls are eternally elevated and rewarded.

Ramchal also writes that when people give up their lives to sanctify

Hashem's Name, the world merits great blessing. Thus, these people served as catalysts for the exponential growth of yeshivos and Torah communities throughout the world in the aftermath of the Holocaust, and their souls are certainly being rewarded immensely for this.

Another element to consider is that the Talmud teaches that even though a righteous person has not himself sinned, he may be punished because he did not rebuke the people of his generation.

When discussing the suffering of the righteous, it is also important to mention the fundamental concept of reincarnation (*gilgulim*), discussed at great length by the kabbalists. Many people are not here on this world for the first time, but have been sent back to complete unfinished work from a previous lifetime.

For example, the Sages tell us that when the Jewish slaves in Egypt could not fill their quota of bricks, the Egyptians placed Jewish infants in the walls to replace the "missing" bricks. The Arizal revealed that those babies were actually reincarnations of the souls of those who had perished in the *Mabul* (the Great Flood), in the days of Noach. Their momentary suffering on this world was what these souls needed to be fully purified and allowed entry into the World to Come.

Similarly, the pious people who perished in the Holocaust may have actually been reincarnated souls in need of achieving perfection, and this enabled them to reach the highest levels of the World to Come.

It is also important to bear in mind that any suffering in this world, as terrible as it may seem, is really only like the blink of an eye when compared to eternal reward. Suffering purifies and sanctifies the soul, so when these people enter the World to Come and look back at their suffering, as difficult as it was, they realize that it was all worthwhile in order to achieve eternal bliss.

In short: The suffering of a pious person can atone for others. It is also possible for a righteous person to suffer for not rebuking the people of his generation sufficiently. Their suffering can also be to perfect their souls from a previous lifetime.

12

I Repented but Had a Terrible Year!

Q ***Rabbi, I have been told that if I repent and pray with all my heart on Rosh Hashanah, I will have a good year. Is that really true?! I did that last Rosh Hashanah and still had a terrible year. And that's what happened to many righteous people who suffered terribly or passed away since last Rosh Hashanah!***

A What you were told is certainly true! Our Rabbis (*Rosh Hashanah* 16b) tell us clearly that Hashem judges every single person on Rosh Hashanah, and the righteous are written and sealed for a good year, while the wicked are decreed to die or suffer. Despite this, as you mentioned, we often witness the exact opposite — the wicked prospering and the righteous suffering — and this causes doubt and confusion. This paradox is dealt with at length by the great commentaries.

Your question also touches on the age-old question of "*tzaddik verah lo*, why bad things happen to good people," a question that was already posed to Hashem by Moshe Rabbeinu.

Although a full understanding of Hashem's ways is well beyond human comprehension, we know that He is just and perfect, and all that happens is part of His master plan. Nevertheless, we can discuss several of the reasons that even someone who was deemed righteous on Rosh Hashanah may still die or suffer during the year that follows.

Firstly, every person is allotted a certain amount of time on this world, and even the righteous don't live forever. The righteous people who passed away may have been taken from this world simply because their time had come.

Additionally, material success such as good health and wealth is not the true barometer of a good or bad year. Good or bad is measured by what really counts — spiritual success and failure. Similar to a painful procedure that saves a person's life, suffering prescribed by the Great Doctor to help someone become a better person is good. Therefore, someone who endured physical hardships that brought him closer to Hashem had a good year.

Furthermore, suffering of the righteous also atones for the generation or completes unfinished work from a previous lifetime (as discussed in "Why Did Pious People Suffer in the Holocaust?").

Another perspective is that a good or bad life is not referring to life in this fleeting world, but to life in the Next World, which is permanent and eternal. Your sincere repentance and prayer were certainly successful in that sense, because they helped you merit a good life in the World to Come. Similarly, any suffering you endured purified your soul, enabling you to receive a better life in the World to Come. So in many ways, you did, indeed, merit a good year.

We must also bear in mind that our vision in this world is limited, preventing us from comprehending Hashem's ways. However, in the World to Come the curtains will part, revealing what was happening behind the scenes, and we will understand in hindsight how everything was for our good.

The Chofetz Chaim compared this to a guest who entered a shul one Shabbos, and expressed his surprise at the seemingly haphazard way people were called to the Torah. The people explained to him that his confusion was only because he was visiting for a single Shabbos. If he would come each week, he would see the entire picture and realize how everything was calculated precisely. Similarly, only Hashem, with His all-encompassing vision of past, present, and future, can design each situation for the precise needs and ultimate good of every person's soul.

In short: There are many ways to understand this: Even the righteous die when their time comes; enduring suffering further purifies a person's soul; "good" and "bad" are measured by spiritual success and failure or by life in the Next World, which is permanent and everlasting. Additionally, many things that seem bad are really for our good.

13

Staying Strong in Face of Challenges

Q ***I sometimes find myself overwhelmed with challenges in my life, and I begin to wonder why Hashem would do this to me. How do I strengthen my belief in Hashem when I'm faced with these challenges?***

A Challenges can certainly feel overwhelming, and we all go through them at some point in our lives. But if you look deeper, you will realize that not only should these situations not cause your *emunah* (belief in Hashem) to become shaky, they should actually strengthen it. Challenges are not intended to be obstacles preventing us from serving Hashem; they are actually tests placed along the way by Hashem Himself in order to stimulate our growth through our efforts to overcome them.

This is an integral part of our mission in this world, and a foundation of Judaism.

Rav Moshe Chaim Luzzatto explains this in the very first chapter of *Mesillas Yesharim*, his classic work on Jewish thought and self-development. Hashem created This World to give us the opportunity to serve Him and overcome challenges, thereby receiving our just reward in the World to Come. If serving Him would not require any effort, our reward would be unearned and of little value to us. Overcoming challenges is what earns us true reward, and thus, the greater the challenges, the greater the reward in the Next World.

This is, in fact, exactly why Hashem created us with a *yetzer hara* (evil inclination). When Hashem finished creating the world, the *pasuk* (*Bereishis* 1:31) tells us that He took inventory of all that had been created, and declared, "*Vehinei tov me'od* — Behold, it was very good." The Midrash comments that "good" refers to the *yetzer tov* (good inclination), but "***very*** good" refers to the *yetzer hara*.

How could the evil inclination, whose job is to entice people to sin, be considered "very good"?

But in truth, it is the *yetzer hara* that actually helps us become great. Without an evil inclination luring us to sin, man would naturally follow Hashem's will at all times. Without overcoming challenges, he would leave the world on the same spiritual level that he entered it, without any growth at all, and he would be just "good." It is because we have a *yetzer hara*, and are constantly faced with challenges to overcome, that we are able to grow and become "very good." This is what brings us close to Hashem and makes us truly deserving of our reward in the World to Come.

This is similar to a bright child placed in a class with weaker children. Not challenged to work hard, he will not use his intellect to its fullest. However, if this same child is placed together with other smart children, he will be challenged and motivated to use his intellect so much more. Similarly, challenges and adversity are for our benefit, as they are the catalysts for us to grow and achieve greatness.

Furthermore, it may be specifically because you are serving Hashem well that He is "raising the bar," and giving you greater challenges! As our Rabbis (*Succah* 52a) tell us, the greater the person, the greater his *yetzer hara*. Indeed, many of our great rabbis and sages were faced with challenges. In fact, *Orchos Tzaddikim* tells us that if we want to know what Hashem is thinking about us, we should check if we are facing challenges. If we are, then we know that we're doing well, but if we aren't, it's not such a good sign.

So when you are faced with challenges, don't lose faith. On the contrary, you should become a greater believer, by realizing that these are Heaven-sent gifts to help you become "very good," and reach great heights.

In short: Hashem sends us challenges to help us strengthen ourselves and become great, thereby deserving greater reward in the Next World.

14

Plagued by Trouble After Becoming a Baal Teshuvah

Q ***As I make great strides in Torah observance, I keep encountering more difficulties, such as family problems, financial loss, or health issues. My non-religious relatives poke fun at me that after sacrificing so much for the will of Hashem, I am suffering so much! Why is this happening?***

A You are a great hero and are certainly very beloved in the eyes of Hashem. Not only should you not be discouraged, this is a sign that what you are doing is very special, as illustrated by the following episode:

An American man had been successful in business, and as he got older, he decided to devote his time to his spiritual growth. With enough money to live comfortably for many years, he moved to the Land of Israel and began to study Torah all day.

Unfortunately, as he was trying to settle down and focus on his studies, things started going downhill. First, his investments began to sour, making it increasingly difficult for him to support himself. Then he was involved in a car accident, where — due to no fault of his own — his car ran over someone who was killed.

The man was devastated, and could not help but wonder if Hashem was sending him a message that, for some reason, He was unhappy with his decision.

Uncertain of how to proceed, he went to a great rabbi for guidance. The rabbi reassured him that Hashem was indeed happy with his noble decision, and he had no reason to be discouraged.

He then offered an enlightening perspective: All of this adversity is nothing but the work of Satan, and the very fact that Satan finds it necessary to do all this proves just how extraordinary your efforts are. Satan's mission in this world is to get people to sin, and Hashem invests him with great powers to accomplish this. Because your exceptional self-sacrifice for the sake of Hashem is so precious, Satan is using his great power to try to make you rethink your decision. The person who was killed was destined to die at that time, and Satan brought about his death through you to try to discourage you.

He pointed to the death of Sarah as proof. Avraham had just reached the pinnacle of his accomplishments, having passed the test of Akeidas Yitzchak, demonstrating his willingness to sacrifice everything — even his beloved son — for the sake of Hashem. Satan had tried unsuccessfully to stop Avraham on the way, but when those efforts failed, Satan didn't let up; he continued to look for a way to get Avraham to fail. He came to Sarah and shocked her by telling her what had just transpired, and overcome with grief or surprise, she died on the spot.

Satan was hoping that Avraham would feel bad that he had caused this terrible tragedy, and some small tinge of regret would creep into his heart, causing him to lose some of the extraordinary greatness he had achieved. However, Avraham rose to the challenge and saw right through Satan's ruse. He remained steadfast in his belief that following the command of Hashem could not have been the cause of tragedy. Surely, the time for Sarah to leave this world had come, and her death was not a result of his actions.

This applies to you as well. The adversity you are experiencing is a test, and the very fact that Satan is placing so many obstacles in your way is a sign that your growth is remarkable, and should inspire you to reach even greater heights.

Another reason you may be having these challenges is that Hashem may be cleansing your soul of any residue left from your earlier sins, purifying you and raising you to loftier levels of spirituality.

In short: Your troubles are the work of Satan, who cannot bear to see you performing such noble deeds, or to cleanse your soul.

15

Terror on Simchas Torah

Q ***Why did Hashem bring such horrors to our nation on Simchas Torah 5784 (October 7, 2023), one of the happiest days of the year, and the culmination of so many days of prayer and repentance, when we have reached such lofty spiritual heights? And is there anything we can do now?***

A Although we don't have prophets and no one can claim to know the exact message Hashem is sending, one thing is clear — He is sending us a very strong wake-up call.

The Jewish people have not suffered a tragedy of such proportion since the Holocaust, and each and every one of us must do something to improve.

At the same time, we must realize that harsh judgment is not meant to hurt us; rather, it is a gift from Hashem, to help us become better and earn much greater reward in the World to Come. Like a parent or teacher who demands more of a child with great potential, Hashem rebukes His special nation because He expects great things from us, and wants us to reach perfection.

The first thing we must realize is that we are all one nation, and what happens to a Jew in one part of the world is happening to all of us. And just as we are all feeling the pain of our brethren in Israel, we must understand that one Jew's good deeds can also elevate the entire nation. So no one can say I live far away and can't do anything to help. The day will come when Hashem will ask every one of us what we did to help our brethren in their time of distress.

So you ask what can we do? We must look at what our forefathers did in times of distress, which was to pray with all their might. Yes, we spent the last two months davening and doing *teshuvah*, but it is quite obvious that Hashem is telling us that we didn't do enough. Hashem is extending Yom Kippur, begging us to do more. We must look back and take a close look at the quality of our deeds and prayers.

Did we truly change and start living higher, or did we already slip back into our old ways?

Were our prayers really heartfelt and sincere, or were they mere lip service? Even if we davened with proper concentration, did we have others in mind, or did we just think about our own needs?

We are certainly davening now with more fervor and concentration and having our Jewish brethren in mind, so let's use this as a springboard for improvement in this area from now on.

Additionally, if we want our prayers to work, we must be extremely careful not to contaminate our mouths. The Chofetz Chaim writes that if a person engages in gossip or other forbidden speech, his prayers become tainted and lose much of their potency.

Every one of us must also add to his Torah study, because that will provide our nation with the greatest form of protection. When Yaakov was running away from Eisav, he spent fourteen years immersed in diligent Torah study. Torah study is our strongest connection to Hashem, and it brings His Presence down to this world, thereby protecting us from our enemies.

The fact that this tragedy happened on Simchas Torah may signify that G-d is sending us a message that we are lacking in "*simchah*," the joy that we are supposed to have for the great gift Hashem gave us — the Torah, and the privilege we have to study and delve into it.

We can also do more acts of kindness and give more charity, which has the power to save lives. We can raise the spiritual level of our Shabbos tables by sharing more words of Torah and singing *zemiros*.

Let us try to recite our blessings with more concentration, thanking Hashem properly for all that He has given us.

These are just some of the things we can work on, and each person knows what he or she can do to improve and become closer to Hashem, protecting and saving us from our enemies.

In short: Hashem is begging us to become better. One Jew's good deeds can elevate the entire nation and help the situation. We must daven with more concentration

and constantly pray for the entire Jewish nation, and also be careful with our speech. Every good deed helps, but studying more Torah is the strongest protection from our enemies.

Section 3

Religion

16

Attitude Toward Non-religious Jews

Q ***What should be my outlook on non-religious Jews? Do they have the same status as those who are religious?***

A It is important to understand that non-religious Jews are Jews like any other Jews. Anyone whose mother is Jewish is Jewish, regardless of his affiliation and level of religious observance.

Additionally, it is worth noting that most Jews who, unfortunately, do not observe mitzvos were never properly exposed to authentic Torah and Judaism. Such Jews have the status of *tinok shenishbah* — "a kidnapped child" who spent his childhood among non-Jews — and they are not held responsible for their religious failings. Many of those who affiliate themselves with non-Orthodox movements — Conservative, Reform, or others — generally fall under this category. At best, most of them think that there are many acceptable types of Judaism, and one has the option to choose the one he wants. Little do they know that if it's not Orthodox it's not Judaism! It is the knowledgeable leaders of these movements, who attempt to falsify authentic Judaism, with whom we take issue.

For example, a basic tenet of Judaism is that the Torah was given to us by G-d on Mount Sinai, and it will never change. This event was witnessed by millions of our ancestors who stood at Mount Sinai, and testimony of it has been transmitted from generation to generation.

However, the spiritual leaders of these movements make the absurd and fundamentally heretical claim that the Torah is not all G-d-given and is therefore subject to change with the times. When their congregants, who know no better, hear this kind of rhetoric, they take it all in, thinking that their leaders are also presenting a legitimate version of Judaism. By teaching this and many other such falsehoods, these leaders are guiding their flocks away from Torah.

The truth of the matter is that today, even many of these leaders are not to be blamed. In most cases, they were raised on these misrepresentations and they, too, know no better. They cannot be blamed any more than their congregants.

I actually experienced this reality first-hand. I once sat down on a plane and the man sitting in the next seat said to me, "Are you an Orthodox rabbi?" I answered, "Yes, I am." He looked at me and exclaimed, "You probably want to run away from me, because I am a Reform rabbi!" I responded, "No, on the contrary, I have been waiting a long time for the opportunity to discuss the Reform views on Judaism."

After a few minutes of conversation, however, my excitement turned to dismay, as it was evident that his knowledge of Judaism was quite shallow. He had never seriously studied even basic Torah literature, such as Chumash and the Talmud, and his entire outlook was based on information he had picked up from some books he had read. So can we really blame such people for being unaware of the Torah-true viewpoint?

Thus, our attitude should not be to distance ourselves from our non-Torah-observant brethren. Rather than shun them, we have to do our utmost to teach them about Torah-true Judaism.

In short: Anyone whose mother is Jewish is fully Jewish. Most of those who are not Orthodox — even many leaders of those movements — don't know any better and are not to be blamed for their views. We should therefore try to help them learn about Torah-true Judaism.

17

Attending an Intermarriage Ceremony

Q ***My non-religious relative is unfortunately marrying a non-Jew, and I'm afraid that if I don't attend the wedding he will be very insulted. Should I attend?***

A You cannot attend the wedding, even if he will be offended and possibly cut all ties with you because of this. Intermarriage is one of the worst sins a Jew can commit, as it breaks the golden chain of our nation, which has spanned thousands of years, and causes the destruction of the Jewish nation. We cannot condone the marriage in any way, and your presence will give the impression that you are not terribly distraught over this horrific sin.

The problem is that many of these lost souls know very little about their Jewish heritage, and have no idea what is so terrible about marrying a non-Jew. So I suggest you explain to him that it is nothing personal, but, as a religious Jew, you cannot participate.

How strong to come across depends on the level of your relationship and if you feel you might be able to have a positive influence on him in the future. While you can't give any impression that you condone or are accepting of his choice, at the same time you don't want to ruin your relationship with him, forfeiting any chance to influence him in the future. But no matter what, you must be clear that this marriage is absolutely unacceptable.

Despite this, you should still keep up the connection with your relative even after they marry. You might find an opportunity to discuss our wonderful heritage, and you may even be able to offer to study Torah with him. If you feel there is the potential to inspire him, you can even invite them over privately, as long as you do not publicly recognize their relationship.

Hopefully, one day he will realize how terrible it is to be married to a non-Jew, and be inspired to return to his heritage — and it is even possible that the non-Jewish spouse will then convert.

I was once involved with a Jewish man who was married to a non-Jew, and I asked Rav Moshe Feinstein if I should try to convince him to divorce his non-Jewish spouse. He told me that since it will be difficult for him to divorce her, it would be better if the non-Jewish spouse converts, as long as it is a proper conversion and they will both keep the Torah and mitzvos. He explained that this would not be considered conversion for the sake of marriage — which is forbidden — because they are already living together.

However, this is very different from a case where a boy or girl from a religious home gets involved in a relationship with a non-Jew. While some feel that the parents should still allow them — accompanied by their "friend" — into their homes, in order to keep the connection with them, this is a big mistake.

Although keeping a connection with the child may sometimes help, the ends do not justify the means, and we can in no way give any impression that their behavior is acceptable. Furthermore, when others see that we are accepting of the situation, it can send the message that such a relationship is tolerable. And, in truth, allowing the child into the home with their partner has a negative effect on the parents and siblings, as well. Witnessing a sin makes us lose our sensitivity and abhorrence to the sin, and is something we must avoid at all costs.

In short: You cannot attend the wedding, as we cannot condone such a marriage. At the same time, try to keep up a connection and teach him more about our wonderful heritage, and hopefully one day he will repent.

18

Why Don't We Proselytize?

Q ***My young son asked me, "If we Jews are G-d's Chosen Nation, why are we a minority, and why don't we seek to add more members to our ranks by converting others to our religion?"***

A Explain to your son that there's nothing wrong with being small in numbers, as spelled out in the Torah (*Devarim* 7:7): "Hashem did not desire and choose you due to your great numbers, because you are the smallest of all the nations." Our special status lies in our closeness to Hashem and our keeping His Torah. Since it is quality that counts and not quantity, simply adding more members to our ranks will not necessarily make us a better people.

Because total commitment to the Torah is extremely difficult, halachah dictates that we actually discourage conversion, and when a person wishes to convert, we generally try to talk him out of it. Although we know how fortunate and fulfilling it is to be part of Hashem's Chosen Nation, we are also aware that along with our status comes awesome responsibility, and it is not for everyone. As Hashem's representatives in the world, He expects us to live up to a very high standard, and if we don't act the way we should, He sends us wake-up calls to help keep us in line. This is why the Jewish nation has suffered untold persecution and oppression throughout our long and bitter exile. We know that this is all because of Hashem's love for us, to help us stay close to Him for eternity.

But a potential convert must realize that it is not easy, and since he will be a full-fledged Jew, he will be expected to live up to his new obligations, and Hashem will hold him responsible for his sins like any other Jew. Someone joining from the outside may find it extremely difficult to withstand the pressure of these enormous responsibilities.

The convert must also realize that it takes time and effort to integrate into Jewish society, and he or she usually faces additional challenges when it comes to finding a marriage partner.

A would-be convert must be aware of all this before making his commitment, because once he has converted there is no turning back, no matter how overwhelming he may find it.

We also explain to him that if he remains a non-Jew who abides by the Seven Noahide Laws, he is fulfilling all his obligations and will earn great reward.

If after all the discouragement he remains determined to become a Jew, we certainly welcome him into our nation with open arms. Indeed, because it can be so daunting to adjust and integrate, our Rabbis (*Bava Metzia* 59b) tell us that there are thirty-six places where the Torah tells us to love a convert and treat him properly. And this is in addition to the mitzvah that we have to love every Jew. Since he sacrificed so much, we must do whatever we can to help him become the best Jew possible.

In short: Quality — keeping the Torah and being close to Hashem — is what gives us our prestige, and not quantity. We don't encourage conversion because the convert may not be able to live up to the high standards expected from every Jew.

19

Attending a Funeral in a Church

Q ***I have had an ongoing and pleasant relationship with my non-Jewish neighbors for many years. One of my neighbors passed away, and the funeral is scheduled to take place in the local Catholic church. Am I allowed to attend the funeral to show my empathy and maintain our relationship?***

A According to Jewish law, it is forbidden to enter a church even if no prayers or religious ceremonies are taking place at the time, as a Catholic church is deemed a place of idol worship. I therefore suggest you join other parts of the funeral, such as the burial, instead. However, if there is no other option, and it is extremely important that you attend, you can, provided that the funeral is not taking place in the sanctuary but in a side room, and only if there is a separate entrance to the building.

There are a number of issues involved in entering a church. Firstly, there is a concept of *maris ayin*. Even a devout and pious Jew is not allowed to do something that can cause others to suspect him of wrongdoing. For example, a person cannot enter an establishment where only non-kosher food is sold, unless it is common for people to enter for other reasons, such as using the restroom. In the case of the funeral, when someone is seen entering a church, he may be suspected of participating in the services in some way.

Additionally, the Talmud (*Shabbos* 149a) writes that one should not stare at idols. Our eyes are the "windows to our souls." Whatever we see has a great effect on our minds and souls, and we must be careful to preserve and maintain our sanctity. For this reason, our Rabbis (*Megillah* 28a) tell us that it is forbidden to stare at the face of the wicked, and some even avoid gazing at non-kosher animals.

Conversely, the holy books write that staring at the face of the righteous can have a positive spiritual effect on a person.

This point is highlighted by a passage in the Torah: When warning the Jewish people not to be attracted to the idols they had seen worshiped by the Egyptians, the *pasuk* says (*Devarim* 29:16), "You saw their abominations and their loathsome idols." But if the idols were so repulsive, why would the Torah need to warn the Jews not to be tempted to serve them?

The Brisker Rav explained that seeing the repulsive idols may have caused the Jews to lose their sense of disgust toward them.

Therefore, if someone goes to a church, he is in danger of seeing something that can have a detrimental effect on him.

In short: It is forbidden to enter a church, but entering a side room through a side entrance is permitted if your attendance is extremely important. It is forbidden to stare at idols, and doing so can have a negative effect on a person.

20

Non-Jewish Commentaries and Translations

Q ***When studying Tanach or searching online for a source or translation, can I use commentaries written by non-Jews or non-religious Jews?***

A Commentaries written by non-Jews or non-religious Jews are full of inaccuracies, and should certainly not be used. When our ancestors stood at Mount Sinai and received the Written Torah from Hashem, they received the Oral Torah along with it, which explains and elucidates the meaning of the Written Torah. This knowledge was transmitted from generation to generation until today. None of this was open for debate, and throughout the generations, those who attempted to change even an iota of this tradition were excommunicated.

Therefore, before we accept any explanation of the Torah, we must be sure that it is based on and conforms with this tradition. For this reason, only works that are written by knowledgeable people who are faithful to that tradition may be used. Works written by non-Jews or non-religious Jews cannot be considered faithful to our tradition and are not to be trusted.

Furthermore, many of these works were written with an agenda, such as to prove the validity of other religions, and they distort the translation to fit this agenda. For example, the Books of the *Prophets* are replete with references to future events, including the coming of Mashiach. Translations and commentaries written by those of other religions falsely translate and explain these references to speak of events that support their religions and beliefs.

It is also important to realize that no translation perfectly reflects the nuance of the original language. Let me share a story that illustrates how the imprecision of even a reliable translation can — unwittingly — misrepresent the meaning of the words of the Torah.

I was once at a farm buying some produce, and the proud farmer was eager to show me the various farm animals he owned. When we passed the pigpen, he made a point of telling me how clean his pigs were, but I couldn't imagine why in the world he felt the need to point this out. It wasn't until I was driving away that it finally hit me.

The Torah writes that we are not allowed to eat pigs because they are "*tamei.*" This farmer must have read a translation that translates the word *tamei* as "unclean," and understood this to mean that they are forbidden because they are "dirty" animals. He therefore made a point to tell me that his pigs were clean and should be permitted.

But this is completely inaccurate, as the word *tamei* has nothing to do with hygiene, and as clean as the pigs may be, we are still forbidden to eat them.

Some translate *tamei* as spiritually impure, but that, too, fails to convey the underlying meaning of the word. The word *tamei* means "blocked," i.e., something that causes an obstruction in our connection to Hashem. We find this meaning in *Parashas Toldos*. The Torah (*Bereishis* 26:15) writes about the wells dug by Avraham, "*sitmum Pelishtim* — the Philistines stuffed them," which Onkelos translates as *tamonun*, which is related to the word *tamei*. Similarly, Hashem, in His infinite wisdom, deemed certain animals not kosher because they cause an obstruction in our connection to Him.

This is a perfect example of a silly mistake and confusion caused by a translation.

If this is true with regard to translations that try to be faithful, how much more so must we be careful not to use elucidations or translations taken from sources that are not based on tradition.

In short: Commentaries written by non-Jews or non-religious Jews should not be used, as they do not follow our tradition and are full of inaccuracies.

Section 4

Bechirah — Free Will

21

Are People Born Evil?

Q ***I have severe anger management issues, and lash out at people easily, almost beyond control. If this is how Hashem created me, I feel that I should not be punished for my actions! Is this true, or am I doomed from the start?***

A Well, let us take a look at Eisav. Even before he was born, there seemed to have been a force pulling him toward evil, as he would try to jump out of his mother's womb when she passed by a house of idol worship. Then the Torah tells us that he was born with an *admoni* ("reddish") complexion, which indicates an inborn tendency toward bloodshed. Can you blame him for becoming the wicked Eisav?

The answer is that every person is created with free will, so while it's possible that some people are born with a stronger tendency toward evil, they are also created with the ability to overcome these challenges. In addition, every trait can be utilized for good, and you can use your anger to fight those who disgrace the Torah or similar causes.

The *pasuk* in *Mishlei* (22:6) teaches, "חֲנוֹךְ לַנַּעַר עַל פִּי דַרְכּוֹ — Educate the child according to his path." The Vilna Gaon explains that if a parent detects a certain negative trait in a child, he should not seek to uproot it from the child; rather, it should be nurtured and channeled toward good things.

He points to the Talmud (*Shabbos* 156a), which tells us that a baby born in the *mazal Maadim* (a "reddish" celestial sign) will have a tendency to shed blood. But, the Gemara adds, he has the ability and free will to harness this affinity and channel it toward good, by becoming a *mohel* or a *shochet*, thereby shedding blood through performing a mitzvah.

So while Eisav was born with an inborn nature for sin and bloodshed, he could have utilized this for good. The *pasuk* (*I Shmuel* 16:12) tells us that King David was also born an *admoni*, just like Eisav. The Midrash (*Bereishis Rabbah* 63:8) tells us that the prophet Shmuel noted this tendency, and was hesitant to anoint him as king. However, Hashem told Shmuel that he need not be concerned. While Eisav utilized this trait to become a murderer, King David would channel it for the good, executing people based on the ruling of Sanhedrin.

Indeed, Eisav's head is buried in the Me'aras HaMachpelah, together with the Patriarchs — a privilege he earned because, intellectually, he was truly great. However, since he succumbed to his body's desires and acted wickedly, the rest of his body was unworthy of being interred there. Although Eisav found his calling in the fields, where he was able to utilize his natural talents to achieve success, he still could have worked alongside Yaakov. Indeed, according to some commentaries, that was precisely what Yitzchak had in mind when he intended to bless Eisav. Bestowing Eisav with material blessings would have enabled him to support Yaakov's spiritual endeavors, similar to the traditional Yissachar and Zevulun arrangement, and Eisav would thereby fulfill his mission on this world and have a share in his Torah study.

So G-d created every person with challenges, but also gives each of us the ability to overcome them. It may take a lot of hard work and perseverance, but it can be done.

A good place to start would be the study of *mussar*, the ethical teachings of the Torah, which will train you to control yourself. There is also a wide variety of trustworthy books, videos, and lectures available on these topics, and they can all help you become more patient and understanding.

In short: Everyone has free will and the ability to overcome challenges and to harness their tendencies to be used for good things.

22

Prayer Not to Have Challenges

Q ***Every morning during Birchos HaShachar (the Morning Blessings), we ask Hashem not to give us tests. Why do we ask for this if the very purpose of life is to face challenges and overcome them?***

A This is a very fundamental question. Indeed, as you note, the very first chapter of *Mesillas Yesharim*, the classic work on Torah ethics, explains that the purpose of mankind is to serve Hashem and to overcome challenges. Hashem created us in order to enjoy eternal bliss in the World to Come, and the way to earn that reward is by performing mitzvos in this world. As the *pasuk* (*Iyov* 5:7) says, "*Adam le'amal yulad* — Man was created to toil." If mitzvah performance would come easily, we would not be earning our reward; we are elevated and earn reward only by overcoming the hurdles that come our way.

That being said, you are correct that it seems counterintuitive to request that we avoid achieving the very purpose of our coming down to this world; it's like traveling overseas on a business trip, and asking Hashem that the clients don't show up!

But in truth, the very question provides the key to the answer: Every situation in life is a challenge. Wherever a person finds himself, he must ensure that every action, every word, and even every thought conforms to the rules of the Torah. Hashem expects us to act, talk, and think in a very specific way, and everything in life must be filtered through the lens of the Torah.

Furthermore, every moment of life is a test, because even when just sitting around, we must constantly seek to grow in our service of Hashem. With every breath of oxygen, we can recognize and appreciate Hashem's greatness and His constant kindness to us. And in every situation we can serve Hashem with more acts of kindness, by studying more Torah, or performing other mitzvos — things that are required 24/7, wherever a person may find himself.

Obviously, then, we cannot understand the request not to face any tests in this world at face value. So what are we asking for?

Although we are here in this world to overcome tests, we must avoid tests that we may not be able to withstand. In this daily prayer, we are asking Hashem that we not be confronted with overwhelming challenges that we may not be able to overcome. But at the same time, if Hashem does send us such difficulties, we must realize that it is because He knows we can overcome them, and it is up to us to rise to the occasion and pass the test.

In short: Every moment and every situation in life is a challenge. We pray not to be given overwhelming, seemingly insurmountable tests that may cause us to stumble.

23

To Err Is Human

Q ***King Shlomo writes in Koheles (7:20): "כִּי אָדָם אֵין צַדִּיק בָּאָרֶץ אֲשֶׁר יַעֲשֶׂה טּוֹב וְלֹא יֶחֱטָא — There is no righteous man on Earth who does good and does not sin." If sin is beyond our control, why is a person ever punished?***

A This question is based on a misunderstanding of the *pasuk*. King Shlomo is not suggesting that sin is inevitable. Indeed, the Talmud (*Bava Basra* 17a) tells us that there were great people who never sinned, and died only because of the curse that man die. Shlomo is merely observing that because the human tendency is to give in to desires and evil inclinations, it is nearly impossible to find someone who never sins.

Furthermore, *Nefesh HaChaim* (1:6) explains that "*cheit,*" usually translated as sin, actually refers to any failure or lack of perfection. Shlomo is telling us that no one is perfect, and even a person who never in his life sinned will not perform every mitzvah with complete perfection.

But there is no question that every person has free will, and one can and must make the proper effort to do Hashem's will in any given situation. If a person does not put in the effort, he will be held liable for sinning, but a person who was truly unable to fulfill a mitzvah is not held accountable.

At the same time, we must remember that Hashem is the One Who sits in judgment of a person, and He knows just what the person was actually capable of. Many people forget this and unfortunately excuse themselves from more than they really should.

Even when the going gets rough and we feel like we are facing insurmountable challenges, we do not give up. We each must try our best, and even make an effort to go beyond our perceived limitations.

In fact, the *Chovos HaLevavos* tells us that if we try our best and ask Hashem to help us, He will endow us with newfound strengths that will help us soar to previously unreachable heights.

This is actually true for every encounter we have with the *yetzer hara* (evil inclination). The Talmud (*Succah* 52a) tells us that the *yetzer hara* is so powerful that we need Divine assistance to withstand his efforts. The Vilna Gaon explains that this means we must do our part, and only then will Hashem help us over the hurdle. By doing our part, the impossible becomes possible.

We see this clearly in the story of Yosef. Yosef found himself in the house of Potiphar, where he was faced with a seemingly insurmountable challenge, day in and day out. Our Rabbis (*Sotah* 36b) tell us that he persevered for a long time, but was finally on the verge of capitulating. Although withstanding this test was beyond his natural abilities, at the last moment, Hashem sent him an image of his father's holy face, which helped him escape the lure of sin. Because he had done all that he could, he merited Divine assistance and overcame the *yetzer hara*.

The Vilna Gaon once used this idea to appease his student, Rav Zalman Volozhiner. Rav Zalman had hurt someone's feelings, and went searching for the man to ask him for forgiveness, but was unable to locate him. When the Gaon heard that his student was distressed over the fact that he was unable to receive forgiveness, he told Rav Zalman that he had no need to be concerned. Since he had done his utmost to seek forgiveness, Hashem would certainly help him and inspire the other man to grant the much-needed forgiveness.

In short: Human tendency is not to be perfect, but we must try our best. In addition, by doing our part, the impossible can become possible.

Section 5

Middos — Character Traits

24

How do I Develop Positive Speech?

Q ***I often find myself speaking lashon hara (gossip) or saying things that are hurtful to others. I know it is wrong, but how can I change what has essentially become second nature?***

A These are certainly terrible sins, and although you think these sins have become part of your character, here are some basic steps you can — and should — take to change.

The first step is learning the laws of proper speech.

Sefer Chofetz Chaim describes in detail the rules and regulations of proper speech, explaining just what is allowed and what is forbidden. If someone doesn't even know the laws, it will be impossible to keep them!

The second step is to understand the tremendous power of our words. Many *mussar* (ethical teachings) works expound on the great ramifications of proper speech. Studying these works will enable you to appreciate the greatness you can achieve by guarding your tongue, as well as the harm caused by improper speech, and you will be inspired to be extra vigilant in the matter. One exceptional choice for this would be another classic work by the Chofetz Chaim, *Shemiras HaLashon*.

Both *Chofetz Chaim* and *Shemiras HaLashon* are available in many formats and languages.

In addition, there is a wide variety of inspirational books, videos, and recordings available on these topics. Each dose of inspiration will empower you in the life-long mission of combating this nature, as well as all the challenges of your evil inclination.

Here is one example of a lesson that can transform you: People sometimes wonder why their heartfelt prayers are not answered. The

Chofetz Chaim points out that — in addition to the many other tragic consequences of sinful speech — it also contaminates a person's mouth, tainting his words and thereby weakening the potency of his prayers. Internalizing this concept can certainly help you be more conscious of what you say and motivate you to be more careful with your speech.

It is also helpful to focus on the positive: Someone who has true *ahavas Yisrael* (love for a fellow Jew) will be unable to talk derogatorily about others. Rav Pam would relate that his mother never spoke negatively about others simply because of her love for every fellow Jew.

On a practical level, spending your time around others who are careful with their speech is crucial. They can actually help you achieve your goal of speaking properly, because if you begin to slip and share the latest piece of news at the lunch table, your friends can call it to your attention. At the same time, you should make sure to steer away from being in the company of gossipers; the evil inclination and your second-nature will take the opportunity to drag you back down, and all your study and inspiration won't be enough to combat your surroundings.

One final tactic is to train yourself not to express every thought that comes to your mind, even things that are permitted. The Chofetz Chaim writes that taking charge of what comes out of one's mouth helps train a person to refrain from prohibited speech. As the great Rav Yisrael Salanter, founder of the *Mussar* movement, famously stated: "Not everything that comes to one's mind should be said; not everything we say should be committed to writing; and not everything we write should be printed."

In short: To change your behavior, you should study the laws and the pitfalls involved; focus on your love for a fellow Jew; choose friends who can help you reach your goal; and restrain from excessive talk.

25

How Far Should I Go to Keep the Peace?

Q ***My neighbor claims I owe him money for a claim that I believe is fabricated, and this disagreement is ruining our relationship. Is it worthwhile to pay him just to keep the peace, or is that just feeding into injustice?***

A If the truth is absolutely clear to both of you, and even your neighbor knows he is simply being malicious, there is no reason to pay him. But if your neighbor is making his claim in good faith, don't dismiss it out of hand.

First of all, there have been many stories where someone was quite certain of the facts, only to later realize that he was the one who was mistaken. But even more importantly, even if your neighbor is totally wrong, you should still try to work things out, since he may never see things your way and will continue to think he is correct, leaving everyone with hard feelings.

The best approach would be to try to do whatever you can to keep the peace. You should try to sit down together to reach a compromise, or find a third party who can help you work things out. And if that is not possible, and you have the means, it would be righteous and praiseworthy to pay him the money he believes you owe him, certainly a worthwhile investment.

One cannot overstate the great significance of keeping peace and harmony. Hashem allows His Name to be erased in order to maintain domestic harmony between a husband and wife (*Shabbos* 116a), and one may even be untruthful for the sake of peace (*Yevamos* 65b). In fact, the Chofetz Chaim writes in a letter (*Michtav* 101): "There is nothing worse in the world than discord, and nothing better than peace."

Indeed, I saw this in the conduct of the venerated Rav Moshe Feinstein, who would avoid disagreements at all costs, commenting that as bad as a situation may seem, generating strife is worse.

One reason harmony is so crucial is because our actions in this world have a powerful effect on the upper worlds and on the extent of our connection with Hashem. As the *Nefesh HaChaim* (1:7) writes in the name of the Midrash, Hashem is like our shadow, and His actions toward us reflect the way we act. Therefore, when we live in harmony with one another, our harmony with Hashem is strengthened. Conversely, if there is discord between Hashem's children in this world, He removes Himself from our midst, and the entire world suffers. Indeed, the Talmud (*Yoma* 9b) tells us that *sinas chinam*, unwarranted hatred, caused the destruction of the Second Temple.

Since quarrels can wreak such havoc, and peace generates such Heavenly blessings, it is certainly commendable to try to work things out, or even go the extra mile, and pay the "extra dollar."

In short: If your neighbor is being malicious, there is no reason to pay him. But if he really thinks you owe him the money, even if you feel he is wrong, try to keep the peace and make a compromise or pay him. This is definitely worthwhile, as the benefits of creating peace in the world are so great.

26

Peace at Last

Q ***A close relative of mine has not spoken to me in many years, apparently because of something I did, although I have no idea what. I have apologized to her over the years, but, decades later, she still won't have anything to do with me. I would love to make peace with her, but I don't know how to do it. Is there anything I can do?***

A Making peace in the world is a great mitzvah, and it is certainly worthwhile to do whatever you can to make it happen. In *Avos* (1:12) we are instructed to be students of Aharon, who not only loved peace but also pursued it, so even when peace is eluding you, you should chase after it. *Avos D'Rav Nassan* elaborates on the innovative methods Aharon would employ to restore harmony between quarreling parties, whether it was a family feud or a friendship that went sour.

As mentioned previously ("How Far Should I Go to Keep the Peace?"), the Chofetz Chaim wrote, "There is nothing worse in the world than discord, and nothing better than peace." As explained there, strengthening peace enhances our connection to Hashem, through which we merit much blessing, and discord weakens our connection to Hashem and the accompanying blessings. So it is definitely advisable to do whatever you can to make peace.

I would suggest you write her a heartfelt letter, articulating how terrible you feel about the situation and offering to do whatever you can to rectify it. I would also recommend that as an expression of your sincerity, you send a meaningful gift along with the letter, such as a homemade challah or cake. You can also mention the fact that you are both getting on in years, and how much it would mean to you to restore the relationship. People tend to soften as they get older, and this point may very well motivate her to come around. These situations don't necessarily repair themselves overnight, so you may need to follow up on it.

If that suggestion is impractical or does not help, you can try to find a third party who can help you work things out.

By showing that you are truly remorseful and want to make peace, eventually harmony will reign once again.

Postscript: Not long after this advice was given, the woman who had asked the question came back and reported how successful it was! In her own words: "Rabbi Mintz, I just wanted to let you know that I followed your advice and it really worked. I sent her a nice gift along with a letter and she actually called me to make up. We were both crying and the air was finally cleared."

I commended her for her extraordinary act, and told her that since bringing peace to the world is so powerful, there is no doubt that Hashem and the angels were crying along with them. We should all learn from this story to do our best to make peace.

In short: Making peace is a great mitzvah. Send a letter expressing how meaningful it would be to reunite, along with a nice gift, or some similar idea. If you persevere, eventually you should be successful in restoring peace.

27

Rude Relatives at a Wedding

Q ***Our wedding day is approaching, and we are planning quite an extravagant affair! We have some relatives who have been quite rude and offensive to us in the past, and they are well aware that they are not wanted at the wedding. Yet we heard that they don't want to miss the "wedding of the century," and are planning to show up uninvited. How do we make sure these people won't ruin our special day?***

A I was really hoping for a different ending to your question, such as, "How can we make peace with these rude relatives?" That would be a much more appropriate question to ask as you prepare to build your new home, and hope for a happy and pleasant life together.

Shalom bayis — having a happy and pleasant home — is the aspiration of every bride and groom, and one of the most important things they should be praying for as they begin their life together. In fact, harmony in the home is the foundation of every marriage, and is stressed in the blessings recited at the wedding and at *Sheva Berachos*, the festive meals that follow. In the last of those blessings, we praise Hashem Who created many different expressions of joy, yet we conclude with "love, unity, peace, and companionship." These expressions are added because true happiness can be achieved only when each one is thinking about and caring for the other.

Unfortunately, this is no simple matter. Sadly, we see so much strife and friction in homes and families today, husbands and wives not getting along, siblings quarreling, and all types of family discord, and you certainly want to avoid that as you and your spouse begin your new lives together. Trying to make peace with your relatives would be a great merit for you and your family to enjoy a peaceful and happy life.

Indeed, in *Avos* (1:12) we are instructed to be students of Aharon, "loving peace and pursuing peace." While living peacefully with pleasant people may not be that challenging, keeping the peace with rude and offensive relatives who are undeserving of your friendship is not as simple. It is specifically in such a scenario that our Rabbis exhort us to "pursue peace," to go the extra mile to create harmony.

One way to clear the air would be with some kind words and actions. As King Shlomo teaches us (*Mishlei* 15:1), "A soft response will relieve anger." In most cases, if you go out of your way to display love and kindness to your relatives, they will slowly come around.

I therefore suggest that you "bury the hatchet," and find ways to make sure they feel welcome and enjoy themselves at the wedding. Perhaps send them an invitation with a message that you are looking forward to seeing them at the wedding. Once they are there, make it your business to dance with them, which will hopefully help change their behavior and create unity.

You can view this as your singular opportunity to restore peace and harmony in the family. There is no question that going out of your way to promote peace will be a great merit for you in your new marriage, helping you achieve a happy and peaceful home for many years to come.

In short: Our Rabbis teach us to pursue peace, and go the extra mile to create harmony. Make them feel welcome at the wedding, and by promoting peace, you will merit a happy and peaceful home.

28

Which Comes First — Derech Eretz or Torah Study?

Q ***We learn in Avos (3:17), "אִם אֵין תּוֹרָה אֵין דֶּרֶךְ אֶרֶץ אִם אֵין דֶּרֶךְ אֶרֶץ אֵין תּוֹרָה — Without Torah one cannot have proper conduct, and without proper conduct one cannot have Torah." That sounds like a catch-22! If I can't have one without the other, where do I start?***

A Character refinement has many levels. One must have basic good character traits in order to study Torah, but can only achieve character perfection through Torah study.

Although a depraved person can become a great mathematician or scientist, a decent character is a prerequisite to Torah study because Torah is the wisdom of Hashem — the epitome of refinement — so someone completely lacking good *middos* is unable to connect to Hashem and His Torah. A person can reach a basic level of character refinement even before he studies Torah, because every Jew was created with inborn good character traits that he can tap into.

Additionally, submitting to his animalistic nature, the source of bad character, will inhibit one's ability to grasp the profound concepts of the Torah. For example, a lazy person will be unwilling to put in the mental exertion needed to grasp an intricate Talmudic discussion. Similarly, an arrogant person will fail to achieve the proper understanding of topics because he will not pay attention to others' insights, or will refuse to admit that their explanations may be better than his own. And someone seeking relaxation and physical pleasure will be unwilling to forgo his comforts in order to study Torah diligently.

But although man was created with innate good character traits, they are raw and need to be developed. In fact, the Vilna Gaon writes that perfecting our character is the very reason we come to this world, and it takes a lifetime to perfect ourselves. This is where Torah study comes in, because the way to perfect one's character is through the study of Torah, for many reasons.

Firstly, when a person studies Torah he learns what true character refinement is all about. Our illustrious ancestors and Sages serve as examples for us, and the ethical topics discussed in Torah works teach us real-life lessons on how to conduct ourselves properly. In fact, the entire Tractate *Avos* is devoted to ethical teachings. And as the Vilna Gaon writes, even when studying other areas of Torah, one who focuses on his studies properly will discover that every word of Torah is replete with lessons and insights to become better people.

Furthermore, as mentioned, proper Torah study requires a person to transcend his animalistic nature and become more and more refined, so the more a person studies, the more refined he will become.

On a deeper level, Torah is the word of Hashem, and when we study it, we connect to His greatness and sanctity. That connection transforms us and makes us more refined and spiritual people.

Thus, although a person must have basic good character in order to study Torah, it is only through studying Torah that a person can fully develop and refine his character properly.

In short: A person must use his inborn basic good character in order to begin studying Torah. But true perfection of character can be achieved only through studying Torah.

29

Rage Rooms and Punching Bags

Q ***There is a form of recreation known as a "rage room" — a room where people let out their frustrations by wrecking partially broken objects. Is this an appropriate technique for one to use if he feels that it will help him be more pleasant afterward to his family and friends? And what about using a punching bag to "let it all out"?***

A Let's start with the rage room. There is no question that destructive activity is repulsive, not Jewish, and really not even human behavior. Someone who has a problem with anger management should work on his character traits, and find a more civilized outlet.

Breaking things falls under the sin of wasting (*bal tashchis*), which includes destroying anything useful. We must remember that everything on Earth was created by Hashem for the purpose of bringing Him honor and serving Him, and ruining His creations clashes with this purpose. In fact, the *Sefer HaChinuch* writes that there were great people who, out of their deep appreciation for everything Hashem gave them, would not even waste a mustard seed. Even if we are not on that lofty level, we should definitely stay away from destructive activities.

One may suggest that this activity is actually constructive — and therefore not considered wasting — because by letting out his rage, one will appease his anger and become a calmer person. This suggestion is actually considered by the Talmud (*Shabbos* 105b), but the notion is then rejected, because by acting this way, a person gives the evil inclination a foothold, and it will then pull him down further and further, until he eventually performs the worst sins. As Rashi explains, destroying objects to calm one's anger does not help. On the contrary, it strengthens the evil inclination and reinforces his animalistic traits.

Unlike the rage room, using a punching bag to let out anger is not destructive and not a violation of *bal tashchis*, so we can't say it's forbidden. Nevertheless, punching is still unrefined, and not in the spirit of Jewish behavior. This falls under what is known as the "fifth section of *Shulchan Aruch*," a reference to concepts that are not spelled out in the four sections of *Shulchan Aruch*, because they should be self-understood. Similarly, the Noda B'Yehudah, the great Torah giant of the 18th century, writes that even if hunting for the thrill of it is technically permitted, it is not an appropriate pastime for Jews.

I therefore suggest that you find other constructive ways to let out frustrations and calm anger, such as exercising or listening to music.

In short: A rage room is repulsive, as it involves destructive activity and will make a person more prone to following his animalistic feelings, and is also wasteful. Using a punching bag is not forbidden, but not refined.

30

Does Hate Have a Place?

Q ***I was taught that we must show our love to every creation of Hashem, spreading His kindness to the world. That being the case, is it appropriate to hate evil people, such as murderers and terrorists? Perhaps our focus should just be on spreading more love in the world.***

A We must certainly hate ruthless murderers! People who murder innocent men, women and children are the epitome of evil, and they and their philosophy are to be hated. King David declared (*Tehillim* 139:21-22), "Indeed those who hate you, Hashem, I hate. I hate them with the utmost hatred." These wicked people are certainly enemies of Hashem, as they are the antithesis of Hashem, the epitome of good, and have no place in the world.

As the great rabbis tell us, every character trait was created by Hashem for a reason, to be used in the right place and at the right time. Hatred was created to be directed against evildoers and those who defy the will of Hashem. As we recite in the Friday evening prayers (*Tehillim* 97:10), "Those who love Hashem hate evil." Those who truly love Hashem cannot tolerate evil and evildoers. And the more a person loves Hashem, the greater the hatred he will feel to evildoers. Feeling love for such people is misdirected, and indicates a lack of true love of Hashem.

Additionally, love for evildoers has a detrimental effect on a person. When we become accepting of wicked people, we come to feel that they are not so bad. This diminishes our disgust for wickedness, ultimately leading us to sanction wrongdoing and corrupting us, making us worse people.

We must be firm in recognizing that these people are wicked and their actions are unforgivable, and they have no place in our world.

Of course, we wish that they would repent and change their ways, in which case we would happily accept and love them, because even the greatest murderer can repent. But as long as they are evil we must hate them, and make sure to have a clear distinction between good and bad. We must not fall for the false ideology of simply loving everyone, no matter what.

In short: Murderers and terrorists are the epitome of evil, and enemies of Hashem, Who is the epitome of good, and we should certainly hate them, unless they change their ways.

31

To Thank or Not to Thank

Q ***My child did something deserving of thanks, but should have done much more. I would like to thank him, but I'm concerned that he may get the message that it's okay to do only half a job and won't do better in the future. Should I still express appreciation even if he may use my thanks to slacken off?***

A Let us first discuss the great importance of *hakaras hatov*, showing appreciation to others. When Moshe was told by Hashem to go take the Jews out of Egypt, he first asked his father-in-law, Yisro, for permission to go. The Midrash explains that although Hashem Himself had commanded him to go, Moshe understood that since he was beholden to Yisro for taking him into his home, Hashem would not expect him to leave without Yisro's permission. Gratitude to others is fundamental to being a good person, and certainly a leader, and the entire Jewish nation would have to wait until Moshe was given the go-ahead from Yisro.

One must even feel indebted to an inanimate object that benefited him. This is why Moshe — who had been saved by being placed in the Nile and was protected by the earth where he buried the Egyptian whom he killed for beating a Jew — was not the one who struck the Nile or the earth to initiate the first three plagues. Similarly, the Talmud (*Bava Kamma* 92b) says, "Do not throw dirt into a well from which you drank." To illustrate this point, the *Shitah Mekubetzes* tells the story of how Rabbi Yitzchak Alfasi (the great 11th-century Torah sage known by his acronym Rif) once fell ill, and made use of someone's bathhouse as part of his treatment. This man later fell upon hard times and was being forced by his creditors to sell the bathhouse. When the Rif was asked to preside over the sale and appraisal of the property, he declined, explaining that it would be lacking in basic decency for him to be involved in the case, since he had benefited from the bathhouse. The *Shitah Mekubetzes* concludes by stating that if this is the feeling one must have toward an inanimate object that has no feelings, one must certainly be careful to express appreciation to people whose feelings can be hurt.

Showing gratitude to others also helps us appreciate the constant blessings we receive from Hashem; conversely, one who fails to show gratitude to others can lose his feelings of appreciation to Hashem.

Because showing gratitude makes us better people and helps our spiritual growth, when someone does something for you, don't just give a general thanks; rather, try to focus on specific details of what they did. For example, after hearing a good class or lecture, tell the rabbi, teacher, or speaker how much you appreciate all the time and effort he or she invested in making the material so clear and inspiring. Or if your wife serves you a delicious supper, don't thank her only for the meal, but also for all her hard work in pulling together the ingredients and preparing a tasty meal. Doing this will help you be tuned in to the many details of Hashem's benevolence, as well.

Having said all this, there is no question that you must express your thanks for everything, big or small, that your child has done. As far as your concern that your child will continue to do half the job, I would not be worried. On the contrary, experience shows that a person who feels appreciated will do even more the next time they are asked. But if you feel that yours is the type of child who will get the wrong message, you can say — perhaps in a joking tone — something like, "Wow, this is so good, imagine how great it would be had you done even more!" If even such a comment will cause him to be disappointed, it would be best to find a different opportunity to convey the importance of performing a mitzvah fully and properly.

In short: You should certainly express your thanks for everything you receive from others. Usually, someone who feels appreciated will do better the next time they are asked, but if you need to say something about the job being incomplete, find a nice way to also encourage your child to improve.

32

How Do You Expect Me to Be Humble?

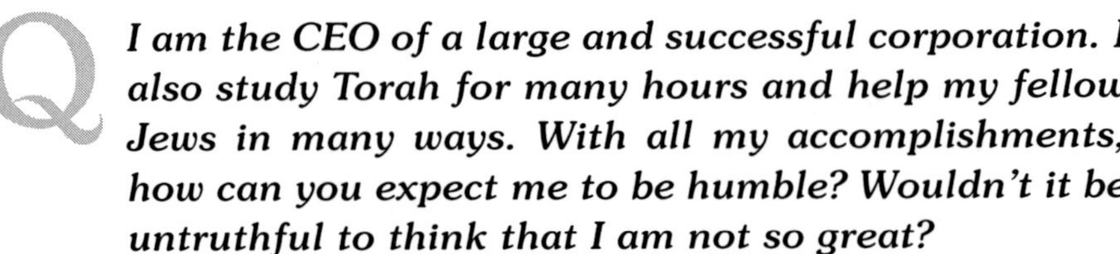

I am the CEO of a large and successful corporation. I also study Torah for many hours and help my fellow Jews in many ways. With all my accomplishments, how can you expect me to be humble? Wouldn't it be untruthful to think that I am not so great?

A I see that there is an important component missing in your schedule. If you'd make some time to study *mussar*, the Torah's ethical teachings, you would realize that the premise of your question has several mistakes. Entire books have been written elaborating on the character trait of *anavah*, humility, and we cannot do the topic justice in just a few lines, but we can touch on some of the points:

Moshe Rabbeinu was the greatest man who ever lived. He led the Jews out of Egypt, spent 120 days in Heaven together with the angels, brought the Torah down to this world, and reached greater spiritual heights than any other human. Yet the Torah testifies that Moshe was the humblest of all men. If he was the greatest person who ever lived, how was he also the most humble? Was he unaware of his talents, accomplishments, and stature?

One basic answer is that Moshe was well aware of his greatness, but didn't take credit for it. Moshe recognized that all his talents and opportunities were gifts from Hashem, to be used to fulfill his purpose on this world. So even if you have accomplished a lot, that doesn't make you great, because everything you have — your money, your talents, and your achievements — are gifts from Hashem.

But this goes even further. Moshe was not only humble before Hashem, the King of kings, he was even self-effacing in front of people who hadn't achieved a fraction of his greatness. When the Jews challenged him in the desert, his response was (*Shemos* 16:7-8), "What are we?" The Talmud (*Chullin* 89a) points out that he considered himself "nothing," an even deeper level of humility than Avraham who referred to himself as dust.

A truly humble person will feel that he is lower than every other person in the world. As the *Chovos HaLevavos* writes, a person should think the following: "If someone is greater than me, I stand in awe of his greatness. And if someone is not as great, perhaps if he had my abilities he would be greater than me, and if I would be in his situation, I would be smaller than he is."

Additionally, since everyone is judged according to his or her abilities, Moshe may have felt humbled by the fact that, considering his outstanding talents, he might not be reaching his full potential. Had he tried harder, he could have achieved much greater heights, and someone else with his abilities might have done better.

Similarly, even though you do many wonderful things, there are certainly areas you can improve in, like fear and love of Hashem. Therefore, instead of holding yourself high, you should realize that there is so much more you can accomplish.

The story is told that one Yom Kippur, Rav Yonasan Eybeschutz heard someone reciting the words "עָפָר אֲנִי בְּחַיָּי — I am dust in my lifetime" with great fervor. He decided to daven next to that man so he would be inspired by his penetrating prayers. However, when it came time for the reading of the Torah, the man received a less prominent *aliyah* than what he felt he deserved, and he began to berate the *gabbai* for not honoring him appropriately.

Rav Yonasan asked the man how this perceived slight to his honor could upset him after he had just finished describing himself as dust. "I am only like dust before Hashem," the man responded, "but I'm greater than all the others here, and deserve to be honored appropriately."

Rav Yonasan then realized that this man was not truly humble, because true humility is when a person feels like dust even before people.

In short: All that you have — your money, your talents — are gifts from Hashem, and your accomplishments are only possible because of what He gives you. Even if you accomplished a lot, perhaps you could have done much more, and others would have done more if they were in your situation. These thoughts should remind you to be humble.

33

Dealing With Cranky Kids and Difficult Neighbors

Q ***I find it hard to deal with my cranky children and my unusual neighbors. I know that I should be more understanding, but that seems to be beyond my capabilities! Are there any practical suggestions you can give me to help develop patience?***

A Obviously, perfecting one's character traits is a lifetime's work, not something you can achieve with the snap of a finger. But I can offer some ideas to help you work on reaching your goal.

To begin with, you should realize that everyone has patience for things they appreciate or enjoy. For example, you may know someone who finds it hard to sit still for more than a few minutes, yet if you give him an interesting book or a show to watch, he can suddenly sit quietly for hours. So if you come to appreciate your situation and understand that this is what's best for you, you won't be so aggravated by your child's crankiness or your neighbor's strange ideas, and you will actually develop patience for them.

One way to achieve this appreciation is by working on your belief in Hashem. This will help you recognize that it is Hashem Who is running the world, and your children or neighbors are not the ones calling the shots.

The *Sefer HaChinuch* writes that this perspective underlies the prohibition against taking revenge. Since everything is orchestrated from Above — for whatever reason Hashem deemed it necessary — the perpetrator was merely acting as Hashem's agent. If Hashem wanted this to happen, even if the perpetrator had done nothing, He would have found some other way for the difficulty to come about. *Sefer HaChinuch* illustrates this point through the story of King David, who was cursed by Shimi ben Geira. David's general Avishai wanted to behead Shimi, but David stopped him, explaining that it was not Shimi cursing, rather "Hashem told him to curse," and there was therefore no reason to retaliate.

Similarly, Yosef assured his brothers that although they subjected him to terrible pain, he bore them no ill will. It was abundantly clear that Hashem had sent him to Egypt to save them from hunger, orchestrating this entire chain of events, and they were not the cause of his pain.

Although a victim still has the right to be upset at the wrongdoer since he chose to bring about the harm, once the victim understands that what occurred would have happened anyway, the hard feelings generally fade away.

Similarly, if you know that your child or neighbor are only Hashem's agents and this stress was coming anyway, it will be much easier to deal with the situation.

Another important pointer would be to remember that such things are to be expected. Kids will be kids, and it is normal for them to be cranky. If you anticipate that your children act this way when they are tired, hungry, or under the weather, you will be able to change your mindset to handle it better.

On a practical level, *middos* are like muscles, and they are built up through exercise. You can slowly build your level of tolerance by delaying when you react, and extending the delay a little more each time, building your "patience muscle" until you eventually become a more patient person.

These same techniques can be used for dealing with the "difficult" neighbor or other interpersonal relationships. Our Rabbis tell us that "Just as every face is different, minds also work differently." Just as you do not get upset if your neighbor doesn't look like you, it should not upset you if his way of thinking and approach to things differs from yours. You are entitled to your opinion, and he is entitled to his. With this in mind, you can learn to appreciate — or at least tolerate — other people's views and attitudes, even when they are very different from your own. This will enable you to take things in stride so that even when you don't see eye-to-eye with others, you can still appreciate them and be friends.

In short: Remember that it is Hashem Who sent you this specific situation, and that it is normal for kids to be cranky and for people to have differing approaches to life and situations. You can also work on slowly developing your patience.

Section 6

Greatness of Mankind

34

Man — Greater Than Angels!

Q ***I heard that every Jew is a "cheilek Elokah mima'al — a part of G-d," and is even greater than angels. Is a person actually part of G-d? And how is it possible that humans — made of flesh and blood — can be greater than the Heavenly angels?***

A Since this concept of "*cheilek Elokah mima'al*" is often misunderstood, allow me to begin by clarifying it: Since G-d is not physical, and He has no "parts," a Jewish soul is not a "part of G-d." Furthermore, Hashem always existed, and souls are His creations, so they are obviously not a part of Him. We express this clearly each morning, when we thank Hashem, saying, "נְשָׁמָה שֶׁנָּתַתָּ בִּי טְהוֹרָה הִיא אַתָּה בְרָאתָהּ — The soul that You placed within me is pure, You created it."

What "part of G-d" really means is that G-d infused our souls with G-dlike powers.

The Torah tells us that man was created *b'tzelem Elokim* — in the "form" of G-d. Since G-d does not have a form, the *Nefesh HaChaim* explains that the meaning of the word *tzelem* in this instance is "resemblance," meaning that Hashem created man with some resemblance to Him. Hashem did not only create the world, He is constantly recreating the entire universe anew, and if He would stop even for a millisecond, everything would simply cease to exist. Man resembles Hashem in this way. Every good deed, word, or thought of a Jew keeps the world going, while his sinful ones destroy the world, Heaven forbid.

We may not be able to see the effects of our actions due to our physical limitations, but if we would have spiritual lenses, we would see how our actions literally impact the world. For example, the

Talmud (*Chullin* 89a) tells us that the world exists in the merit of someone who remains in control of himself and does not respond during a dispute. Although we are unable to perceive this, that is the reality.

Only humans have this tremendous power. Angels, on the other hand, are merely agents of Hashem and do not have their own power to affect the world. This is what makes us greater than the angels.

A Jewish soul is also loftier and more exalted than angels, because we are taught that it originates from the highest places in Heaven, right by Hashem's "Holy Throne." As Rashi writes (*Bamidbar* 23:23), there will come a time when even the angels will ask the "insiders" — the Jewish people — when they wish to find out what is happening in G-d's inner chambers.

The reason you are having a hard time accepting that man is greater than angels is because you think of man in terms of his body. But in truth, it is your soul that is the real "you." Because a soul is too spiritual to be exposed to this physical world on its own, it is sent clothed in a physical body. Just as you wouldn't say your clothes are you, you shouldn't think your body is you. I often explain to people who are grieving excessively at the burial of a loved one that it is only his physical "clothing" being buried, but the real person — the soul — is very much alive and will live on for eternity.

In short: A Jewish soul is not "part of G-d," but it resembles G-d, because it is invested with the G-dly power to build or destroy the world. This makes man greater than angels. Additionally, the soul is greater because it originates from next to Hashem's Holy Throne.

35

I'm Only Human!

Q ***Rabbi, I'm only human, so why do you always tell me to jump out of bed in the morning like a lion?***

A You may be human, but you possess the power of a lion!

Man is an "*olam katan*," a microcosm of the world, because he is comprised of all the different powers that are contained in the universe. Before creating Man, Hashem said, "Let us make Man" (in the plural form). The *Nefesh HaChaim* (1:6), based on the *Zohar*, explains that this was not just a proposal to create Man. It was a call to each element of creation to impart its unique characteristic into Adam, empowering him with the ability to accomplish all that he needs to in this world. Adam was created with these powers, which then became the DNA of mankind for all generations.

We can now understand the advice given in *Avos* (5:23): "Be bold as a leopard, light as an eagle, swift as a deer, and strong as a lion." These are not mere metaphors, but a directive to discover the hidden strengths within ourselves and tap into them in order to better serve Hashem.

Knowing and appreciating our true abilities is crucial for our mission in this world.

Mitzvos cover all facets of human existence, and different mitzvos require us to call forth feelings or perform actions that seem contradictory. Some mitzvos — such as performing kind deeds — require benevolence, while others — like eradicating Amalek — require an opposite emotion. How are we expected to perform actions that are polar opposites?

The answer is that man is multi-faceted — peaceful as a dove yet strong as a lion — and is therefore capable of performing actions that seem to contradict each other. On the one hand, he has inborn sympathy and compassion, which he can channel toward helping others. But, at the same time, he possesses unyielding strength of character, and when faced with difficulty and challenges, he has the power to persevere. Only by recognizing the extent of our strengths and abilities will we be able to maximize our potential and rise to great heights.

In short: Mankind is empowered with all the forces in creation, so tap into your inner strength of a lion and jump out of bed!

36

Becoming Great at an Old Age

Q ***I know that Rabbi Akiva first started studying Torah at 40, yet grew to become one of the greatest Torah scholars of all time. But I am almost 60, so is there any hope for me to still become great in Torah?***

A It is never too late to achieve greatness! Let me share a real-life account of someone like you, who started studying Torah at your age, yet grew to great heights in Torah.

A father of a student in our yeshivah did not merit receiving a Torah education and did not even know how to read Gemara. But after witnessing his son's growth in Torah, he was inspired to start studying Torah and strive to become a Torah scholar, despite his advanced age.

He joined our yeshivah, and every day he would approach a different student and ask that he teach him a few lines of Gemara. He would write the translation of every word in his Gemara, and then sit down and review it over and over again, until he knew it fluently. He would then call over another boy to test him, until he was sure that he knew it all clearly. He would repeat the process, finding yet another boy to teach him another few lines, and continue doing this all day, every day, until he covered a lot of ground.

This man was diligent, persistent, and stubborn, and after he continued this practice for quite a while, he amassed great amounts of Torah knowledge. Indeed, when he passed away, Rav Moshe Feinstein instructed the family to inscribe on his tombstone that the deceased began to study Torah late in life, yet merited to become very knowledgeable in Torah.

This beautiful story illustrates that no matter when one begins studying Torah, with enough patience, perseverance, and hard work, it is still possible to become a Torah scholar.

Additionally, even if someone is not capable of comprehending the more complex areas of Torah, he can still study the simpler subjects, such as the weekly *parashah* and practical halachah. And even someone incapable of studying Torah can still connect to the greatness of Torah. By providing financial support to Torah scholars and enabling them to devote their time to the study of Torah, benefactors share in the reward of what was learned. Furthermore, in the Next World — where Torah knowledge really counts — the supporters will actually be proficient in the areas of Torah studied by those they supported.

In short: With perseverance, a person can become an accomplished scholar, even if he starts learning at an advanced age. Additionally, by supporting others, he has a share in their Torah.

37

The Power of the Individual

Q ***With so much strife and tragedy in the world, it seems that we need a massive teshuvah movement for the entire Jewish nation to better their ways. Being that I am incapable of changing the world, is there anything "little me" can do, as an individual, that would make a real difference?***

A Of course, it would be most powerful if everyone in the world would change. But never underestimate the power of even one individual, and even if you can't get anyone else to change, "little you" can still change the world! The Talmud (*Kiddushin* 40b) tells us that Hashem judges the world as a whole, and at a time when the world is half-worthy and half-guilty, one person's good deeds can tip the scale for the entire world. Additionally, one person's repentance can invoke a measure of forgiveness for the entire world (*Yoma* 86b).

Furthermore, our Rabbis teach us (*Sanhedrin* 37a) that Hashem created only one person — Adam — to teach us that the entire universe was created for the sake of even one individual. Every person has the ability to change the entire world, and so, in a certain sense, the world was created for that individual. As Rav Shach once commented: "If one tyrant can cause so much destruction, murdering six million Jews, one righteous person can certainly uplift and inspire many more, since the power of good is much greater than the power of evil."

Indeed, many innovations that have changed the Jewish world and that we benefit from today were initiated by individuals. For example, Rav Meir Shapiro introduced the concept of Daf Yomi, a daily study of one page of the Talmud, which has helped thousands of people worldwide complete the entire Talmud every seven years.

Sarah Schenirer created the Bais Yaakov movement to educate Jewish girls, and Rebbetzin Vichna Kaplan established the first advanced Bais Yaakov school in America, resulting in tens of thousands of Jewish women remaining committed to Torah and establishing observant families. In fact, Rav Aharon Kotler credited these women for ensuring the renaissance of Torah in America, for without girls with a true appreciation for Torah, his students would have had no one to marry and with whom to build Torah-true homes.

But this is in no way limited to great leaders. Many organizations and initiatives that have become household names in the Jewish community were started by regular people. Hatzolah, Bikur Cholim, and *chesed* organizations of all sorts, to name a few, have all come about through the efforts of one man or woman who worked hard to bring it to fruition. Many simple individuals are responsible for Torah revolutions across the globe, through study programs they initiated or through the use of technology to disseminate Torah to the masses.

And the change doesn't have to be large-scale; even bettering your shul, your block, or just your own family can uplift the world.

Additionally, we must appreciate the immense power contained in every mitzvah. When a person does a mitzvah here on Earth, we don't see anything significant taking place. But if one would be given the opportunity to take a glimpse at what is transpiring at that moment in the higher spheres, he would observe the powerful effect our actions have in Heaven. Every mitzvah and every word of Torah studied causes an overwhelming reaction in Heaven, and can impact the entire universe.

So no one can say, "Who am I?" as we can never know the true impact one person's actions can have on the universe. One person's *teshuvah* or good deeds may be sparing one person, ten people, or even thousands from tragedy. And even just saving himself or his own family is a great accomplishment.

In short: Even one person can tip the scale for the entire world, and everything we do makes a difference. Every mitzvah causes an overwhelming reaction in Heaven. Many changes in the world were initiated by individuals.

Section 7

Torah Study

38

Does Torah Study Change a Person?

Q ***I heard that studying any area of Torah makes someone a better person. I find that hard to believe! How would learning about some intricate Talmudic topic change a person? Additionally, if Torah study does make someone better, why have I encountered Torah scholars who are not so refined? What happened to them?***

A There are many ways that Torah study makes a person better, and I will mention a few.

First of all, there are lessons to be learned from any area of Torah, even if the messages are not always clearly spelled out. While those messages are more obvious when learning things like *Chumash* or *Pirkei Avos*, one who focuses properly will usually be able to glean life-lessons from almost anything studied.

This point is discussed in the *sefer Maalos HaTorah*, written by Rav Avraham, the brother of the Vilna Gaon. He quotes his illustrious brother, who maintained that although the Talmud (*Makkos* 23a) tells us that there are 613 mitzvos in the Torah, they are just referring to the 613 main categories. In reality, however, every word in the Torah is a mitzvah, and is replete with lessons and insights for us to grow from.

Additionally, toiling over Torah helps a person transcend his animalistic nature. Studying Torah properly requires diligence and exertion to grasp its intricacies, and it requires a person to consider and submit to others' opinions, making a person become more refined.

Furthermore, every word in the Torah emanates from Hashem, Who is the epitome of goodness and holiness. When we study His words, we connect to His greatness and sanctity, and our souls and bodies are uplifted. In addition, the Torah is called *Sefer HaYashar* (The Book of the Straight) because it contains the ultimate truth. Simply studying Torah makes us become upright people — both in mind and in action.

As far as how there can be people who study Torah diligently yet remain unrefined, it is likely that the Torah did improve them. Even if they are still far from perfect, just imagine how much worse they would have been without the impact the Torah had on them!

It's also important to understand that the Torah only refines people who want to become better. If someone wishes to remain unrefined, the Torah won't change him against his will. Although Hashem wants us to follow His lofty path and become refined, we still have freedom of choice, and no one is forced to change.

In short: There are lessons to be learned from any part of Torah. One who studies Hashem's Torah also connects to Him and will be uplifted. Toiling over Torah also helps a person transcend his animalistic nature and become more refined. Torah refines everyone on some level, but only someone who wants to become better.

39

Making Use of My Limited Time for Torah Study

Q ***Between work and helping at home, my day is pretty packed, leaving me with only one hour for Torah study. I have been studying Daf Yomi — two sides of a page of Gemara each day — which is taking the full hour, leaving me no time to study other topics. Should I rather cover less ground and devote some time to other topics?***

A This is reminiscent of a question posed to Rabbi Yisrael Salanter, the founder of the *Mussar* movement — the study of the ethical teachings of the Torah. Someone with limited time for Torah study once asked him if he should use the half hour he had available to study *mussar*, or focus on more fundamental parts of Torah, such as Gemara and *Shulchan Aruch*. Rabbi Salanter famously responded that he should use it to study *mussar*, which will inspire him to reevaluate his priorities, and he will discover that he really has much more than half an hour a day to study Torah. So if you study *mussar* daily, you may find that you have more time for Torah study.

But more importantly, the *Mishnah Berurah* (603:2) quotes the Arizal and the Vilna Gaon, who assert that the study of *mussar* is vital for every G-d fearing Jew, and the only way to ensure we serve Hashem properly. He also rules (1:12) that a person must study *mussar* every day, referencing the Talmud (*Kiddushin* 30b) that Hashem tells the Jewish people, "I created the *yetzer hara* (evil inclination) and I created Torah as the antidote," a reference to the words of *mussar* found in the Torah.

You should also keep in mind that while a husband must certainly help at home, a true *eishes chayil* (woman of valor) will encourage her husband to study Torah as much as he can. Doing so makes her a partner in his Torah, and she shares in the great reward in the World to Come. Thus, if you are truly committed to your Torah study, your wife will hopefully extend herself, and allow you more time to learn.

But if your time is truly limited, it is indeed a good idea to cover less ground each day, such as learning and reviewing an *amud* (one side of a page) a day in 30-40 minutes, instead of a whole daf in an hour. Learning a little slower and reviewing will give you the opportunity to retain the material, making the learning more enjoyable. This schedule will also leave you time each day for studying ten minutes of *mussar* and ten minutes of practical halachah.

Giving yourself time to study halachah daily is extremely important. The Chofetz Chaim (*Mishnah Berurah* 155:3, *Sheim Olam* 7:2) rules that one is obligated to study basic halachic works in order to keep the laws of the Torah properly. He cautions working men who "only" have three or four hours a day to study, not to be satisfied with only the study of Gemara, but to be sure to include the study of halachah. Torah study is not just an academic venture, but a means of learning how to live correctly. As Chazal tell us at the conclusion of Talmud Bavli (*Niddah* 73a), "Whoever studies two laws every day is assured of a place in the World to Come."

You should also make sure to learn *Chumash* and some *Nach* every day, or at least once a week. You are certain to find that the timeless, fiery messages of the prophets will penetrate your heart and mind.

In short: Make time every day for the study of mussar. By doing so you may also realize that you actually have more time for Torah study. Cover less ground each day, and use some of the time to review the material. Set aside time for studying practical halachah, and some Chumash and Nach at least once a week.

40

The Best Place to Study Torah

Q ***I have been learning with my chavrusa (study partner) over the phone or via Zoom, but he recently suggested that we learn in person. I am happy studying from the comfort of my home, which also gives us more time to study, because we don't have to waste time on driving and parking! And if meeting in person is better, should we just meet in one of our homes or in shul? And if we go to a shul, should we choose one with many sefarim (books), or rather one that has more people studying?***

A Learning in person is preferable for many reasons, even if it takes some time to get there. First of all, when each of you is in your own home it is easy to get distracted, but when you are together, you can each make sure the other one is focused and involved.

In addition, facial expressions and body language are valuable tools, as you communicate your message with greater clarity; and as you watch your partner's reactions, you can gauge whether he fully grasps what you are saying.

Furthermore, joy and excitement is integral to Torah study, and the contagious smiles and joyful expressions are missing when you study over the phone. Indeed, when we learned with masks during the coronavirus pandemic, I felt hindered by the inability of my students to see my expressions, and my inability to see theirs.

As far as where to learn, a shul or *beis medrash* is certainly recommended. Firstly, "the comfort of your home" that you mentioned is precisely the reason not to learn at home. When it comes to physical pursuits, results are all that matter, but in spiritual endeavors, the effort itself is part and parcel of the mitzvah. When it comes to Torah study, effort is even more essential, as our Rabbis tell us that the essence of Torah study is toiling over Torah, and is a necessary ingredient for properly comprehending and acquiring.

A *beis medrash* is also a miniature Temple, a place infused with Hashem's Holy Presence and holiness. Studying Hashem's Torah in a place full of spiritual energy will elevate the Torah study to a higher level, helping you learn with more enthusiasm and gain a better understanding of what you are studying.

There is an additional benefit to learning in a *beis medrash* where others are learning. Since any mitzvah performed as a group is more powerful than one done individually, learning in a place where other people are studying will add great spiritual power to your learning. This is particularly true with regard to Torah study, because whenever we study Torah, Hashem is there teaching us His holy word, and the Mishnah (*Avos* 3:7) teaches that the more people learning, the greater the concentration of the Divine Presence.

Choosing between a quieter *beis medrash* with a lot of *sefarim* and one with a larger crowd would depend on where you think you can study better. If your learning will be enhanced by having the benefit of the resources, then go for the place with the *sefarim*. But if the pulse of a vibrant *beis medrash* — where the excitement and vibe are tangible — will keep you energized, that would be the better choice.

In short: Learning in person keeps people focused and allows for facial expressions, which enhance the learning. Leaving the comfort of home is usually recommended, because toil is essential to Torah study. Studying in a beis medrash full of spiritual energy will enhance the learning, and learning in a group setting is much more powerful. Whether to learn where there are more sefarim or where there are more people would depend on each individual's needs.

41

Divine Presence When Studying Over the Phone

We learn in Avos (3:3) that when two people study Torah together, the Shechinah, Divine Presence, joins them. What if someone studies over the phone with a study partner or a TorahMate, does that also invoke the Divine Presence? And if so, to which one of them does Hashem come?

A We must be ever thankful to Hashem for these wonderful modern inventions, enabling us to reach out to and study with others who may not have access to in-person study partners. This kindness especially manifested itself during the coronavirus pandemic lockdowns, when many people were unable to meet in person and technology helped keep the flame of Torah burning.

As far as the Divine Presence joining, in truth, the Mishnah later (*Avos* 3:7) adds that the *Shechinah* joins even a person who is studying on his own. This is true because whenever we study Torah, it is Hashem Who is there with us teaching us His holy word.

So what is special about two people studying? The Mishnah actually mentions other size groups studying together — ten, five, or three — because each one represents a different level of *Shechinah*. The more people learning, the more intense the spiritual level and the greater the degree of Divine Presence.

In fact, my rebbi, Rav Yaakov Yitzchak Ruderman, Rosh Yeshivah of Yeshivah Ner Yisroel in Baltimore, quoted the following fascinating statement from the holy books: When ten Jews are together — even if they are not studying Torah, as long as they are not involved in forbidden activities — the room is infused with so much sanctity that even an angel is unable to enter. And if the ten people are learning Torah, the spiritual energy is exponentially greater.

Similarly, although Hashem is everywhere, there are certain places that are more spiritual and contain a more heightened degree of Divine Presence, such as a shul or a *beis medrash*. This is one reason that one should study and pray in these places whenever possible, because this higher degree of Divine Presence makes the Torah and prayer there much more powerful. The same is true with Eretz Yisrael, the Holy Land, and even more so the Kosel (Western Wall), the last remnant of the Beis HaMikdash (Holy Temple), which was — and continues to be — the source of all sanctity in the world.

Torah study with a partner is certainly on a higher spiritual level, even if the partners are located at two ends of the world. In addition, on a practical level, when people study together — even if not in person — they will usually gain more clarity, and connect to the Torah on a deeper level. Therefore, their Torah study will certainly invoke a greater concentration of Divine Presence.

As far as to where the Divine Presence goes, since Hashem is Omnipresent, He can surely come to both of them no matter where they are.

In short: The greater the number of people learning together, the stronger the concentration of spirituality and the more intense the level of the Divine Presence, even when they are not in the same place.

42

Studying Torah With an Angel

Q ***I heard that some great rabbis in previous generations were taught Torah by angels, while others turned down such opportunities, choosing to work hard for their Torah. How does this apply to me on a practical level? Should I go to a class or learn from an ArtScroll Gemara, which will help me cover more ground, or is it better to work hard figuring out the Gemara on my own, even if that means covering less ground?***

A It is well known that the Beis Yosef, author of the *Shulchan Aruch*, was taught secrets of the Torah by an angel, which he later compiled and published in his *sefer Maggid Meisharim*. On the other hand, Rav Chaim Volozhiner testified that when the Vilna Gaon received such an offer he turned it down, because a person must toil over Torah and not take the easy way out, being spoon-fed words of Torah. Although at first glance these great rabbis seem to disagree about taking shortcuts, perhaps there is a basic difference between the scenarios.

There is no doubt that toil is an essential ingredient of Torah study, as Rashi explains the words, "אִם בְּחֻקֹּתַי תֵּלֵכוּ, If you will follow My decrees" (*Vayikra* 26:3), to mean "that you should engage in intensive Torah study." The only way a person can properly comprehend and acquire Torah is through blood, sweat, and tears. Therefore, when it comes to areas of Torah that are within human reach, a person must do whatever he can to learn and understand them on his own, which is why the Vilna Gaon turned down the angel.

However, there are areas of Torah that are sublime and beyond human comprehension. It is quite possible that this is what the angel would teach the Beis Yosef. In fact, the Vilna Gaon himself would receive Divine revelations while sleeping, and he would then share those teachings with his students. He would say that although these are special gifts from Heaven, they don't compare to Torah that was attained through hard work.

Since toil is so vital to Torah study, it is generally preferable to expend the effort when studying Torah and not take the easy route. Therefore, if you are capable, you should certainly exert yourself, and take the time and effort to learn on your own, as this will make your Torah study much greater, even if you cover less ground.

But a most important consideration is that a person has to enjoy and be excited about his learning. So if you enjoy the challenge of working through the intricate nuances of the Gemara, that is certainly a good option. However, if you find this exertion strenuous and difficult, it is not a good idea, since you may lose your enthusiasm, or even give up learning altogether. In that case, it would be advisable to attend a class, where there is a live person teaching, and perhaps even some lively interaction between the participants, thus enhancing your understanding of the Gemara. If such a class is not available, learning from an ArtScroll Gemara or something similar is certainly a wonderful option.

Acquiring Torah knowledge and studying the entire Talmud is also an important factor, and in some cases that would be a reason to attend a class or use an elucidation that will help you cover more ground.

In general, it is also important to have a rebbi from whom to learn, since Torah must be transmitted from rebbi to student.

In short: One must toil over Torah and not seek shortcuts, but concepts beyond human comprehension can be learned from an angel. If you enjoy working hard to understand Gemara, you should certainly do so. If not, attend a class with live interaction. If that's not possible, a Gemara with commentary and explanations is an option. The need to acquire broad Torah knowledge must also be factored into your decision.

43

Study of Kabbalah

Q ***I always had a great thirst for the mystical dimensions of the world found in Kabbalah, and in fact, it was one of the reasons I became a baal teshuvah. Then I was told that I would have to wait until I am 40 and also finish the entire Talmud! Yet I don't see any older Torah scholars studying Kabbalah either, so was that just an excuse? Why is Kabbalah so strongly discouraged?***

A Before we can discuss the study of Kabbalah, let us first clarify what it is.

Many people have a misconception that Kabbalah is a study of magical powers, giving a person the ability to perform miracles. The true meaning of Kabbalah is the study of the mystical secrets of the Torah, based on the *Maaseh Merkavah,* Divine Chariot, described in the Book of *Yechezkel* and expounded on by the *Zohar* and other kabbalistic sources. For those on the level of understanding it properly, Kabbalah offers a deeper understanding of the methods Hashem uses to run the world.

However, for the simple person, these sublime concepts are beyond comprehension. Trying to study them before mastering the revealed parts of the Torah would be like trying to teach Einstein's theory of relativity before having basic knowledge of arithmetic. It may sound exciting, but it's impossible to properly understand it before one is fluent in all the necessary mathematical concepts. Similarly, one who tries to study Kabbalah without a thorough knowledge of the revealed parts of the Torah is missing the proper background, which could cause confusion, and very possibly a warped understanding of halachah and *hashkafah*, correct Torah view.

For this reason, before delving into these esoteric studies, one must be well-versed in Tanach, Talmud, and *Shulchan Aruch*. Mastering these topics can take a lifetime, and that is why they remain the focus of study for most Torah scholars.

This system of proper Torah study is spelled out by Rambam (*Yesodei HaTorah* 4:13). He writes that before trying to grasp the hidden parts of the Torah, one must first "fill his belly with bread and meat," i.e., be well versed in the revealed parts of the Torah. This refers to studying the laws of the Torah, what is permitted and what is forbidden, something that everyone can study and comprehend. He adds that studying these topics also develops the mind, making it more capable of grasping the abstract concepts of Kabbalah.

Age is also an important factor, as the Mishnah (Avos 5:25) tells us that there is a certain level of understanding that cannot be reached until the age of 40. Therefore, even if someone has already studied much Torah, it is generally assumed that the mind is not capable of fully grasping the lofty concepts of Kabbalah before then.

In addition, only a holy person, who lives on a higher spiritual plane and is close to Hashem, is allowed access to these Divine secrets, and anyone not on that level has no right to delve into them. Just as the president will only disclose top-secret information to his cabinet and close advisors, as such highly confidential information is not meant for the public, Hashem will share His secrets only with those who are close to Him and worthy of this profound knowledge. That is another reason why many Torah scholars shy away from the study of Kabbalah, out of fear that they may not be on the elevated spiritual level necessary for its study.

In short: Kabbalah is the study of the mystical secrets of the Torah and of the methods Hashem uses to run the world. It is only for the elite few, who are well versed in all the revealed Torah and on a lofty level of piety, not for simple laymen.

44

What Is So Significant About a New Torah Scroll?

Q ***I recently attended a Hachnasas Sefer Torah — the celebration upon the completion of a new Torah Scroll — and the dancing was as lively as a wedding! Being that we already have many Torah Scrolls, I couldn't help but wonder why this is such a joyous occasion.***

A Even if you already have many Torah Scrolls, something very extraordinary takes place with the completion of each and every new one. Torah is the very purpose of creation and the lifeblood of every Jew, and is called the "Fiery Law" (*Devarim* 33:2). Just as fire brings warmth and light to its surroundings, Torah infuses our dark, cold world with an abundance of spiritual warmth and light. Since the Sefer Torah is the embodiment of the Torah, each new Torah Scroll brings untold holiness and blessing to the world.

In addition, the relationship between Hashem and the Jewish nation is compared to that of a bride and groom, a connection forged through the Torah, Hashem's wisdom. Hashem and His Torah are like one, so every Torah scroll brings more of the Divine Presence to the world. Furthermore, the holy books tell us that every Jewish soul is linked to a letter in the Torah. With each new Torah, our connection to our Groom and His Torah is strengthened, and we therefore celebrate this occasion with the fanfare of a wedding.

But in truth, every Torah Scroll contains far more spirituality than we can perceive, so there is much more that we celebrate. Rashi writes that the "Fiery Law" refers to the Torah that was in Heaven, in a lofty spiritual dimension, long before it was given on Mount Sinai.

That Torah was "black fire on white fire," alluding to the two components of Torah — the Written Torah and the Oral Torah — and is the reason a physical Sefer Torah must be written in black ink on white parchment. The words of the Torah are written in black, with very specific rules regarding the writing of each letter. This represents the Written Torah and all its mitzvos, which have precise rules and regulations, and cannot be changed even one iota. The parchment of a Torah Scroll is white, and appears deeper than the black letters, symbolizing the Oral Torah, which expands extensively on the written words, and is much deeper than the written Torah.

Furthermore, halachah dictates that each letter be surrounded on all sides by empty parchment, that every line must have spaces before, after, on top, and under it, and there must also be margins on all sides. This indicates the great depth and breadth contained in every word and even every letter of the Torah. We must strive to uncover the precious gems that are "between the lines" and beneath the surface. Indeed, the Vilna Gaon would demonstrate how every law in the Talmud is alluded to in the Written Torah. Thus, every Sefer Torah contains the endless wisdom in Hashem's Torah — both the Written and the Oral Torah — and we rejoice upon the arrival of this spiritual treasure.

But the true celebration doesn't end once the Torah is inducted into the shul. Every time we read from the Torah Scroll, we connect to His Torah on a deeper level, and our souls are reignited. We may not feel this spiritual surge because of our physical limitations, but one who studies Torah diligently will sometimes feel some of this spiritual energy, and in the Next World we will all feel it.

In short: A Torah Scroll contains Hashem's wisdom and is a spiritual fire, bringing us great spiritual warmth and light, and intensifies the Divine Presence in this world. It also strengthens our connection to Hashem — our Groom — and it is therefore celebrated with the joy of a wedding.

Section 8

Prayer

45

Using a Phone During Davening

Q ***Is there anything wrong with praying from a smartphone instead of a siddur? On a similar note, is it appropriate to take out my phone to learn Torah while I am waiting around for the chazzan to continue the service?***

A I don't think a phone belongs in shul at all.

Since prayer is the "service of the heart," it requires *kavanah* (concentration), and we must do whatever we can to maximize our ability to concentrate properly. In fact, there are many laws in *Shulchan Aruch* intended to minimize distractions during davening (prayer). Even before there were cell phones, we had enough distractions that made it extremely difficult for us to concentrate properly. Having a phone in one's hand — or even in one's pocket — is certainly a distraction. Feeling the phone vibrate or taking a quick glance to check for missed calls or messages are just some examples of how a phone detracts from our focus as we speak to Hashem. That's why having cubbies outside the shul for people to leave their phones in is a wonderful idea.

Even if one can use his phone in a way that it won't cause any distractions, praying from a siddur is still preferable. We try to maximize the potency of our prayers. We are taught that when a person davens with a pure mind and mouth it adds sanctity to his prayers and brings them to a higher level, making them more accepted by Hashem. The same is true for davening in a shul because of the holiness that permeates the shul.

Similarly, a siddur has a special holiness because the Name of Hashem and the words of the davening are printed permanently on the page. Davening from a siddur infuses one's prayers with an extra dose of holiness. A phone — even if it contains the entire Torah — does not have any holiness, since the words merely flash on the screen temporarily.

Pulling out a phone in the middle of davening is also not advisable. Phones are generally used for business or pleasure purposes, and people may not realize that you are using it for the right reason. This is known as *maris ayin*, doing something that appears to be wrong — even if it is really appropriate — and is therefore forbidden. Additionally, when people see you looking at your phone during davening they may follow your example, using their phones, but for something inappropriate during davening.

Of course, if one doesn't have a siddur handy, it would be okay to use his phone instead.

As far as having something to do while waiting, I suggest you plan ahead. By having a good *sefer* available next to you, you will have what to do as you wait for the chazzan to resume the prayers.

In short: One should daven from a siddur, if possible. In general, a phone should not be used at all during davening, even for studying Torah, since people may get the wrong message and there are other ways one can study.

46

Praying for Things Hashem Didn't Give Us

Q ***We believe that Hashem can and does provide us with all our needs, and every situation a person finds himself in was tailor-made for him by Hashem. If so, how can someone pray for something he lacks, such as health or livelihood, if Hashem, in His infinite wisdom, determined that he shouldn't have it?***

A This is an excellent question, and the answer requires a better understanding of how *tefillah* (prayer) works. When a person lacks something, it does not mean that Hashem wants him not to have it. Hashem is the epitome of good, and wants to shower us with goodness. But in order to be able to receive this goodness, we need to have a close relationship with Hashem, the Source of all blessing. When a person is distant from Hashem, he is removed from the source of blessing and his ability to benefit from His goodness is diminished.

Prayer is the vehicle that brings us closer to Hashem. Prayer is not merely an opportunity to approach Hashem with a list of our requests. It is primarily a means of internalizing the belief that Hashem is the only one Who can help us, thereby making us worthy of having our prayers answered. When we turn to Hashem for help, we affirm this belief. For this reason, the *Shemoneh Esrei* prayer begins with praises of Hashem, to help us reinforce our recognition that He alone is the address to turn to.

When a person prays for his needs, he is not asking Hashem to change His will. Rather, he is reinforcing his connection to Hashem, making him worthy of receiving the blessings that Hashem always wanted to bestow on him. In fact, there is actually a mitzvah to pray, because Hashem wants us to turn to Him in our time of need, and the very purpose of the person's troubles may be to arouse him to reconnect to Hashem.

Another perspective into why we may pray for what we lack is that troubles are often Heaven-sent punishments for sins. Through physical pain and suffering, a person becomes more spiritual, which helps atone for his sins. When he prays, he achieves that very holiness and heightened spiritual level, eliminating the need for his suffering. Since he no longer needs to suffer, his situation can now improve.

We should keep in mind that prayer is a great mitzvah as well as a practical expression of numerous other mitzvos, such as *emunah,* belief in Hashem and Divine Providence; and *bitachon,* implicitly trusting Hashem. Thus, prayer has the power to elevate a person and bring him to a much higher spiritual level.

In truth, every mitzvah has the power to make a person more spiritual, and the most potent mitzvah of all is Torah study, which is why the Talmud (*Eruvin* 54a) recommends Torah study as the remedy for any pain or illness. A strong dose of the Torah's greatness and spirituality raises a person greatly, enabling him to transcend his troublesome situation and reach a new level of existence, one that is more worthy of Heavenly blessings.

In short: Turning to Hashem in prayer expresses our belief that we are in His hands. This brings us much closer to Hashem, the Source of all blessing, and makes us worthy of receiving His goodness. In addition, prayer — or any mitzvah — elevates a person spiritually, removing his need to suffer.

47

Praying With Tears

Q *I have heard that the "Gates of Prayer with tears" in Heaven are never closed. What is so powerful about tears? Additionally, I'm not an emotional person and don't cry when I pray, so does that mean that my prayers will not be answered?*

A Tears are exceedingly powerful. Our Sages tell us (*Bava Metzia* 59a) that although the "Gates of Prayer" were closed when the Beis HaMikdash (Holy Temple) was destroyed, the "Gates of Tears" remained open. Similarly, Rashi (*Bereishis* 29:17) writes that Leah had initially been destined to marry Eisav, but through tearful prayer she was able to have the decree annulled, and merited marrying Yaakov and bringing six of the twelve tribes into the world.

But what is so special about tears? The Talmud (*Taanis* 2a) teaches that prayer is a service of the heart. This means that prayer is not merely reciting the words, nor is it just a mental exercise recognizing and acknowledging the power of Hashem. True prayer must include emotion that resonates within the heart. When a person prays with feeling, fully aware that he is standing before the King of all kings and that He alone provides him with his needs, it is human nature to become emotional and even cry. Such heartfelt prayer brings a person closer to Hashem, making him or her truly worthy of having their prayers answered.

But this does not mean that genuine, heartfelt prayer recited without tears will go unanswered. As the commentators explain, it is not the physical tears that accomplish; it is the sincerity and heartfelt emotion of the prayer — which generally arouse the person to tears — that invoke Heavenly mercy. To illustrate this point, we can refer to a famous question: If the "Gates of Tears" are never closed, why are there gates in the first place? The answer is that the gates are closed to keep out insincere tears. Tears that are not the result of a person truly beseeching Hashem for mercy will not achieve the desired result. So as long as one prays with true feeling and the emotion appropriate for his or her personality, his or her prayers will be answered, whether or not they are accompanied by actual tears.

With this background, we can appreciate something my rebbi, Rav Yaakov Yitzchok Ruderman, Rosh Yeshivah of Yeshivah Ner Yisroel, once told me. He and the Mashgiach, Rav Dovid Kronglas, were once discussing some former students, and they noticed an intriguing phenomenon. Many students who did not seem to have a promising future went on to become great, while many students who seemed destined for greatness never realized their potential. One of the factors they pointed to was the power of prayer that can truly change the trajectory of a person's life.

Although the weaker students were really not blessed with the capabilities needed to achieve greatness, through sincere prayer they were able to achieve much more than they were originally capable of. On the other hand, students who may have had inborn qualities and an inherent potential for greatness tended to rely on their talents to achieve greatness, and failed to sincerely pray for Heavenly assistance to succeed, thereby forfeiting their ability to attain these levels.

In short: When someone truly pours his heart out to Hashem, it is natural to cry, but it is not the tears per se that are answered. Any prayer recited with feeling and emotion that is appropriate for each person's personality is answered.

48

Should I Ever Stop Davening?

Q ***I have been praying very hard for something for a long time without results, and it seems that Hashem is not willing to grant my request! Even Moshe eventually stopped requesting entry to Israel when he realized his prayers wouldn't be answered. Should I also stop praying?***

A You should never stop praying! There is no limit to the amount of times one can ask Hashem for something. Even if you prayed for something many times and were not answered, that doesn't mean that you will never be answered. King David tells us (*Tehillim* 105:4), "Seek out His face constantly," and the Talmud (*Berachos* 32b) teaches that if one's prayers went unanswered, he should pray again. It is possible that Hashem wants one more heartfelt prayer from you, which will make the final breakthrough.

Even the great Moshe's prayers were not always answered immediately. When the Jewish nation sinned by worshiping the Golden Calf, Moshe beseeched Hashem for their forgiveness. He prayed for forty days and nights until his request was finally granted. Imagine the tragedy if he would have given up after a week or even thirty-nine and a half days of intense prayer! He knew the secret of prayer's effectiveness, and he persevered until they were granted forgiveness.

Although Moshe stopped praying to enter the Land of Israel, that was an exception to the rule. In that case, Hashem had a specific reason why his request could not be granted and asked him to stop.

Even if Hashem, in His infinite wisdom, doesn't grant your specific request — because it may not be good for you or for whatever reason — no prayer goes to waste. At times, Hashem stores our prayers or tears in His special storehouse, and pulls them out when they are needed. This can happen years — or even generations — later.

The Chazon Ish once explained the phenomenon of the baal *teshuvah* movement that began in his days, shortly after World War II. He pointed out that as some Jews started drifting away from Judaism, their parents and grandparents cried out to Hashem to save them. Even though these souls unfortunately went astray, the prayers were not lost. Decades later, Hashem took out those tearful prayers, and used them to ignite a spark of *teshuvah* (repentance) in their descendants.

In addition, even if we don't receive what we asked for, prayer is never a waste a time. Our davening is not just an opportunity to ask G-d to grant our requests. Every heartfelt prayer is an end unto itself, expressing our firm belief that Hashem is in control, and that He is the only place to turn to for all our needs. Through this, we are performing some of the basic mitzvos of the Torah. Hashem derives great pleasure from seeing us turn to Him, and this brings us closer to Him, for which we will be greatly rewarded.

In short: Never stop praying! One more heartfelt prayer can be a breakthrough, or may be put to use at a later time. In addition, prayer expresses our belief that Hashem is the One to turn to for all our needs, and brings us close to Him.

49

Should I Pray for Someone Who Is Deathly Ill?

Q ***Someone I know is deathly ill, and the doctors give him no chance of recovering. Should we still pray for his recovery, or should we just accept the situation and pray that he pass on without too much pain?***

A We must never give up hope! No matter how grim the situation may seem, things can turn around at any moment, and many people have lived for many healthy and productive years long after medical professionals had given up on them. Although Hashem gives doctors permission to heal, they do not have the power to write a person off. As our Rabbis teach (*Berachos* 10a), "Even if a sharp sword is against a person's neck he should not cease to beseech Hashem for mercy." There may be a discovery of a new medicine or a mistaken diagnosis.

Rav Moshe Feinstein once applied this to a situation similar to yours. A woman was racked with cancer from head to toe, and the family asked me to ask Rav Moshe if they should continue to pray for her recovery. Rav Moshe responded that he personally knew of people alive and well many years after receiving such a prognosis, so they should never stop praying. At the same time, he added, one is permitted to pray that the patient should experience only minimal pain, but not to mention death, because we don't "open our mouths to [arouse] Satan."

Even some doctors realize the power of our prayers. I once heard about a group of doctors who were discussing statistics of patients with various illnesses and diseases. One of the doctors proclaimed, "Don't bring data from Jewish patients into this discussion! They are a category of their own, as time and time again I have seen them defy doctors' predictions and prognoses through the power of their prayers."

I heard a story about this from a rabbi I know, who, unfortunately, had to spend a lot of time in the hospital tending to his sick child, and with time, he became somewhat friendly with the doctors.

While he was there, a non-Jewish baby was born with a condition that made it impossible for him to urinate. The mother came crying to the rabbi, telling him that the doctors told her there was nothing they could do, but suggested she ask the rabbi to see if he could help. He told the woman, "Pray, but be sure to pray to the right G-d — Hashem, the G-d of the Jews! He is the one and only G-d, Who controls the entire universe, and only He can help your child."

The woman fell to the floor, crying her heart out to Hashem, begging Him for mercy, and merely a few hours later, the baby had the first wet diaper of his life!

Just this past year, a student of mine was in a terrible accident, and was told by top doctors that he will never be able to walk again. Well, not only is he walking, he is actually dancing, shocking the doctors beyond belief!

A rabbi I know was in a coma for four months due to Covid, with the doctors giving up on him a few times, and he is now alive and well.

So even if it looks like the end is near, we must pray with all our hearts. And even if our prayers don't save the person's life, they may at least prolong his life or ease the situation in some way. As Jews, we know that every minute of life in this world is extremely precious, an opportunity to perform mitzvos or complete our mission in this world in some way, thereby bringing more honor to Hashem.

In short: We must continue to pray with all our heart, and never give up hope, as things can turn around at any moment. The prayers may also prolong a person's life or help ease his situation.

Section 9
Mitzvos

Mitzvos Bein Adam LaMakom

50

Tefillin Questions

Q ***I am excited to wear my brand-new pair of tefillin, graciously sponsored by Oorah after I committed to wearing them daily. I have several questions: I know they are considered very holy, but to me they just look like plain black boxes. I was also wondering why there are hairs sticking out of the box. And if tefillin are so special, why don't we wear them on Shabbos and Yom Tov?***

A In this case, you have to think "in the box"! Although there are many laws that apply to the boxes, what makes tefillin holy is primarily not the box, but what's inside — scrolls with four fundamental portions of the Torah written on them. The first two portions talk about how Hashem miraculously redeemed us from bondage in Egypt and thereby acquired us as His nation and servants. The other two are the first two portions of *Shema* that we recite every morning and night, which contain the fundamentals of our faith: the declaration that Hashem is the One and only G-d Who controls the entire universe, that we accept Him as our King, and that we commit to fulfill all His mitzvos.

Wearing tefillin, containing these portions of the Torah, helps us internalize these fundamental concepts. Placing them on the arm — and specifically on the muscle — reminds us that Hashem redeemed us with His "outstretched arm," and all that we accomplish with our hands is from Hashem Who gives us strength, not our muscles and arms. Placing them near the heart shows that we are submitting all our feelings and desires to Hashem. By wearing them by our brain, we are subjugating our intellect — both our thoughts and our actions that are controlled by the brain — to G-d's will.

Thinking about these ideas when donning tefillin is not just a virtuous practice, but actually a requirement spelled out in *Shulchan Aruch* (*Orach Chaim* 25:4). Even the word "*totafos*," used in the Torah for tefillin, carries this message. As Rashi (*Shemos* 13:16) explains, "*totafos*" is an expression of speech, because seeing tefillin reminds us of Hashem's miracles, and inspires us to discuss them. Indeed, many people recite the prayer printed in the siddur prior to donning tefillin, which spells out all these concepts. However, this should not be mere lip service, but a means of truly thinking about these concepts while wearing tefillin.

The hairs you mentioned customarily come from a calf, and are tied around the parchments that contain these words of the Torah, to remind us of and to atone for the sin of the Golden Calf. Since through the mitzvah of tefillin we are internalizing our belief that Hashem runs the world, we can atone for the lack of belief in Hashem displayed when we worshiped the Golden Calf.

We don't wear tefillin on Shabbos or Yom Tov because the very essence of these days is acknowledging that Hashem is the Master of the world and is the greatest submission to G-d's will, negating the need for any other reminder. This is a central theme emphasized throughout Shabbos and Festivals. By refraining from work, we affirm that it is not we who accomplish anything in this world — it is all Hashem. The expanded morning *Pesukei D'Zimrah* and *berachos* before *Shema* describe at length the wonders of Hashem's creation. And we begin the festive meals with Kiddush, where we acknowledge that Hashem is the Creator of the universe and chose the Jewish nation with love.

In short: Tefillin contain scrolls that describe the miracles Hashem performed when we left Egypt, and our acceptance of His reign and His mitzvos. By wearing them, we subjugate our hearts and minds to Hashem's will. This helps atone for the sin of the Golden Calf, represented by the calf hairs. Since Shabbos and Yom Tov are themselves proclamations that Hashem created and runs the world, tefillin are unnecessary.

51

The Mystical Power of a Mikveh

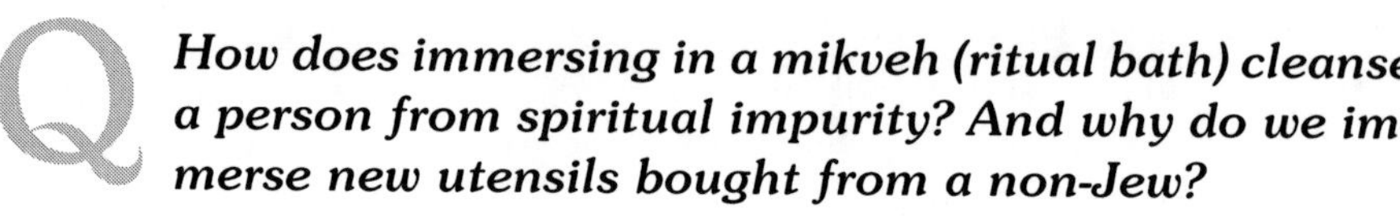

Q ***How does immersing in a mikveh (ritual bath) cleanse a person from spiritual impurity? And why do we immerse new utensils bought from a non-Jew?***

A In order to appreciate the mechanics of a *mikveh*, it is important to step back and take a look at the source of impurity. We will then understand what this immersion is meant to accomplish.

All spiritual impurity is a result of sin and the contamination of this world. As the holy books write, when Adam and Chava ate from the Tree of Knowledge, their sin brought great contamination to humanity, as well as to this entire universe.

This sin also brought death to the world, which is a primary source of *tumah* (spiritual impurity), for a corpse contaminates anyone or anything that comes in contact with it — or even comes under the same roof. Similarly, *tzaraas* (a leprosy-like disease) is inflicted on someone who speaks *lashon hara* (gossip) or related sins. Other impurities also stem from, or are related to, sin and physicality, although a comprehensive discussion of the topic is beyond the scope of this work.

Because the root cause of impurity is antithetical to sanctity and purity, one who is impure has no place in the Beis HaMikdash, the source of all holiness in this world, and he is thus forbidden to enter there. We find (*Esther* 4:2) that Mordechai found it disgraceful to enter the king's palace in sackcloth, so one must certainly not enter Hashem's home with an impure soul, for this would be a disgrace to the King of kings.

With this understanding of *tumah*, we can begin to appreciate the purification process of a *mikveh*. Since human beings cannot survive in water, a body of water is considered a world unto itself. By completely immersing oneself in water — down to the last hair — a person is removing himself from the evil and impurities of this world. After undergoing this process, he is ready to return to this world, clean and pure.

Immersing new utensils can also be understood along these lines. A utensil bought from a non-Jew needs to undergo a transformation from non-Jewish to Jewish ownership. This is similar to a convert, who must immerse in a *mikveh* as part of the conversion process, in order to become a "new person." Immersion in water removes the convert or utensil from this world, subsequently returning renewed and transformed.

Indeed, even the slightest obstruction preventing the water from reaching every part of the body or utensil invalidates the immersion, because true purification and renewal can be attained only with total detachment from this world. Similarly, the *Sefer HaChinuch* states that this physical cleansing is intended to arouse a person to reflect on his spiritual status, and to refresh and rejuvenate himself, ready to serve Hashem with renewed vigor.

In short: Since humanity cannot survive in water, total immersion in water is a way of removing the person or utensil from the evil and impurities of this world, allowing him to return new and pure. It also arouses a person to rejuvenate spiritually.

52

How Does an Offering Bring Someone Close to Hashem?

Q ***In Sefer Vayikra, we read a lot about the various korbanos (offerings), a topic I don't find to be very relevant in our times. Yet, I have heard that the word "korban" in Hebrew is actually derived from the root kareiv, which means to come close. How does sacrificing animals bring one close to Hashem?***

A It is beyond the scope of these few lines to give a comprehensive explanation of the profound meanings and concepts behind the *korbanos* (offerings), but we can discuss some of the basic ideas involved.

Offerings are a very powerful way to connect with Hashem. In fact, we can tap into their power even today, because our Sages teach that reciting and studying the Torah portions and laws of the *korbanos* is equivalent to actually offering a *korban*.

Korbanos are fundamentally different from the sacrifices offered by idol worshipers. Pagan philosophy held that the gods enjoyed the gift of the sacrifices, and would reciprocate in kind, showering blessings upon the ones who offered them. This is obviously not the case with *korbanos*, because Hashem is the epitome of perfection and completely self-sufficient. He has no need of our service in any way, shape, or form. The sole purpose of every mitzvah — including *korbanos* — is for our benefit, to help bring us closer to Hashem, the very purpose of why He created us.

Every person is comprised of a body and a soul. The real person is the soul, whereas the body is just the "clothing" of the soul, and when a person dies, only this outer layer is laid to rest, while the real person lives on in the World of Souls.

The body is earthly and made up of animalistic characteristics, which pull us toward physicality — the pursuit of materialistic pleasures, stinginess, laziness, and arrogance. Our mission in this world is to take control of our inborn animalistic characteristics and channel them into spirituality, by using every part of our body to serve Hashem. Indeed, every mitzvah infuses us with spirituality, as we recite in the blessing before performing a mitzvah, "*asher kideshanu b'mitzvosav* — Who sanctified us with His commandments."

Offerings contain an even greater focus on spirituality. By slaughtering and sacrificing an animal, we show that we want to slaughter and subdue the animalistic traits that pull us away from Hashem, and we choose to have our intellect take control of our desires. In addition, each *korban* has its specific message. For example, when we read about the *olah*-offering, which is completely burned on the Altar, we should be inspired to destroy our animalistic desires. The *shelamim*-offering, which has parts that are eaten by the Kohanim and the owner, represents partaking of this world for the sake of Heaven. Similarly, the *nesachim* (libations) of wine and oil demonstrate that even physical pleasures are to be channeled toward the service of Hashem.

These concepts are relevant today more than ever, as much of society is unfortunately preoccupied with the exact opposite — using their intelligence to pursue material pleasure. Indeed, every time we control our desires and subdue our animalistic traits for the sake of Hashem, we are offering a true sacrifice, connecting to Him for eternity.

In short: Korbanos help us connect to Hashem. This is true even today, because reciting the Torah portions about korbanos serves as a reminder to subdue our animalistic traits and devote all our abilities to serve Hashem.

53

Shemittah Only in the Holy Land

Q ***Why is Shemittah (the Sabbatical year) only observed in Israel? In addition, I have received many requests from different organizations asking for financial support for Shemittah-observant farmers. Since the Torah clearly promises a bumper crop for those who observe Shemittah, why would they need my help?***

A The greater a person is, the more Hashem expects from him. For this reason, certain members of the Jewish nation have more mitzvos than others, depending on their spiritual level. For example, when the Holy Temple stood, the Jewish people were on a higher spiritual level, and many more mitzvos applied. Kohanim are imbued with extra holiness even today, and they therefore were given more mitzvos than the rest of us.

The same concept can be applied to Shemittah. One of the reasons for this mitzvah is to give the farmers time off to focus on spiritual endeavors and come closer to Hashem, just like our weekly observance of Shabbos. People who live in the Land of Israel live on a higher plane than those living in the Diaspora and are therefore more worthy of this unique opportunity to come closer to Hashem. Indeed, there are many mitzvos that apply only in the Land of Israel, and missing out on all these opportunities is a great loss for those living in the Diaspora.

As far as helping these farmers, it is definitely a great form of charity. If all the farmers would keep the laws of Shemittah there would certainly be bumper crops, as promised in the Torah. The problem is that there are those who don't put their trust in Hashem that that is what is going to happen, and they are afraid that if they don't plow and plant they won't have what to eat. So they plow and plant, and since all Jews are connected, this makes it difficult for everyone else. That's why Hashem's promise of a bumper crop did not and does not happen. Not to mention that your financial assistance may be the very method Hashem is using to fulfill His promise to provide for the farmers.

Additionally, supporting these farmers is for your benefit. It provides you with an opportunity to partner in this mitzvah even though you don't own land in the Land of Israel and are incapable of observing Shemittah. A similar concept is found in the Talmud (*Bava Basra* 10a) with regard to charity. The Roman general Turnus Rufus asked Rabbi Akiva, "If your G-d wanted the needs of the poor to be taken care of, why didn't He provide for them Himself?" Rabbi Akiva responded that He made them needy for our benefit, in order to give us the opportunity to provide for their needs and thereby merit a share in the World to Come.

There are also times when Hashem does miraculously provide for the heroic farmers who strictly follow the laws of Shemittah, a phenomenon I witnessed first-hand on a trip to Israel during the recent Shemittah. We went to visit a settlement where the laws of Shemittah were being observed and a farmer proudly showed us his barren fields. He then pointed to some wild grass that had miraculously grown on the barren Shemittah land, which he declared was Heaven-sent to provide food for his cattle. Although his usual source of income was missing, Hashem had sent him grass to feed his animals, thereby helping him recoup some of his losses.

In short: Shemittah is an opportunity to come closer to Hashem, exclusive to those living in the Holy Land. Since Hashem doesn't usually perform open miracles, we must pitch in to help the farmers, which also provides us an opportunity to connect to this mitzvah.

Interpersonal Mitzvos

54

Why Is There a Need for Logical Mitzvos?

Q ***Many mitzvos seem so basic and should be self-understood. For example, any decent person understands that it is wrong to murder or steal. Why is there a need for the Torah to command us about things so obvious?***

A The key to the answer lies in the very words of your question.

Yes, there are many mitzvos that seem logical and we may have performed them even without being commanded to do so. But that is not why we do mitzvos. We do mitzvos because Hashem told us to, whether we understand them or not. Fulfilling the will of Hashem is our purpose in the world, and even when we keep mitzvos that are logical, we do so because that is the will of Hashem.

In addition, even if it is logical to be nice to others, and certainly not acceptable to hurt others in any way, we cannot be sure that we will always act properly. We find this concept in the Torah, when Avraham arrived in Gerar and, out of fear for his life, denied that he was Sarah's husband. When King Avimelech discovered that she was actually Avraham's wife, he confronted Avraham, asking him why he had lied to him. Avraham responded that this land had no *yiras Shamayim,* fear of Heaven.

As the commentators point out, he was telling Avimelech that although their society appeared refined and civilized, since this was not rooted in fear of Heaven, they could not be trusted. Without fear of Hashem, the finest "gentlemen" can commit the greatest atrocities, as indeed transpired during the Holocaust. When people are gripped by a burning desire or hatred, they can come up with philosophies and excuses to justify anything.

Additionally, even if certain mitzvos may seem logical, every mitzvah has many subcategories, some of which are not so obvious. For example, our Rabbis (*Berachos* 43b) tell us that embarrassing another person is akin to murder, which is why Tamar was willing to be burned at the stake rather than shaming Yehudah publicly (*Bereishis* 38:25). Similarly, the Talmud (*Bava Kamma* 119a) says that stealing even a very small amount is like taking a person's life, because it can cause a poor person to lack his basic needs and eventually lead to his death.

The Torah's command against stealing also has many subcategories that are not so obvious, such as making noise that prevents someone from sleeping, or failing to ensure that one's animal doesn't cause damage to other people's property.

These subcategories and many others are all included in the mitzvos of the Torah, and had Hashem not given us these commandments we would not have thought of them on our own.

In short: We must perform mitzvos because Hashem told us to do so, not because they are logical. Additionally, without Hashem's command, we cannot be sure that a person will always act properly. There are also many subcategories included in these mitzvos that are not obvious.

55

What's so Great About Giving Charity?

Q ***Rambam (Matnos Aniyim 10:1) writes that one should be extremely vigilant when it comes to the mitzvah of tzedakah (charity), even more than with any other mitzvah. He adds that one who gives to others is a true tzaddik, an indication that he is following in the footsteps of our forefather Avraham, and that charity is the key to the ultimate redemption. What is so significant about giving someone some money?***

A Before exploring the greatness of charity, let me add another, related question: When Hashem told Noach that the people of his generation were wicked and they were going to be destroyed by the Great Flood, He mentioned that their fate was sealed specifically because they were stealing from each other. What is so terrible about theft that it would be the "nail in the coffin," bringing an end to civilization?

The answer to both these questions is that giving is the very essence and purpose of creation. Hashem doesn't need anything from us, so when He created the world, it was not for us to give to Him, but for the sole purpose of benefiting His creations. Because He is the ultimate Giver, He created a world where He would constantly provide His creations with everything and anything, culminating in His ultimate benevolence — the World to Come, where we will merit to bask in His presence.

Thus, giving to others is emulating the way of Hashem, and through this we connect with Him and make ourselves worthy of eternal reward. This is why giving charity and performing acts of kindness are the very purpose of creation, as the *pasuk* states (*Tehillim* 89:3), "עוֹלָם חֶסֶד יִבָּנֶה — The world was created for kindness." Indeed, the

Chofetz Chaim writes that one should not let a day go by without doing at least one thing for others.

On the opposite end of the spectrum is theft, which is the antithesis of the purpose of creation. When a person steals, he is unjustly taking that which belongs to others — undermining the very foundation of creation.

This is what happened at the time of the Flood. Although they had been doing many wicked things, theft is what deemed the world unworthy to continue to exist.

With this perspective, we can better understand a seemingly puzzling action taken by Avraham Avinu. In the beginning of *Parashas Vayeira*, as he was recuperating from his *bris milah* (circumcision), Avraham received a very special guest: Hashem Himself. Yet, while basking in the Divine Presence, he noticed three wayfarers whom he assumed to be Arabs, so he excused himself from the Almighty in order to take care of them. How could Avraham possibly walk away from Hashem to go feed some simple travelers?

The answer is that Avraham understood that although conversing with Hashem is a very great spiritual experience, doing for others is emulating Hashem, and will bring a person much closer to Him and to much greater spiritual heights. Indeed, our Sages explain (*Shabbos* 127a) that the episode of Avraham teaches that hosting guests is even greater than greeting the Divine Presence, because the host is actually fulfilling the very purpose of creation.

In short: By giving to others one is emulating Hashem, fulfilling the very purpose of creation and bringing him close to Hashem, making him worthy of eternal reward.

56

Charity Priorities

Q ***I am constantly bombarded with requests for charity from so many worthy causes — in person, in the mail, or via text and email! I am by no means a rich man, so how do I divide my limited funds, and which causes should I prioritize?***

A Of course, it would be ideal to give a generous amount to each cause. But for the average person who has a limited amount of funds available to donate to charity, this is usually not feasible. While some try to respond to each request with a small donation, others feel that doesn't really accomplish much and prefer to give larger amounts to fewer causes, thereby making "a difference." But which ones should be on the top of the short list?

The *Shulchan Aruch* (*Yoreh De'ah* 251-252) discusses the guidelines as to who comes first. Without going into all the details, here are some of the causes that are more worthy and therefore take precedence:

First and foremost, a collection to help save the life of someone in danger — such as a person in need of a life-saving surgery — takes precedence over all other causes, as saving a fellow Jew's life overrides all other mitzvos. Additionally, if a needy person approaches you personally, you cannot turn him away empty-handed, and you must give him something, even if it is a minimal amount. A close relative, followed by the needy of your own city — or organizations that supply locals with basic needs — also come ahead of other causes.

As far as responding to requests beyond those categories, the primary consideration should be supporting Torah study. As the Chofetz Chaim (*Ahavas Chesed* II:19) explains, aiding needy Torah scholars and Torah study is among the highest levels of charity, and comes before most other causes. Since Torah study is the greatest mitzvah, supporting Torah takes precedence over providing financial support for other mitzvos. Furthermore, without Torah study the world would cease to exist, so by supporting the study of Torah, you have a share in keeping the world going.

Moreover, as the *Nefesh HaChaim* discusses at great length, Hashem runs the world based on our actions, and the mitzvos we do provide the spiritual energy for His blessings to reach the world. Since Torah study is the greatest mitzvah, it produces the most spiritual energy and generates an abundance of blessing in all areas of life. This means that when you give money to support Torah study, you are also helping all worthy causes, by bringing the blessing that helps the needy with their financial needs, the sick to merit a recovery, those in search of a marriage partner to find one, etc.

To help bring out this point, I like to quote one of the directors of a camp for seriously ill children. At the beginning of each summer season, he tells me, "Please do a good job teaching Torah to the children in your camp. The Torah they learn will surely bring an abundance of blessing to the world, which will help heal sick children and alleviate the need for them to come to our camp."

In short: Charity to save a life takes precedence. If a needy person himself requests help, you must give him something. Close relatives or the needy of your city have priority over others. Supporting Torah comes before most other causes, because Torah study is the greatest mitzvah, and because supporting Torah is in essence helping all other causes, as Torah study brings an abundance of Heavenly blessing.

57

Kidney Donation

Q ***I am always looking for ways to help others, and lately I have been hearing about people who have donated a kidney to help save the life of someone with renal failure. Is this something I should explore, or perhaps I should be concerned about going under the knife, or other health concerns? And if I do donate, is there any preference to whom?***

A Giving away of oneself — literally — to save someone's life is a wonderful display of benevolence and a fantastic mitzvah. At the same time, you cannot put yourself in danger to help others. So you can only do this if your health is up to par and your doctors are confident that this will not adversely affect your health in any way.

Additionally, such a great act of selflessness cannot be performed at the expense of others. Therefore, it is only appropriate if the donor is fully comfortable and confident with this monumental decision, and it is preferable that he or she receive the permission and support of his or her spouse and parents.

Saving a life is a very great mitzvah. The Mishnah tells us (*Sanhedrin* 37a) that Hashem created Adam alone to teach us that the entire universe was created for one person, and "one who saves a life is considered as if he saved the entire world."

Perhaps this is a reason for the name the Torah uses for our great leader — Moshe Rabbeinu. Moshe was not the name given by his parents at birth; they gave him the name Tovyah, which means "goodness of G-d." Moshe, which means "removing," was the name Basya the daughter of Pharaoh gave him, to express that she saved his life by removing him from the Nile. By perpetuating the name given to commemorate this act, the Torah is teaching us just how great her action was. Although it may have seemed to be a relatively small act of saving one little baby — only one out of many others who perished — by saving his life she saved the entire Jewish nation, impacting world history.

As far as your question about preference, we would apply the same rules we have for any act of kindness or charity. The *pasuk* says (*Yeshayahu* 58:7), "Do not ignore a blood relative," meaning that there is a special requirement to help close relatives first. And as the saying goes, "Charity begins at home." So when one has limited time or resources, priority should be given to those close to him, with the closest relatives coming first. Similarly, when it comes to kidney donations, it goes without saying that a close relative comes before others.

It is also important to speak it over with a rabbi, as there may be other factors to take into consideration, such as who needs it more and who has a better chance of surviving.

In short: Donating a kidney is a great mitzvah and a wonderful act of kindness, assuming it does not pose any danger to your health. Someone who needs it more or a close relative comes first. Other priorities should be discussed with your rabbi.

Section 10

Marriage and Family Life

Marriage

58

Throwing Candy at the Chassan

Q ***I was wondering about the aufruf and the Shabbat Chattan, where the groom is called to the Torah on the Shabbos before or after the wedding, and the congregation throws candy at him. Isn't it disrespectful to throw food, especially in a shul, and especially since it may hit the Torah Scroll?***

A Let us take a step back and understand this tradition. One of the reasons a groom is called to the Torah is based on the Talmud (*Yevamos* 62b) that tells us that an unmarried man "is living without Torah." Since Hashem and His Torah are perfect, it is impossible to achieve perfection in Torah until after marriage, when the person becomes complete. Calling a groom to the Torah illustrates that he will now be capable of studying Torah on a much higher level.

The custom to throw candy is to symbolize that in the merit of these newfound levels of Torah learning, Hashem will shower the couple with sweet blessings. Originally, the candy was not thrown by the men or boys, but by the women who were high up in the gallery, symbolic of the blessings that come from Above. They would also use soft items, so no one would get hurt. Afterward, the children would pick up the bags gleefully and walk away with big smiles on their faces.

Practiced in this refined manner, it is a beautiful tradition, and this is indeed how it is still practiced in some shuls. Since the entire ceremony is in honor of the Torah and a demonstration of the blessings that come from the Torah, and the Torah itself is covered with a *tallis*, it is not disrespectful, even if some candy falls on it.

However, nowadays, many women's sections are located in the back of the shul, so the women can no longer throw the candy down from above. They are also too far away from the groom and obstructed by a *mechitzah* (partition), so the boys took over. Sadly, in some places it has turned into a contest of who can hit the groom the hardest, with hard candies added to help people aim. It has also become a free-for-all, with boys picking up the bags from the floor and throwing them again and again. Some adults also join the fun and act like little children, turning it into a Purim-like atmosphere.

A shul is a "miniature Beis HaMikdash," and as the *Shulchan Aruch* (*Orach Chaim* 151:1) states clearly, must be treated with great respect, and is certainly not a place for such games. Such behavior is even more disgraceful in the presence of a Torah Scroll — the testimony that Hashem chose us as His people and gave us His Torah — where halachah (*Yoreh De'ah* 282:1) obligates us to conduct ourselves with great awe and reverence.

How wonderful it would be if this custom would be practiced properly — with just bags of soft candy tossed at the groom. In this way, this beautiful tradition can be carried on while maintaining the proper decorum and respect required for a shul and the Torah Scroll.

In short: Throwing candy is a beautiful tradition, symbolizing Hashem showering the new couple with blessing in the merit of the Torah. But when done improperly it becomes disrespectful to the shul and the Sefer Torah, and such behavior should be stopped.

59

Bringing Joy to the Bride and Groom

Q ***Why is it such a great mitzvah to bring joy to a bride and groom? After all, no one is happier than a newlywed couple, so why the need to add more joy? And what about during the week of Sheva Berachos, is there an obligation to have a nightly party, or can we skip some of them?***

A The purpose of a Jewish marriage is to build a home for the sake of serving Hashem. Indeed, we bless every bride and groom that they build a *bayis ne'eman*, a loyal home — loyal to Hashem and His Torah. Furthermore, our Rabbis teach us that when a couple follows the proper path, they merit to have the Divine Presence in their home. Thus, when a man and woman marry, they are building a miniature Beis HaMikdash (Holy Temple). This is why bringing joy to a bride and groom is akin to rebuilding one of the ruins of Jerusalem (*Berachos* 6b), and why, in the *Sheva Berachos* blessings, we pray for the rebuilding of the Beis HaMikdash.

The wedding is the foundation of this wonderful holy edifice, and we want to make the foundation as solid as possible. Starting their married life amid great joy and celebration can help carry the couple over the many hurdles and challenges that will inevitably arise during their long life together. So although it's true that a new couple is already in high spirits, the happier we make them the stronger the marriage will be. Indeed, the Talmud (*Kesubos* 17a) tells us how even the greatest Tannaim and Amoraim would perform all kinds of antics to add to the merriment of the bride and groom, thereby empowering them to establish a life filled with joy.

This is similar to the impact the various holidays have on the Jewish calendar. Each Yom Tov has its own unique flavor that is meant to uplift us and bring us close to Hashem and the Torah, recharging our "spiritual batteries" to help us remain connected to Hashem throughout the rest of the year.

For a bride and groom, the wedding is a once-in-a-lifetime opportunity to infuse them with joy and elation that will hopefully keep them going for the rest of their lives.

But it is not only the wedding itself that sets the tone for the marriage; the seven days of festivities that follow are also part of the foundation. These seven days correspond to the seven days of inauguration celebrated at the time the Mishkan in the desert was erected. Those days were also meant to infuse a level of spiritual elation to last for the entire "lifetime" of the Mishkan.

In the same vein, the young couple's miniature sanctuary is inaugurated with great fanfare and doses of spiritual energy provided by the *Sheva Berachos* recited throughout these days, infusing it with sanctity and blessing.

Thus, although having a nightly party is not a requirement, it is certainly worthwhile, as the *Sheva Berachos* help launch their marriage with great joy and spiritual energy.

In short: The happier we make the bride and groom, the stronger the marriage will be for their future life together, helping them rise above challenges that may come their way. The Sheva Berachos recited throughout these seven days infuse their new home with great spiritual energy.

60

The Most Important Ingredient in Marriage

Q ***What is the most important thing to focus on in marriage, and why?***

A *Shalom bayis,* maintaining a happy and pleasant home, is the most important ingredient in a marriage. But this takes effort, and a husband and wife must both do whatever it takes — within the bounds of halachah — to ensure that peace reigns in the home. One way to do this is by focusing on the needs and wishes of your spouse, and not just on what is good for you. Be easy-going and willing to overlook situations that may not have turned out the way you would have liked or expected.

Peace and harmony are the foundation of marriage, and are stressed at the very onset of every Jewish marriage. In the last blessing recited at the wedding ceremony and at the *Sheva Berachos* celebrations, we praise Hashem Who created "joy and happiness, groom and bride," and a whole list of additional expressions of joy. Yet the list concludes with "love, unity, peace, and companionship." Although these are not expressions of joy, they are included because they set the tone, at the very onset of the marriage, for achieving true happiness.

Why is this the most important ingredient in marriage? On a simple level, a peaceful home is the ideal environment — physically, emotionally, and spiritually — for a couple. Our Sages (*Yevamos* 62b) tell us that "an unmarried man lacks happiness, blessing, goodness, Torah, protection, and peace," and only through marriage can a person fully attain these wonderful things. The stronger the bond between the couple, the more they will be able to enjoy these qualities, and since a strong bond can be created only through peace and harmony, these are the essential ingredients in a marriage.

This atmosphere is also crucial for the children. Children who grow up in a happy home will be emotionally secure and empowered to succeed in life both physically and spiritually. This will make the home the place it is meant to be — one where people serve Hashem properly and joyfully. Conversely, friction in the home causes negativity and ill will, and makes everyone lose out.

But a deeper understanding of a Jewish marriage will give you a more profound appreciation for the importance of *shalom bayis* and the impact it can have, in Heaven and Earth. As the *Nefesh HaChaim* states, all our actions in this world invoke a Heavenly reaction, and when we live in peace with each other, Hashem is at peace with us.

This is all the more so when it comes to a Jewish marriage. The Jewish nation shares an intimate relationship with Hashem, and — as the *navi* tells us (*Yeshayahu* 62:5) and as we recite in *Kabbalas Shabbos* — when we are worthy, Hashem rejoices with us as a groom rejoices with his bride. So when a husband and wife strengthen their connection to each other, Hashem's connection to His people is strengthened. This is the reason the Talmud (*Sotah* 17a) teaches that when a husband and wife establish a proper home together, the Divine Presence dwells with them, for their harmonious marriage is bringing His Presence into our world.

So by focusing on how to live in harmony with your spouse, you will not only be helping yourself and your family, you will be strengthening the Jewish nation's intimate relationship with Hashem. This is the greatest merit you can have for a happy, successful life together, and the best thing you can do for the world.

In short: Shalom bayis — ensuring that peace reigns in the home — is the most important ingredient in a successful marriage, because a peaceful home is conducive to serving Hashem properly and joyfully. And when a husband and wife live in harmony, they strengthen the intimate relationship we have with Hashem.

61

The Boss in a Jewish Marriage

Q ***Who is the boss in a Jewish marriage?***

A A Jewish home does not have a "boss." While the man is generally considered the head of the household, he is by no means the boss. Hashem created men with the nature to be more of a leader, and women with a more passive nature. In addition, a man spends time studying Torah, and is expected to be more knowledgeable in Torah law (halachah) and Torah perspective (*hashkafah*), and therefore should be the one to make decisions in running the home according to the Torah. Indeed, most girls I speak to express their desire for a husband who will be a leader and set the tone in the home.

At the same time, there are areas in the home that a wise husband will understand belong to his wife. The Talmud (*Bava Metzia* 59a) tells us that although the husband should take the lead role in spiritual matters, when it comes to domestic matters he should defer to his wife. The physical aspects of the home are usually the woman's area of expertise, making it logical for her to be the one in charge of them. This includes which foods to serve, the type of clothing the children wear, and the setup of the home.

And of course the main goal of a Jewish woman is to bring children into the world and raise a healthy, wholesome family of G-d-fearing Jews. She accomplishes this by creating a peaceful and warm atmosphere in the home, so that all members of the family can bring out their qualities and capabilities to the fullest in serving Hashem. Indeed, many great women throughout the generations have played critical roles in helping their husband and children reach great spiritual heights. And the great Torah giant, Rabbi Akiva Eiger, writes about the long discussions he had with his wife on topics of *yiras Shamayim* (fear of Heaven) until late into the night.

But that doesn't mean that either of them should be "bossy." On the contrary, they should discuss any difference of opinions they may have, with each one respecting the other's opinions and trying to accommodate them. Indeed, Hashem gave the wife the ability to use her feminine touch to help her husband appreciate and follow her perspective.

This amazing system — the husband taking the lead role, but encouraging his wife to take charge of her area of expertise — makes a perfect and harmonious partnership. And even as he leads, she has her impact. But if for whatever reason they can't figure out how to work things out peacefully, they should speak it over with a rabbi who can guide them.

There is one more important ingredient needed for the special formula of a Jewish marriage. A husband must use his position as the head of the household to provide all of his wife's needs. For this reason, a husband is required to write a *kesubah* (marriage contract) accepting upon himself to provide his wife with all her physical and emotional needs. In fact, the Talmud (*Yevamos* 62b) teaches that a husband should love his wife like his own self and respect her even more than his own self. This includes taking care of her and being attuned to her needs and wishes, such as spending more money on her clothing and any other things that are important to her. Following these guidelines is sure to bring peace and happiness to the home.

In short: There is no boss in a Jewish marriage. While the husband is the one who runs the home according to the Torah, the wife should be in charge of the physical aspects of the home, because this is her area of expertise. But neither of them should be bossy or force their opinions on their spouse.

62

Marriage Relationship

Q ***Rabbi, you have said that in a Jewish marriage, the husband has more of a lead role, while the wife has more of a supporting role. Why did Hashem create marriage like this? Why can't they both be equal?***

A As we have discussed in the past, a "ship can only have one captain," so having one leader is a wonderful recipe for *shalom bayis*. And it is logical for it to be the husband, since men are usually more knowledgeable in Torah as well as natural leaders, whereas women have a more passive nature and are more accepting of their husband as the leader and provider.

But on a deeper level this setup helps us understand our relationship with Hashem, as every relationship in this world mirrors an aspect of our multifaceted relationship with Hashem. Hashem is our King, Father, Master, and Groom, but without real-life examples, we would not be able to truly comprehend these relationships. Each of these human relationships — husband and wife, parent and child, master and servant, king and his subjects, etc. — helps us understand our relationships with Hashem.

For example, without a parent-child relationship in this world, we would not be able to grasp the concept of Hashem being our Father. As my friend told me, when he became a father he looked lovingly at his baby and declared, "If only I had realized that this was the love my father felt for me when I was a child." Only after experiencing his own paternal love was he able to understand what this feeling really was. Similarly, without kings and masters in this world, we would not know how to accept Hashem as our King, and to be true servants of our Master, Hashem.

This brings us to the unique relationship of husband and wife. As described in *Shir HaShirim*, Hashem is the Groom and the Jewish nation the bride. He has abundant love for us and provides us with all our needs. This concept is brought to life in marriage, where the husband has great love for his wife and accepts responsibility to provide her needs. And the husband acting as leader with the wife in the background reflects our marriage with Hashem, where we are humble and unassuming before Hashem, our Leader. The couple playing their roles in this world brings out our wonderful relationship with Hashem, making them worthy of great reward.

Furthermore, in a physical marriage, the man plants the seed, which develops into a child in the woman. Similarly, Hashem "implanted within us eternal life — *vechayei olam nata besocheinu*." He gave us the Torah, which is completely spiritual, and our mission is to study and expand upon its meanings and to perform the mitzvos written in it, thereby giving the Torah physical expression.

Taking this idea a step further, every marriage relationship affects our connection to Hashem. As the *Nefesh HaChaim* states in the name of the Midrash, Hashem is like our shadow and acts toward us in the way we interact with each other. Therefore, when a couple conducts their marriage the way they're supposed to, with the husband supporting and caring for his wife while she accepts his leadership, Hashem's leadership and blessings to the world are also strengthened.

In short: Men are natural leaders and usually more knowledgeable in Torah, the ideal setup for a successful marriage. This also helps us understand our relationship with Hashem. Just as a husband is the leader and provider, Hashem is our leader and provides all our needs, and gave us the Torah for us to develop.

63

Household Responsibilities of a Husband

Q ***As a wife and mother, I feel as if the bulk of the work around the house falls on my shoulders, and my husband is not doing his part. How can I get him to help out more?***

A This question is really unfair and impossible to answer properly, because I am only hearing your side of the story. Perhaps, if your husband would have a chance to offer his side, he would present the facts quite differently. For example, perhaps his work schedule does not leave him the time or strength to pitch in around the house. Or maybe he really is doing his part, and it's you who is being unreasonable.

But let's assume that the picture is painted accurately, and your husband is really not doing as much as he should; instead of putting the kids to sleep or helping with other household chores, he just loafs around and checks his phone for the latest news. What would likely work for such a husband is to have someone he respects speak to him and explain to him that he is not living up to his responsibilities.

Every Jewish marriage begins with a husband accepting the responsibilities of the *kesubah*, marriage contract, wherein he obligates himself to support and honor his wife properly and to "hold her in high regard." Included in this is respecting her and doing things to make life easier for her. After it is read under the *chuppah* (wedding canopy), the *kesubah* is given to the wife, and she must keep it in a safe place throughout their married life together.

The *kesubah* is a contract, and he must honor his obligations.

But a husband must be prepared to help even in areas that are not technically part of his responsibility. There are times that he might have to help with the domestic chores his wife usually handles. In a Torah-true home, the husband and wife will look for ways to help ease one another's burden, not try to get away with doing less.

Additionally, a husband must realize that his wife often helps him with his responsibilities, so he must help with hers. One example of this is working to support the family. Ever since the sin of Adam, when G-d cursed man and said, "By the sweat of your brow you shall eat bread," the responsibility to financially support the family has fallen on the husband's shoulders, and every husband accepts this responsibility, as spelled out in the *kesubah*. Yet, in many cases, the wife shares this responsibility and also works to bring in more income. So if a husband says he's not interested in helping around the house because that's the wife's domain, he may find her responding that she will stop helping share the financial burden.

Marriage is a working relationship, with husband and wife helping each other with their responsibilities, even when it means going beyond the call of duty. Living this way will bring harmony and stability to the home.

In short: Someone the husband respects needs to tell him to live up to the responsibilities he accepted upon himself when they got married. And a couple must understand that even when things are not technically part of their responsibility, a husband and wife should seek to help each other.

64

Telling Your Wife You Don't Like Her Food

Q ***My wife served a meal that I didn't particularly enjoy. Should I tell her in a nice way that I didn't like it, or should I lie and tell her how delicious it was so that she won't feel bad? Even if it's worth lying to keep the peace, perhaps I should be concerned that she may eventually find out that I don't really like the food, and then feel even worse that she served it so many times. In addition, I don't really want to be stuck with this menu for the rest of my life!***

A Generally, this can be compared to a discussion in the Talmud (*Kesubos* 17a). What should one say to a newlywed about his new wife, who is not particularly pretty? Or what should one do if a friend purchases new clothing that doesn't look particularly nice on him? The Gemara rules that you should praise the bride or the purchase. Since this is what your friend chose, it obviously fits his taste and is good for him, so it is not untruthful to say she is pretty or that it looks nice on him. Similarly, even if the food was not the way you like it, there is no question that you should tell your wife how good the food was, and praise her for her culinary talents.

In addition, even if her cooking is not very good, you would be allowed to tell her that the food was delicious, in order to make her feel good. This is because *shalom bayis,* domestic harmony, is so important that, when necessary, one should even deviate from the truth in order to keep the peace. The Talmud (*Yevamos* 65b) proves this from an exchange at the beginning of *Parashas Vayeira* (*Bereishis*

18:13), when Hashem Himself altered the truth. When the angel informed Avraham that he and Sarah were going to have a child, she expressed doubt, and thought to herself, "Can an old man like my husband still father a child?!" But when Hashem reported her reaction to Avraham, He quoted her as saying "I am old," rather than referring to Avraham as old, in order to preserve the harmonious relationship between them.

Depending on your wife's personality and sensitivity, after complimenting her on the meal, you might add that you prefer some of her other delicious dishes to this one. In fact, some wives would prefer knowing that right away. But if you have a doubt about how she will handle your saying that, I would suggest you simply stick with the compliment.

As far as whether or not you should be concerned that she may find out, that is indeed a legitimate point, and I actually heard of such a case. There was someone who didn't like tuna fish, but when his wife served it, he pretended that he did, so she continued to serve it regularly. Years later, his mother came to visit, and she asked her daughter-in-law why she was serving tuna fish if her son dislikes it!

I have a simple suggestion that would avoid offending your wife and might help you get your desired menu as well. Find an occasion when she hasn't invested so much time and energy in her cooking, and mention which foods you really do enjoy. Assuming you have a healthy relationship, not only will she not mind your telling her, she will even appreciate the opportunity to please you by cooking the food you like in the future.

In short: You should definitely praise your wife at the time the meal was served, and you can find a different occasion to mention your preferences.

65

What a Marriage!

Q ***Rabbi Akiva's wife Rachel sent him away to study Torah shortly after their marriage, and he was away for twenty-four years. While she may have done a very noble act, what type of marriage did she have, living a lonely life and not seeing her husband for decades?***

A While this is not recommended for any of us, don't be concerned about their marriage. Simple people like us, who live a physical life, understand marriage on a physical level and would consider this a lonely marriage. But Rabbi Akiva and Rachel were spiritual giants who lived life on a different level and understood that marriage is not merely a physical connection, but a spiritual bond of two souls that share each other's accomplishments in this world and for eternity. This is certainly true in the case of Rachel, as it was to her credit that Rabbi Akiva went to study Torah and became a Torah giant.

As the daughter of one of the wealthiest Jews of the time, Rachel could have easily married any prestigious Torah scholar. Yet when she detected great potential in Akiva, her father's ignorant shepherd, she offered to marry him if he would go study Torah. Her father was incensed and drove her out of his house, subjecting her to a life of abject poverty. By marrying Akiva, she helped him develop into one of the greatest sages of all time, as well as one of the primary transmitters of Torah for all generations, and thus was a true partner in all his spiritual attainments.

Rachel obviously understood that it was only through the combined spiritual energy of their souls that Rabbi Akiva would be able to achieve what he did. And because she was on such a high spiritual level, she knew that sending her husband away to study would be her greatest achievement and make their marriage the most successful one, even while physically far apart.

As the Talmud (*Kesubos* 62b) relates, Rabbi Akiva actually returned after twelve years and was about to enter his home. But then he overheard someone rebuking his wife for letting her husband stay away for so long, leaving her to live the life of a widow, to which she replied that if it were up to her, he would stay for another twelve years. When Rabbi Akiva heard this, he turned around and returned to his studies for another twelve years, becoming an even greater Torah scholar and teacher.

Only a woman like Rachel, who truly appreciated the greatness of what she was accomplishing with every fiber of her being, could give such an answer.

Indeed, Rabbi Akiva himself understood quite well that all he had accomplished was to Rachel's credit. When he finally returned, accompanied by his 24,000 students, she went out to greet him, but was pushed away by his attendants, who did not realize who she was. Rabbi Akiva told them to allow her through, declaring that all his accomplishments, and theirs, were possible only because of her encouragement and sacrifice, saying "Mine and yours are all hers."

So while they were physically apart for all those years, they certainly felt spiritually connected the entire time, and they continue to be together for eternity. They had a wonderful marriage and continue to live "happily ever after," reaping the fruits of their labor.

This is something every one of us can take to heart, each on our own level. Even if we cannot live on such a high spiritual plane, we can still encourage each other to make our homes and our marriages more spiritual, and together reap the benefits for eternity.

In short: Rabbi Akiva and his wife were on an extremely high spiritual level and understood that marriage is primarily a spiritual and eternal bond. Their marriage was the happiest one possible — then and for eternity.

66

Saving a Marriage

Q ***Unfortunately, our shalom bayis (domestic harmony) has seen better days, and we feel that it may be time for divorce. How far should we go to remain married? And should we continue to live in misery just for the sake of the children?***

A Obviously, every case is different, and it would be best to discuss your situation with a rabbi who can guide you based on the specifics of the situation. But generally speaking, a couple should certainly try to do whatever they can to save their marriage, and reawaken the fondness they had for each other when they first got married. With proper help, many such couples have been able to take the right steps to rectify the situation, and their marriages are once again flourishing.

But even if a couple tried and was unsuccessful, it may still be noble for them to stay together for the sake of the children, as it is important for children to have a home with both a father and a mother. But this is only true if they can keep the quarreling to themselves, and maintain a healthy and happy atmosphere in the home. Indeed, for the sake of their children, many couples manage to stay together for years, divorcing only after their children have moved on in life. But if there will be constant strife, with the children experiencing the tension and misery, they may be better off if the parents are not together.

It is also important to realize that although there are circumstances that call for divorce, breaking up a marriage is far more than a private matter between husband and wife. Marriage is not merely a physical relationship, but a spiritual bond of souls, and separating these souls is not a simple task. For this reason, a *get,* halachic bill of divorce, has many rules and regulations, with an entire tractate in the Talmud, *Maseches Gittin,* dedicated to these intricate details.

In addition, every relationship in this world — and certainly the deep-rooted relationship of marriage — has a ripple effect on our connection to Hashem. Indeed, the Talmud (*Sotah* 17a) tells us that when a husband and wife build a proper Torah home, the Divine Presence dwells with them. Similarly, in the blessings recited at a wedding and at each of the *Sheva Berachos* celebrations, a primary focus is prayers for the rebuilding of Jerusalem, because Jewish marriage invokes the intimate relationship we share with Hashem.

We see this concept in the words of the *navi*, who tells us (*Yeshayahu* 62:5) that when the Jewish nation is worthy, Hashem rejoices with us as a groom rejoices with his bride. Indeed, our Rabbis (*Berachos* 6b) tell us that gladdening a groom is akin to rebuilding the ruins of Jerusalem, because this harmonic unification of souls strengthens our connection to Hashem, bringing us closer to the rebuilding of Jerusalem!

This is why, in the final words of Tractate *Gittin*, our Sages tell us that when a divorce takes place, even the *Mizbei'ach* (Altar) cries. Just as a *korban* (offering) offered on the Altar brings a person, along with the entire universe, closer to Hashem (the root *kareiv* means close), every couple living in harmony brings Hashem closer to this world. Conversely, when there is strife and divorce, the entire universe suffers and is distanced from Hashem, and this is why the Altar — the vehicle meant to bring us close to Hashem — sheds tears. It is therefore imperative for a couple contemplating divorce to keep in mind the great damage this will cause to the entire Jewish nation.

In short: Couples should do whatever they can to restore peace and harmony to their marriage. It is noble to stay together for the sake of their children as long as they can maintain a healthy and happy atmosphere in the home. When there is strife and divorce, the entire world suffers.

Family Life

67

Juggling Responsibilities — Who Comes First: Parent or Wife?

Q ***I often find myself torn between the responsibilities I have to my parents and to my wife. When there is a conflict between helping and spending time with my wife or my parents, who takes precedence?***

A Honoring parents is a great mitzvah — one that is compared to honoring Hashem — and we can never overemphasize a child's obligation to show appreciation to his parents for all that they do for him. Furthermore, a spouse is also obligated to honor his or her in-laws and be understanding of their needs. For example, if your spouse and parents or in-laws are at the dinner table with you, you should certainly serve your parents or in-laws first.

One must realize that their spouse did not grow up in a vacuum, and the mere fact that parents brought their child into the world is reason enough to require their children and children-in-law to honor them. How much greater is that obligation when we consider that they cared for that child until marriage and, as they quite often do, continue to help in various ways after their marriage. Therefore, every husband and wife must understand that their mindset should be to try to allow their spouse to help his or her parents whenever possible, even if it comes at the expense of their own needs.

However, as great as the mitzvah of honoring parents is, there is a notable exception: *shalom bayis,* domestic harmony. The Torah tells us that Hashem even allows His Name to be erased in order to uphold harmony between husband and wife. And, as discussed elsewhere ("Honesty for the Cooking Spouse"), *shalom bayis* is so important that, when necessary, one should even deviate from the truth in order to keep the peace.

For this reason, when there is a conflict of interest and your help is needed by both your wife and your parents, your parents' needs should generally come first. But if tending to their needs will cause your wife to be upset or resentful, *shalom bayis* takes precedence. Of course, whenever possible, a wife should try to let her husband be available to help his parents.

In short: A wife is also obligated to honor her in-laws and be understanding of their needs, and should try to allow her husband to help his parents. But in case of conflict, if ignoring her needs would infringe on their shalom bayis, the wife's needs take precedence.

68

Honoring Absentee or Abusive Parents

Q ***I had a very difficult childhood. My mother was abusive and my father abandoned us. Are we still expected to honor and respect them?***

A In general, a child must certainly continue to respect and honor his parents. However, there are some rare situations where a child might be guided by a competent and experienced halachic authority to limit his interactions with his parents.

One of the basic reasons for the mitzvah of honoring parents is *hakaras hatov*, showing appreciation for all that parents do for their children. Even if, at first glance, it seems as if your parents didn't do much for you, and even if they may have caused you pain, there is no question that they did do a lot for you, and you are still obligated to respect and honor them.

In fact, my illustrious rebbi, Rabbi Dovid Kronglas, Mashgiach in Yeshivah Ner Yisroel, once made the following bold statement: Even if parents abandoned their child at birth and never lifted a finger for the child, the mitzvah of honoring parents still applies, simply because they are the ones who brought the child into the world!

He brought proof to this from the Mishnah (*Bava Metzia* 33a), which states that one must honor and have gratitude to his father "who brought him into this world." This teaches that the mere fact that a parent brought the child into the world — and never did anything else for the child — is enough reason to be grateful.

In most cases, however, one's parents did perform countless acts of kindness for them from the moment the child entered the world. We must consider the things we take for granted, like tending to the needs of the house, cooking, nursing sick children back to health, and earning a livelihood.

While an abusive parent must certainly rectify his wrongdoing, the child is still obligated to be appreciative of all he received. Even if your parents had only selfish motives in mind when they provided for you, you must still be thankful to them. The beneficiary of unintentional kindness — or one who is helped by even an inanimate object — should be incapable of doing something hurtful to his benefactor. For this reason, Moshe, who was saved as an infant in the Nile, could not smite the Nile to initiate the plague of blood. So you should certainly feel obligated to show your appreciation to your parents for all you received.

In short: Parents perform countless acts of kindness for a child. But even if a parent never did anything for the child, the mitzvah of honoring parents still applies, because they are the ones who brought him into this world.

69

Calling In-laws "Mom and Dad"

Q ***Many of my friends call their parents in-law Mom and Dad, or Mommy and Totty. Is it correct to honor them in this way, or perhaps it is wrong, as it shows a lack of respect for one's own parents? Has this always been done, or is it a modern invention? And does it make a difference if my parents are not happy with my doing so?***

A Referring to in-laws with the same title as parents is by no means a new thing, and has always been an accepted practice among the Jewish people. The *Shulchan Aruch* (*Yoreh De'ah* 240:24) rules that a person is obligated to honor in-laws, and as cited by the *poskim*, the source is from King David, who called his father-in-law Shaul, "my father." In fact, some *poskim* prove from here that one is required to honor in-laws just as much as biological parents. And even more telling is that the source is from David, whose father-in-law was out to kill him. So we see that the practice of calling in-laws by the same title as parents is actually rooted in halachah.

As the *poskim* explain, the requirement to honor in-laws is based on the concept of *ishto kegufo* — one's wife is like oneself. When a couple marries, the Torah tells us (*Bereishis* 2:24), "*Vehayu levasar echad* — They shall become one flesh." A husband and wife are not just partners, they are soulmates, and the holy *Zohar* teaches that the souls of a husband and wife are linked together like two halves of one soul. Therefore, a spouse's father and mother are like one's own parents, and deserve the same titles we use for parents.

You may wonder that if in-laws are to be regarded like parents, perhaps you should use this title exclusively, even in formal settings.

For instance, if you are the *gabbai* calling people up to the Torah, you should call up your father-in-law as "*avi mori* — my father, my mentor," just as you would for your own father. Or if you are leading the *bentching* in his home, you should say, "*Bershus avi mori* — With the permission of my father, my mentor." However, this is not the case. Calling your father-in-law "father" is a way of showing endearment and respect, but when it comes to formal settings, you refer to him by his formal title, which is "father-in-law." This is similar to someone who is known as Dave, but it is not the name used to call him to the Torah.

As far as parents objecting to their children calling their in-laws by their own titles, I have never heard of this, and I believe it would be wrong for them to feel that way. On the contrary, I believe that most parents are pleased to see their child happily married, enjoying a close and loving relationship with his or her in-laws. But if they do indeed object, you should find a different title for your in-laws, as you are not allowed to upset your parents.

In short: It has always been an accepted practice to refer to in-laws like parents, because a husband and wife are like one. I have never heard of any parent objecting, but if they do object, you should use a different title.

70

Is Cleanliness a Virtue?

Q ***How important is it for me to keep my home and clothing neat and immaculate? And is it a mitzvah to hire cleaning help?***

A Yes! Cleanliness is definitely a mitzvah and a great virtue, which includes hiring cleaning help, if needed. The Midrash (*Vayikra* Rabbah 34:3) relates that when the great Hillel was heading to the bathhouse, he told his students that he was on his way to perform a mitzvah. When the students wondered why he considered bathing a mitzvah, he told them the following: "If a statue of the king is washed and scrubbed to ensure it remains clean, certainly we, who are created as a *tzelem Elokim* (form of G-d) must stay fresh and dignified." Indeed, the Talmud (*Shabbos* 50b) tells us that washing ourselves daily is a method of honoring Hashem.

The Shelah HaKadosh adds that this virtue of cleanliness applies not only to the body, but to clothing and the home as well. As he explains, cleanliness and proper hygiene make a person feel respectable, which will make him want to be pure from sin. Just as members of the royal family understand that certain improper behavior is beneath their dignity, similarly, all Jews are *bnei melachim* (princes) and have to act accordingly. Proper dress reminds us of our prestigious status, and helps keep us focused on living for a higher purpose.

This is important not only on a personal level; it can actually change the world. People often form their impressions of others based on their appearance. The Jewish nation — and certainly those who study Hashem's Torah — represents Hashem in this world. Thus, as His ambassadors, our external image can go a long way in bringing people closer to Hashem or, G-d forbid, turning them away from Him.

Taking this concept to the next level, Shelah writes that cleanliness is relevant not only in the physical realm. Since our bodies and souls are connected, physical cleanliness actually evokes spiritual purity. Furthermore, our Rabbis list *nekiyus,* cleanliness, as one of the rungs on the ladder of reaching spiritual greatness (as elucidated by the *Mesillas Yesharim*). Although this is commonly understood as spiritual cleanliness, *Sefer HaChinuch* writes that simple hygiene is included, and can serve as a stepping stone toward attaining the lofty level of Divine Inspiration (*ruach hakodesh*).

In short: Cleanliness is a mitzvah, as it brings honor to Hashem, raises a person spiritually, and helps us act the way we should. This includes hiring cleaning help, if needed. In addition, our external appearance has the ability to bring people closer to Hashem.

71

Dealing With Peer Pressure

Q ***My children often complain that they don't have what "all" their friends or neighbors have — the latest gadget, the nicest vacation — things I feel are not appropriate or not affordable for us. What can I do to help my children — and the adults too — deal with this peer pressure?***

A It is important to realize that in the world we live in, this is quite a common phenomenon, and parents deal with this all the time.

The first thing you must know is that more often than not, it is not really true that all — or even most of — the friends and neighbors have it. It's just that the hype created by the few who do have it creates the illusion or the feeling that everyone has it.

But even if others do really have something that your child doesn't, you can still emphasize the positive. Show your children all the good things they do have in life and all the nice places they do go. Although "the grass is always greener on the other side," it is quite possible that, in many ways, your children are the ones who have a better life. And, if necessary, you can compensate for their "lack" with other items or trips that do fit your budget and lifestyle.

If your children are a little older, you should share with them the Torah-true perspective, and help them appreciate that there is no reason to gauge their needs based on what others have. They should be taught to appreciate that whatever they have or don't have is orchestrated from Heaven specifically for them.

We see this concept clearly in the blessing we recite every morning, "*she'asah li kol tzarki*," thanking Hashem for providing us with all our needs. At first glance, one may wonder about this blessing. If you would ask a group of people if they have all their needs, such as money, clothing, and a nice house, many will respond that they don't. If that is the case, how can they honestly recite this blessing daily?

The answer is that each person has an individual mission in this world, and Hashem provides him with precisely what he needs to accomplish it, no more and no less. Therefore, if someone lacks certain things, it's because this is precisely the situation he needs to be in to accomplish his task. This blessing is a daily opportunity to reinforce this truth and ingrain this concept in our psyche.

This is also the explanation given for the mitzvah of "*lo sachmod* — do not desire what others have." When a person lives with the reality that everything is specifically earmarked for each individual, he will realize that what others have will not benefit him at all, and the desire to have what others have will dissipate. Armed with the clarity that whatever one has — or doesn't have — is Divinely customized for his individualized mission, a person will find it much easier to be happy with his lot, with no need for what others have.

In short: Show your children all the good things they have, and if necessary compensate them with other, affordable things. You can teach the older ones that each person has exactly what Hashem has given them, and what others have will not benefit them. This will help them to live their lives content with what they have.

Section 11

Role of Women

72

Updating the Role of Women in Today's Society

Q ***What is the Torah outlook on modern feminism? Many laws in the Torah seem to relegate women to the sidelines, such as being placed behind a mechitzah (partition) in the synagogue or not counting in a minyan. Since women in today's society are more on par with their male counterparts, shouldn't their status be updated?***

A Your very premise that women are second-class is unfounded. According to the Torah-true outlook, women were never inferior, so we have no reason to change their status. Rav Yisrael Salanter (*Even Yisrael, Derush* 8) quotes the Midrash (*Tanna D'Vei Eliyahu Rabbah* Chapter 9), which states that a woman who keeps her mitzvos faithfully can reach the greatest spiritual heights.

As far as why women don't seem to "count," perhaps a better appreciation of a woman's unique mission in this world will help you understand this as well. Hashem created men and women differently, each one with a very specific physical and emotional makeup, tailor-made for accomplishing their specific mission in this world. Women were created with the capability of bringing children into the world and, with their loving touch and special intuition, raising a healthy and wholesome family, and this is what Jewish women have proudly been doing for millennia.

In fact, Yocheved and Miriam are called Shifra and Puah in the Torah, referring to the fact that they took care of the newborn children in Egypt. Although they were righteous women and leaders of the nation, the Torah uses specifically these names, because there is no greater accomplishment for a Jewish woman than bringing up the next generation of G-d-fearing Jews. That role is far more significant than any career or corporate success. This has always been the case, and it will continue to be so forever, even if "modern" society thinks otherwise.

Since women are occupied with this noble task of raising precious souls, they are not expected to commit to attend the daily *minyan*, and were never given this mitzvah. While they are welcome to attend, because they are not obligated to do so they are not counted toward the *minyan*.

It is so unfortunate that many women today do not appreciate the innate greatness of being a caring wife and mother, and falsely believe that prestige can be attained only by having an accomplished career. When women prioritize their careers over their families, they and their families suffer.

As statistics show, when parents are too busy and preoccupied with their careers to give proper care and attention to their children, their children are much more prone to drug use and juvenile delinquency, and will often need emotional help. Even if a mother must work to help support her family, her focus should be on her family, not on her career. A home with a loving, nurturing mother, who places her family above all else, offers the children much more stability and security. The rate of divorce, drugs, and juvenile delinquency is much lower among those with the traditional Jewish family way of life. So instead of bringing Judaism "up to date," let's bring "date" back to Judaism, the tried-and-true method for happy and healthy families.

As far as the *mechitzah*, it is not there because women are inferior; rather, it serves as a partition between the men and women. Prayer is "the service of the heart" and requires concentration. We are human, and both men and women can be distracted by the presence of members of the opposite gender.

In short: Women are not inferior in Judaism, so there's no need for change. They are preoccupied with the exalted task of raising a family, and not expected to attend minyan. The partition in the synagogue is there to help maintain the proper focus on the prayers.

73

Bat Mitzvah Questions

Q ***Should we celebrate our daughter's bat mitzvah with a lavish celebration, as we do for a bar mitzvah? Also, why does a boy become bar mitzvah at 13 and a girl bat mitzvah at 12? And why does a father recite a blessing only when his son becomes bar mitzvah and not when his daughter becomes bat mitzvah?***

A Let us first understand what this celebration is all about.

The Torah only obligates halachic adults to keep the mitzvos, and not minors, because children are not mature enough to truly understand right from wrong and to control themselves and resist temptations. While children are also required to perform mitzvos, this is only a Rabbinic requirement to train them to perform mitzvos when they reach adulthood.

Bar or bat mitzvah is the age when the Torah considers a boy or girl an adult, obligating them to now keep the mitzvos. Since a girl matures at a younger age than a boy does, she is capable of accepting this awesome responsibility at a younger age.

When a child reaches this tremendous milestone, we celebrate to show how excited we are that this child has attained this distinct honor and status. Since a girl is as privileged as a boy, we should certainly celebrate this wonderful occasion. Indeed, many great rabbis celebrate a bat mitzvah with a special dinner at home together with grandparents and close relatives, and this is how we celebrated with our daughters.

The reason not to make a large, more public party for a girl is because Jewish women and girls are princesses, and "כָּל כְּבוּדָּה בַת מֶלֶךְ פְּנִימָה — The dignity of a princess is within" (*Tehillim* 45:14). *Tznius,* modesty, is not just a dress code, but applies to all areas of behavior.

This is why Jewish women seek to stay out of the limelight and not take center stage, preferring to be active from behind the scenes. But it is important for your daughter to remember that a party is not what makes her an adult, and the lack of public festivities doesn't minimize the great significance of her reaching this milestone.

The father's blessing you mentioned is an expression of thanks to Hashem that he is no longer solely accountable for his son's sins. Training one's child to perform the mitzvos is an awesome responsibility, and if the father doesn't do so properly, he is held accountable for his child's sins. The blessing was instituted only for a boy who becomes bar mitzvah, because, for reasons discussed elsewhere, males have many more mitzvos than females have, which makes the father's responsibility much greater.

But even after a child reaches halachic adulthood, the parents must still be involved in the *chinuch* (education) of their children. In fact, I once heard Rav Moshe Feinstein state emphatically that parents — and even grandparents — are never exempt from the mitzvah of *chinuch*.

In short: You should certainly celebrate your daughter's bat mitzvah, albeit not with a large, public celebration, because girls stay out of the limelight. Girls mature at an earlier age than boys do. The blessing is recited only for a boy because males have many more obligations than females, and the father is relieved of a greater responsibility.

74

Women Staying Up on Shavuos Night

Q ***The focus of the festival of Shavuos seems to be on celebrating our receiving of the mitzvah of Torah study, as the men customarily study the entire night to show their enthusiasm for the Torah. But we women are not obligated to study Torah, so is it appropriate for us to stay up, or is this holiday just for men?***

A First of all, your assumption that Shavuos is merely a celebration of our receiving the mitzvah of Torah study is a fundamental mistake. On Shavuos, we express our appreciation that Hashem chose us as His nation and gave us His Torah with all 613 mitzvos, something men and women celebrate equally. While it is true that Torah study is the greatest mitzvah, equivalent to all the other mitzvos combined, it is still only one of the many mitzvos we received.

Although women are not obligated to study Torah, they are still very much connected to the mitzvah in many ways. Firstly, women recite the daily blessing for Torah study, since they have an obligation to study the parts of Torah that pertain to them and they fulfill a mitzvah when they study any Torah subject.

Secondly, when a woman helps others learn Torah, she becomes a partner in their Torah study and shares in the reward. She can do this in a number of ways. She can provide financial assistance, such as by working to support her husband learning in kollel, or donating her own money to support yeshivos. She can also give emotional support through creating a happy atmosphere in the home, enabling her husband and sons to concentrate on their studies, and by encouraging them to delve into their studies.

Finally, as with many mitzvos, being part of the collective efforts of the entire Jewish nation connects every person to every mitzvah, even those that he or she cannot personally perform. Certain mitzvos apply only to Kohanim, some only to men, and some only to women, yet as one nation we all have a share in all of them. The same is true with Torah study — when each person does his or her share, every member of the nation connects to the entire Torah, and we all celebrate equally.

Since men have a mitzvah to study Torah, they express their enthusiasm and love for this great gift by studying through the night. But an equally important component of this holiday is showing enthusiasm for receiving the Torah, expressed through the festive meals we eat — something both men and women can enjoy. Although, when it comes to other holidays, some opinions maintain that one may devote himself entirely to spiritual pursuits, all agree that on Shavuos one is required to enjoy festive meals in order to demonstrate delight and pleasure in having received the Torah (*Pesachim* 68b).

Even more, being that food preparation is typically the woman's domain, this dimension of the festivities is particularly applicable to you. Thus, a woman who prepares and enjoys a delectable meal, with delicious cheesecakes and blintzes, is expressing her appreciation and excitement for being part of the Chosen Nation, and for the Torah and all the mitzvos we received. So women have their special way to express their enthusiasm for this holiday. Certainly, though, a woman may stay up to learn, as long as it is not at the expense of her other responsibilities.

In short: Women share in the celebration of receiving the Torah on Shavuos, as well as in the mitzvah of Torah study, and express their excitement by enjoying and preparing festive meals. However, they may certainly stay up and study.

75

How Much Are Women Worth?

Q ***Rabbi, I have heard you claim that Judaism does not consider women inferior, but I'm not so sure about that! When a person pledges to donate someone's value to the Holy Temple, the Torah gives a price tag, depending on age and gender, with the female always being cheaper than her male counterpart. Similarly, if a man and a woman are in danger, the rule is (see Horayos 13a) that the man's life takes precedence. Doesn't that show that the Torah considers males superior?***

A This is an excellent question, and it is actually posed by Rav Yisrael Salanter (*Even Yisrael, Derush* 8). In fact, this question is similar to the age-old question about the blessing "*shelo asani ishah*," which is recited by men, thanking Hashem for not being created a woman — and his answer will address both questions.

Although, at first glance, the implication might be that females are inferior, that is simply incorrect.

The blessing recited by men each morning is an expression of thanks to Hashem for the many mitzvos — and especially the great mitzvah of studying Torah — that only men are commanded to perform. The fact that only men have this mitzvah of studying Torah is also why their value is higher.

But, as Rav Yisrael Salanter points out, this is a value that applies only in our fleeting world. He illustrates this by citing a fascinating narrative related in the Talmud (*Bava Basra* 10b): Rav Yosef took ill and fell into a near-death state, but then came back to life. When his father, Rav Yehoshua, inquired about his otherworldly experience, he responded that he had seen an "upside-down world," where people who were considered great in this world were "on bottom," while lowly people were "on top." His father responded, "No, my son, you saw a true, accurate world."

This seems quite puzzling. Why was Rav Yosef so shocked? Didn't he know that people hide their good or evil in this world and are exposed only in the World of Truth?

Rav Salanter explains that the people Rav Yosef considered "great" and "lowly" had truly earned their status in this world based on their achievements. But accomplishment is a barometer only in our world. In the World of Truth, a person's status is based on how much effort he expended.

That is the truth Rav Yosef saw. People who exerted themselves in this world to serve Hashem — even though they accomplished less — were more prominent in the World of Truth than those who accomplished more, but who had not tried as hard.

The same is true for a woman who faithfully fulfills her mission during her lifetime. In this world, a man has more mitzvos and is obligated to study Torah, which is why a man is measured differently. However, in the World of Truth, a woman who did all she could to serve Hashem may be much higher than her male counterparts, who did not.

But this goes even further. Rav Salanter quotes the Midrash (*Tanna D'Vei Eliyahu Rabbah* Chapter 9), that every man and woman who serves Hashem faithfully can reach the greatest spiritual heights.

The Midrash tells the story of Devorah, the prophetess and judge who was chosen to become the leader of the Jewish people, even though Pinchas, who was many years her senior and who was a grandson of Aharon HaKohen, was still alive. Devorah's husband, Lapidos, was an unlearned man, so she suggested they make wicks and he bring them to be used in the Menorah in the Mishkan. They took this task seriously and prepared thick wicks that would give off much light.

Because she acted with the purest intentions and did her utmost to increase the light of the Menorah, Hashem declared that she would be recognized by the entire Jewish nation.

The female's price is still cheaper, just as in a play, where there are actors with main parts and others with supporting roles. Even if the lead actor has a higher price, it doesn't mean he is better. An actor with a lesser part, who performs his part to perfection, can be just as important. Similarly, the relationship between male and female mirrors the relationship between Hashem and the Jewish nation, with the man taking the "lead role" and the woman having the "supporting role," thereby mirroring our subjugation to Hashem.

In short: Men have a certain value in this world because of the many mitzvos they perform. But a woman who fulfilled her mission can be on a higher spiritual level and receive greater reward in the World to Come.

Section 12
General Life

Daily Life

76

Path for Life

Q ***Some people devote their lives to helping others by studying and teaching Torah, while others focus on outreach or performing acts of kindness. Which path is more correct?***

A The answer to this depends on a person's circumstances, capabilities, and personality.

Some people find within themselves the drive to study Torah, dedicating their lives to constant growth in Torah and devoting all their energy to becoming great scholars, thereby helping themselves and the entire world through their study. They find a means to support their families, either through a wife who willingly works to facilitate her husband's pursuit of Torah, or through a regular stipend, investments, an inheritance, or some other method.

Other people like to study Torah, but also want to share what they learn with others. Such people can become teachers, for young people or for adults, depending on their personality. Teaching Torah to children takes a certain type of personality, as not everyone is capable of bringing himself to their level — presenting the material in a way that they can understand, while maintaining their interest. This is a method of serving Hashem by teaching Torah, while at the same time also doing a kind act to help others.

Some people who enter the field of education possess leadership qualities, and become school principals, while others choose to remain in the classroom with the children.

There is also the matter of circumstance: Sometimes people are forced into a position because they are needed there, not necessarily because that would be their choice. For example, a teacher may prefer to remain in the classroom, but because he has the necessary skills and talents, he is chosen to become principal. Indeed, for some people their calling is to move to a city where there's not much Judaism, and they are needed to teach, or to fill some other position.

Then there are those who devote much of their time to helping others. Some donate money to charities of various causes — above all to yeshivos, helping them keep the flame of Torah burning. Others get personally involved in different worthy organizations. Today there are countless chesed organizations — Hatzalah, Chaveirim, and Bikur Cholim to name a few — one can choose to get involved in. Some people devote much time and energy to these causes, even accepting leadership roles or helping with fundraising.

Of course, in addition to circumstances, capabilities, and personality, a key component to success is taking pleasure in what you're doing, so a person has to be involved in something he enjoys.

So to answer your question as to which path to follow, a person should consider all the factors we mentioned and then discuss their options with a rebbi, mentor, or someone who knows them well.

Of course, there are many variables, but these are some of the main points to consider.

In short: The answer depends on circumstances, capabilities, and personalities, and enjoying the path one will choose.

77

The World's Wonders and Enjoyments

Q ***It is often quoted in the name of Rabbi Shamshon Raphael Hirsch that Hashem will ask, "Did you see My Alps?" Yet in Avos (3:7) we learn that one who interrupts his Torah study and exclaims, "What a nice tree this is!" is considered as if he forfeited his soul. That sounds like it is wrong to be involved in the beauties of the world, even for praising Hashem. So should I be enjoying the world's wonders or not?***

A Partaking of the pleasures of this world does have value. In fact, Rav Hirsch reportedly quoted the teaching of Talmud Yerushalmi (*Kiddushin* 4:12): "One will have to give a reckoning for not enjoying permissible foods that he saw in this world." However, as you note, this seems to contradict the many instances where our Sages stress the importance of abstaining from worldly pleasures.

This apparent inconsistency is addressed by the *Mesillas Yesharim*, who explains that it depends on a person's intentions. Enjoying this world for the sake of Heaven — such as to praise Hashem or for physical or emotional well-being — is commendable, because it helps us serve Hashem better. However, simply indulging in physical pleasures to satisfy one's desires is not correct.

In addition, one is expected to partake only in those worldly pleasures that he encountered, and there is no need to go around the world sightseeing. Rabbi Hirsch probably had to travel to the Alps for health reasons, and once there, he added that Hashem would want him to enjoy and be inspired by His creations.

Truth be told, there is no need to travel to the Alps to find Hashem's wonders, as you can see great wonders from the comfort of your home. Just look at your own body! Indeed, Iyov (19:26) declared, "From my flesh, I see G-d." Every breath and every step you take, and even just contemplating the many wondrous and complex systems inside your body, should leave you speechless over G-d's wonders.

But an even greater way — actually, the greatest way — to come close to Hashem is through the study of Torah and the performance of mitzvos. Which brings us to the Mishnah you mentioned: If someone sees a beautiful tree and praises Hashem for His beautiful world, it is truly commendable. But this should not be at the expense of Torah study.

The depth and breadth of Torah is by far the greatest wonder Hashem created, and someone who stops in middle of studying Torah to express his excitement over a nice tree is showing that he lacks full appreciation for the magnificence of Hashem's Torah.

Imagine someone visiting the Grand Canyon for the very first time. He would be completely mesmerized by the breathtaking view, and a beautiful tree on the side wouldn't even catch his attention.

The same should be true when it comes to Torah study. If one properly appreciates the greatness of the Torah and the positive effect it has on the world, he will understand that even the greatest wonders of the world should not attract his attention. That is why someone who interrupts the great wonder of Torah study to look at the more "simple" world Hashem created is criticized.

In short: One should only seek to enjoy this world for the sake of Heaven, and there is no need to run around searching for pleasures. One who appreciates the greatness of the Torah will not become distracted by the wonders of the world.

78

Best Place for Vacation

Q ***We have money set aside for vacation, and two options of where to go. We can either go to Israel and use up all the money, or we can go to Orlando, which will cost only half, and then we can use the other half for charity. Which option is better?***

A That is an excellent question!

I believe we can find the answer in the following story. Rabbi Yisrael Salanter, the great sage and founder of the *Mussar* movement, elaborated on the paramount importance of devoting time each day to the study of *mussar*, the ethical teachings of the Torah.

After hearing about the initiative, a man came to Rabbi Salanter and told him that as much as he would love to join, he simply didn't have the time. He worked very hard, barely eking out a living, and also had many other family obligations, which left him with only a half hour each day for Torah study.

Wouldn't it be more appropriate, he maintained, to dedicate this limited amount of time to the study of the Talmud, a basic obligation for every Jewish man, and the foundation of the Oral Law? In addition, shouldn't he spend the time studying *Shulchan Aruch* (the Code of Jewish Law), so he can properly observe the laws of the Torah? How could he possibly study *mussar* during the small window of time he has available?

Rabbi Salanter responded that he should indeed spend that half hour on the study of *mussar*. The study of *mussar* teaches a person what is important in life and what is not, and by studying *mussar* he would discover that not all the things he was doing with his time were really that important. With this fresh perspective, he would learn to spend his time wisely, and come to the realization that he actually had more time to study the other parts of the Torah as well.

We can apply this lesson to your situation as well. While it may be true that your vacation to Orlando will leave you with extra cash to give to charity, that will only be a one-time donation. On the other hand, if you travel to the Holy Land and visit some of the holy places there, you will receive a boost of spiritual energy, inspiring you to climb to greater heights in your service of Hashem.

This will help you become more involved in Torah study and mitzvah performance, and will be well worth the investment. You may also gain a new appreciation for spending time on spiritual endeavors and rethink how you spend your money, leading you to spend less money on unimportant items and more money on charity!

In short: By going to the Holy Land, you can become inspired to greater heights in serving Hashem, and in the long run, you may even give more charity!

79

Midwinter Vacation Plans

Q ***With war still raging in Israel, should we cancel our midwinter vacation plans? And on the topic of vacations, I heard that there is a charity that helps fund vacations for families that can't afford them, so their children won't be embarrassed of their friends when they return to school. Should we support this cause?***

A Let us first understand the purpose of vacations according to the Torah, and which vacations are appropriate.

As our rabbis tell us, materialistic pleasures are not an end unto themselves, but rather a means to help us serve Hashem better. Food is eaten to give us strength, cars help us travel to our destinations, and homes are for shelter and hosting guests. Similarly, vacations are for resting up and recharging our batteries so we can continue to live a life of serving Hashem. So vacations that help our physical or emotional well-being have a place in a Torah way of life, but extravagant and exotic vacations just for pleasure do not, even at times when there is no suffering in the world.

Additionally, the Torah does not want us to spend a lot of money on things that are not important. Therefore, going on an exotic midwinter vacation simply for thrill and excitement is incorrect, even for someone who can afford it, and certainly for someone who cannot. Collecting money to support this craziness is a terrible thing to do, as we are just teaching our children to be copycats and "keep up with the Joneses." If we collect money for vacations today, tomorrow it will be for the latest style of clothing, and the next day for something else.

Instead of going on exotic trips, you can find ways to give your family a good time without going overboard. Some children may initially give you a hard time, but little by little, this truth will penetrate their minds and hearts and begin to resonate with them, and they will be proud that they follow the ways of the Torah.

In truth, this is not an issue only when it comes to vacations. In general, we must train our children not to gauge their happiness based on others. This is terrible *chinuch*, as when they are adults they will continue to need everything their neighbors have or do. True *chinuch* would be to instill in our children a satisfaction in what we have and what we do, a feeling of joy without extravagant vacations, and pride in following the Torah.

This is the Torah perspective for vacations under normal circumstances. But at this time, when the lives of so many of our brethren in the Holy Land are in danger — soldiers, hostages, people in danger zones — and so many families have been displaced by the war, we should certainly feel their pain, and refrain from vacations. I can't say it's forbidden, but it is certainly noble not to go on a vacation.

Even President Bush, as Commander in Chief of the American army, stopped playing golf while his troops were at war. It is certainly proper for us to do the same and make ourselves a little uncomfortable while so many Jewish families are suffering and under so much stress. However, if the vacation is needed for health reasons, or to alleviate the pressures and stress of life, or to recharge your batteries, and you won't be able to function properly without it, there would be nothing wrong with going.

In short: Indulging in worldly pleasures is wrong, and we should certainly not support it. We must teach our children to do what's correct and not just copy others. It is noble not to take vacations while so many of our brethren are suffering, but if the vacation is a real need, there would be nothing wrong with going.

80

Hitchhiking

Q ***In my community, it is common for young yeshivah boys to hitchhike, and I often wonder if I should stop for them. On the one hand, I want to help others. On the other hand, stopping can disrupt traffic and even be dangerous, especially if there is no shoulder. In addition, in some states it is actually illegal to hitchhike. Should I be offering rides if it is dangerous, inconveniencing others, or against the law?***

A I don't think this is as complex as you make it sound.

Giving rides is a fulfillment of the great mitzvah of *chesed* (kindness), and you definitely should do so if you can, as long as there is no danger involved. Obviously, if you can pull over to the side of the road and not inconvenience others, you should do so. Additionally, these boys should be taught how to get rides safely and without disrupting traffic.

But even if there is no place to pull over and you need to stop for a few seconds, I don't see any issue, as long as you are not doing anything dangerous. Under normal circumstances, people do not get upset by having to wait a few seconds, especially if it is obvious that you stopped for a valid reason.

I know of places in the city where there is no room to pull over, but it has become accepted practice for people to stop for a moment to pick up a passenger or package. And if the driver behind you starts to honk unreasonably, there is no reason to be concerned.

As far as the legal aspect is concerned, I would suggest the following perspective. Obviously, these boys take rides only from people who are identifiable as religious Jews and who seem safe. That being the case, it should not be called hitchhiking. No one would consider picking up a relative who was walking along the road to be hitchhiking. Since all Jews are brothers, giving these boys a ride is like giving a ride to a relative, and should not be an issue.

In short: If you can pull over to the side, you should. But there is nothing wrong with stopping for a few seconds to pick someone up, as long as it is not dangerous and only for a few seconds. Since all Jews are brothers this should not be considered hitchhiking.

81

Sweet Dreams!

Q ***Are people more spiritual when they sleep? Recently, I have been having interesting dreams, including visions of deceased relatives and future events, and I remember the dreams vividly when I wake up. Should I take these dreams seriously? Might I be receiving revelations from another world?***

A We generally assume that dreams are meaningless, even when they seem to be real and contain an important message. The Talmud (*Berachos* 55b) explains that dreams are usually a manifestation of thoughts people had during the day, and they should not be taken seriously. Rabbi Moshe Chaim Luzzatto, in his *sefer Derech Hashem*, adds that dreams are usually meaningless because a person's intellect is inactive while sleeping, allowing the imagination to go wild and enabling him to entertain irrelevant or even ridiculous thoughts. Indeed, over the years, many people have shared with me their concerns about their dreams, but after discussing it, they realized that they were actually caused by what they had been thinking about during the day.

However, there are rare occasions where a dream may be communicating a message, and such dreams are usually identified by their recurrence. In these infrequent instances, the matter should be discussed with a competent rabbi who can help decipher the meaning.

Kabbalists explain the phenomenon of communication from the deceased and the revelation of the future during dreams: When a person goes to sleep, the soul disconnects from the body and ascends to Heaven, where it is in contact with spiritual beings that are privy to information about future events not available in our physical world.

The soul "hears" some of this and sometimes remembers it even after returning to the body.

In fact, the Vilna Gaon explained that one reason Hashem created people with the need for sleep — which seems to be a waste of so many precious hours of life in this world — is to allow the soul to make this journey to Heaven. He noted that certain lofty concepts cannot be grasped while the soul is confined within the physical body; they can be comprehended only when the soul is freed from the shackles of the physical body and can ascend to the spiritual spheres. Indeed, the Arizal and the Vilna Gaon were known to express deep and profound Torah insights that had been revealed to them in their sleep.

At the same time, while the soul ascends to Heaven and disconnects from the body as we sleep, a person lacks much of his spirituality, making him more susceptible to the evil spirits that prevail during the night. These impure spirits can cling to a person as he sleeps, and for this reason we recite *Shema* and other special prayers before going to sleep. Indeed, one reason we wash our hands in the morning is to remove any trace of these impurities.

Just as we start the day accepting Hashem's kingship with the recital of *Shema*, and declare our allegiance to Him for the entire day, we do the same at the end of the day, which helps shield us from evil. The common custom is to also recite special verses before going to sleep, to infuse us with sanctity and help us maintain pure thoughts throughout the night, warding off these evil spirits.

It is also beneficial to go to sleep with the proper intentions: that one wants to "recharge his batteries" to serve Hashem with renewed strength the next day. This will transform a person's sleep into a service of Hashem, and help maintain his purity throughout the night.

In short: Dreams are usually meaningless, a result of thoughts people had during the day, and because the intellect is dormant during sleep. However, there are rare occasions that a person may receive revelations, the result of his soul having been in Heaven.

82

The Power of Segulos

Q ***I am constantly bombarded with texts and emails exclaiming, "If you recite these chapters of Tehillim, or if you give a certain amount of charity, you will merit good children." This week's message was to say the parashah of the manna as a merit for sustenance. Is there any meaning to all this, or is it just hyperbole?***

A Although there is a basis for *segulos* — rituals done as merits for success in specific matters — they clearly have become overdone. *Segulos* have become ever more popular over the past several years, and it has come to a point where people think, "just do this or that and everything will be fine." This is unfortunately causing people to ignore the greatest and most effective *segulah* of all — belief in Hashem, the Source of all sustenance, and the need to turn to Him for all our needs.

In truth, *segulos* are not a new phenomenon. There are several places where the Chofetz Chaim decries the practice of spending large sums of money on *segulos* to merit children. He writes that people would do themselves a great favor if they would follow the advice of the Torah: putting their time and effort into studying more Torah, davening with greater concentration and intensity, and performing acts of kindness, as the Torah and Talmud teach us that these are the greatest *segulos* of all.

We often hear of people who are facing distress and turn to *segulos* to achieve salvation. For example, as soon as they encounter a challenge, they will immediately check their mezuzos or tefillin to make sure they are valid. However, our Rabbis have a different recommendation. The Talmud (*Berachos* 5a) tells us that one who is suffering should inspect his deeds, and try to become a better person. Our behavior is the true source of any situation we find ourselves in, and distress is Heaven-sent, a wake-up call to better ourselves.

But it may be appropriate — from time to time — to perform a *segulah* that comes from a great *tzaddik*. And even if there are times when one should check his mezuzos or tefillin, it would be far more powerful to check ourselves, and see if we are fulfilling the mitzvos contained in the mezuzah or tefillin, such as love of Hashem and Torah study. In fact, having a kosher mezuzah on your doorpost, or even kissing it every time you pass by, is not the full fulfillment of the mitzvah. Rambam writes that when one passes the mezuzah, he is to be reminded of Hashem's constant involvement in our lives, which will help keep him focused on serving Him properly.

There is a story of someone who was in need of a salvation, and after having gone to a *tzaddik* (righteous sage) numerous times for his blessing, with no results, the great man told him that it seems he is unable to help. The man then cried out to Hashem, "What should I do now? Even the *tzaddik* can't help me! If no one can help me, then You will have to help!" The *tzaddik* turned to him and exclaimed, "Now I know you will be helped! My powers are limited, but once you turned to the Source of all salvation and relied only on Him, you will be answered!"

In short: The greatest segulah is belief in Hashem. He is the Source of our sustenance, and turning to Him for all our needs and keeping His Torah better will bring the best results. While a segulah that is from a great tzaddik can be done once in a while, many other segulos that have become popular make people forget to turn to Hashem, and should be avoided.

83

Celebrating Birthdays

Q ***My birthday is coming up, and my friends and relatives keep reminding me to make sure to give them blessings. Is there any source to this claim that a person has special powers to bestow blessings on a birthday? And is there anything else I should be doing on my birthday?***

A I am not aware of any source for giving blessings on a birthday, but I would suggest that it is based on the idea of a birthday being a day of good *mazal* (fortune) for this person.

The Talmud (*Megillah* 13b) tells us that when the lot to destroy the Jews fell in the month of Adar, Haman rejoiced. Since Adar is the month in which Moshe died, he assumed it was an unfavorable time for the Jews. Indeed, a parent's *yahrtzeit* (anniversary of death) is considered an ill-fated day for the family, and this is one of the reasons many have the custom to fast on that day. The Gemara goes on to tell us that Haman didn't realize that Moshe was also born in Adar, making it a favorable time for the Jewish nation.

We see from this that a birthday is a propitious day, because it is the day on which Hashem decided to bring this person into the world and shower him or her with an abundance of blessing. Because it is a day of abundant blessing for this person, perhaps they have the ability to share it with others.

But as far as I know this is a new phenomenon, only becoming popular in recent times, and although there may be some merit to it, the idea — like so many *segulos* and similar ideas — has certainly become terribly exaggerated. Today, people seem to constantly be looking for the latest innovation and quick fix, and they tend to forget the tried and true methods for receiving Hashem's blessings, handed down to us from our Sages. The Chofetz Chaim already bemoaned this trend, wondering why those in need search for new methods to receive Hashem's blessings. For example, he notes that it would be more beneficial if people would focus on strengthening their Shabbos observance, because Shabbos is the source of all blessings, and on guarding their speech, which King David declared is the recipe for a long, good life.

Similarly, we see so many advertisements offering trips to all corners of the globe in search of merit and blessings. While these may have some value in certain situations, we must not lose sight of our ability to take our requests straight to Hashem, the Source of all blessings. These excursions are often the evil inclination at work, attempting to distract us and make us forget about the power of our own prayer.

As far as what a person should think about on a birthday, I would say that a person should be both thankful and hopeful. He should express thanks to Hashem for the wonderful gift of another year of life and all the blessings he received, giving him the honor and privilege to use the world to serve Him and accomplish. And he should then pray for another, even better year, with the ability to serve Hashem in an even greater way.

In Short:* *A birthday is a day of good mazal and blessing, which can perhaps be shared with others. But this seems to be a new trend, and people should be more focused on receiving blessings directly from Hashem. A birthday is a time to be thankful for the past and pray for the future, to serve Hashem even more.

84

Color War

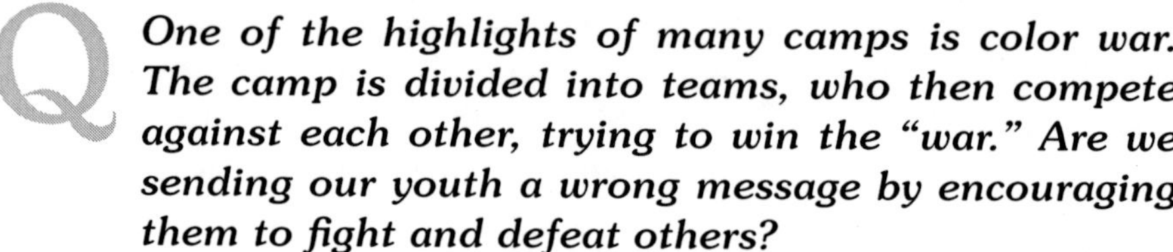

Q ***One of the highlights of many camps is color war. The camp is divided into teams, who then compete against each other, trying to win the "war." Are we sending our youth a wrong message by encouraging them to fight and defeat others?***

A I believe that color war — when conducted properly — is a very healthy experience for children. Many people go through life never developing — and often never even discovering —wonderful talents and abilities they possess. Color war provides a great opportunity for children and young adults to discover, express, and nurture their inborn talents.

On a similar note, Rabbi Shammai Blobstein recounted how, when he was a yeshivah student, he ran a learning program in a summer camp. When it came time for color war, he sent someone to ask Rav Moshe Feinstein if the yeshivah students should participate or if they should refrain because it would take away time from their Torah study.

Rav Moshe answered that it would indeed be a good idea for them to take part. He explained that during the school year, boys are busy with their Torah studies so they don't usually have time to develop their talents. Color war gives them a chance to bring out their hidden talents in a wholesome way.

Color war is not meant to encourage fighting; rather it is a means of promoting healthy competition and challenge, which can be used to bring out the best in every camper and counselor. When under pressure to produce, people tap deeper into themselves and suddenly discover skills and energy they never knew they had.

For example, many young men and women discover their

leadership qualities during color war, whether by leading a choir, teaching groups of campers to work together, or assigning the right job to the right person. Some discover or develop their artistic or musical talents by painting a banner or writing a song. Others learn to speak publicly or even to teach young children. And yet others work into the wee hours of the morning on their team's song or play, discovering their ability to focus on a project diligently for hours on end, a strength that can be channeled into great accomplishments later on in life.

At the same time, the children — and the counselors — must be coached to compete in a healthy way. For example, while cheering adds a good vibe and infuses your team with positive energy, mocking the other team is wrong.

It is also a great opportunity for the staff to teach the children the proper way to win and lose. There is nothing wrong with the winning team displaying their excitement, but they must be careful not to get carried away or gloat at the expense of the losing team. They should teach campers how to handle success in all things in life, explaining to them that the credit for any achievement goes to Hashem, since it is He Who gives us the talents to succeed.

Learning how to lose is also an important skill. Everyone will encounter failure and disappointment at some point in life, and it is crucial for a person's development to learn how to cope. Have the senior staff guide campers and younger staff members on how to be content in every situation and not to fall apart when things don't go as expected. They can also discuss with them what true success is, and that winning or losing anything materialistic in this fleeting world is not a real accomplishment or loss.

In short: Color war — when conducted properly — is a good thing, as competition brings out hidden talents. Children should be taught not to mock the other team and the correct way to win and lose — giving credit for their achievements to Hashem, and dealing properly with failure and disappointment.

Dress and Looks

85

Tzitzis or Yarmulke

Q ***My TorahMate has been growing slowly in his Torah observance, and he recently expressed interest in taking on something new, specifically regarding his attire. What would be better for him to start with, wearing tzitzis or a yarmulke? Then his question got me thinking about a similar question that applies to me as well: When I get dressed after a shower, should I first put on my tzitzis or my yarmulke?***

A Let us first discuss the question of sequence when getting dressed. Wearing tzitzis is a fulfillment of a Biblical mitzvah, whereas wearing a yarmulke is not, so — when practical — you should put on your tzitzis before your yarmulke.

However, when it comes to a *baal teshuvah*, it would be better for him to start with wearing a yarmulke. Although wearing tzitzis is a mitzvah and a yarmulke is not, in the greater picture, wearing a yarmulke has the potential to influence his whole way of life. Everyone recognizes a yarmulke as an identifiable symbol of being Jewish, whereas many people don't notice tzitzis or even know what they are. By wearing a yarmulke, he will feel recognized as a religious Jew, which will make him more conscious of his Jewish identity.

A yarmulke also makes the Orthodox Jews around him recognize him as Jewish and "one of theirs," which will make them warm up to him and help him break in. Seeing someone with tzitzis and no yarmulke, on the other hand, looks unusual and does not give the same impression.

In addition, our Rabbis (*Shabbos* 156b) teach us that covering the head infuses a person with fear of Hashem, and even young children should be trained to do so. Wearing a yarmulke reminds us that Hashem is above us at all times, and that our mission in this world is to serve Him always. Some even say that the origin of the word yarmulke is the Aramaic expression "*yarei malka*," fear of the King.

Every mitzvah should be done with feelings of love and fear of Hashem, as well as profound joy over the golden opportunity we have been given to serve the King of all kings. These feelings elevate a mitzvah, bringing it to a much higher level. Since wearing a yarmulke increases one's fear of Heaven, it would be appropriate for him to start with a yarmulke, because this will make all his subsequent mitzvos much greater.

In short: When practical, tzitzis should be donned first, as wearing them is a Biblical mitzvah. A baal teshuvah should start with a yarmulke, because it is a stronger identification of Jewishness, and it will have a greater influence on him.

86

"Black and White" Orthodox Dress Code

Q ***Why do many Orthodox Jewish men dress in black hats and white shirts? Shouldn't life be more exciting and colorful, not just "black and white"?***

A The way a person dresses can have a tremendous impact on his behavior. The Talmud (*Shabbos* 113a) relates that Rav Yochanan would refer to his clothing as "*mechabdusai* — those that honor me." The Gemara adds that wearing nice clothing is a form of honoring Shabbos.

If you take a visit to the offices of major corporations, you will notice that executives and high-ranking employees dress in respectable clothing to show their status. On the other hand, someone walking around in a tee shirt and jeans does not come across as respectable, and is unlikely to be hired for a prestigious job. As members of the Chosen Nation, we are prominent employees in Hashem's corporation, and dress accordingly.

But this concept goes even further. A Jewish body is very holy, since, as long as it is alive, it is the home of a Divine soul, and it is also the vehicle for mitzvah performance in this world. In addition, our bodies and our souls are each comprised of 613 elements, with each one corresponding to one of the 613 mitzvos we perform with our body and soul. Every mitzvah we do infuses holiness into the corresponding part of the body and soul. We therefore show honor and respect to our bodies by dressing in a fashion that befits its noble status. Indeed, there are even many laws regarding respect for a dead body, because it is the vehicle for mitzvah performance in this world.

But our focus is not just on the external. Part of why we wear prestigious clothing is to remind us of our greatness, and then be sure to act accordingly. Unfortunately, some people disgrace their bodies by pursuing their animalistic desires, and dressing respectably can remind them to keep themselves and their bodies holy.

Dark clothing is also conservative — elegant, but not too flashy. As members of Hashem's nation, Jews humble themselves before Him, and prefer to stay out of the limelight, wearing clothing that has class but is not too loud.

This holds true even more when it comes to yeshivah students, who spend their days and nights in Hashem's presence, studying His Torah. They are like a person who has an audience with the king or president, who would certainly dress formally, as appropriate for the occasion. As part of the elite group that spends time with the King of all kings all the time, it is appropriate for their mode of dress to be more formal.

In short: Orthodox Jews are executive employees of a very important "corporation," and therefore dress more formally. We also dress with class — but not flashy — to show honor to our bodies that perform mitzvos and study Hashem's Torah.

87

Ponytails

Q ***I have a male acquaintance who sports a ponytail. He says that he searched through all of Torah literature and found nothing wrong with a man having a ponytail, and he wants to keep his hairstyle. Is he correct?***

A We can't say he's wrong, because, technically speaking, there is no Torah law against a man having a ponytail. But if he is open to hearing a deeper view on life, you may want to suggest to him to be honest with himself and understand why he insists on keeping it.

More often than not, a person will choose an ostentatious hairstyle or mode of dress as a way of rebelling against the establishment, a declaration that he is "out of the box" and not confined by the norms of society. He is announcing to the world: "Look at me! I am different and I want everyone to know it!"

That attitude is troubling for a number of reasons:

Firstly, a person should seek to be "in the box" and part of Jewish society, not seeking to be different from everyone else. Also, a Jew must strive to be constantly aware of the presence of Hashem. One who senses Hashem's presence at all times will realize how insignificant he really is, and will not call unnecessary attention to himself, shying away from the limelight.

In addition, a Jew should get his excitement from spirituality and intellectual accomplishments. We seek to make our mark on the world through positive actions, such as studying Torah or giving charity, not through dress or external trappings. Those who seek thrills from such outer trimmings are acting in a way that is rather shallow, and it generally indicates a lack of spirituality. The more a person spends time doing mitzvos, studying Torah — which is the wisdom of Hashem — and talking to Hashem through heartfelt prayer, the closer he will feel to Him. People who have this true excitement in life don't need artificial ways of attracting attention.

So I would recommend to your acquaintance that he tap into his spirituality and connect to Hashem through authentic Judaism and Torah study. If he does, his ponytail will probably disappear on its own.

In short: While there is no Torah law against having a ponytail, Jews try to shy away from the limelight, and seek fulfillment from spiritual and intellectual accomplishments, not external trappings.

88

Prominent Position for the Physically Impaired

Q *I am physically impaired, and I've heard that according to Torah law, a Kohen with certain physical imperfections cannot perform the service in the Holy Temple. Does that mean that I cannot have any prominent position in serving Hashem?*

A The Torah tells us that the Mishkan (Tabernacle) and the Beis HaMikdash (Holy Temple) were built with gold and silver, along with various splendid and regal colors. Similarly, the Kohanim who perform the service there are required to wear special garments "for honor and splendor." Obviously, none of this was done for the sake of Hashem, Who needs none of these physical enhancements. Rather, it is done for us humans, who are impressed and inspired by external beauty. The impact of seeing Hashem being served by people adorned in exquisite clothing in such a magnificent edifice leaves an indelible impression on its beholders, ingraining in us the great importance of the *avodah* (service) in the Beis HaMikdash.

This is one of the reasons the Kohanim — or even the animals used for sacrifices — are not allowed to have imperfections. Keeping everyone and everything in perfect condition helps preserve the honor and prestige of the *avodah* performed in this holiest of places at the highest level.

However, this does not mean that all positions of prominence are exclusive to those who possess external beauty. In fact, quite the opposite is true. The Talmud (*Taanis* 7a) tells the story of a great sage who was very unattractive and was approached by a princess, who asked him how it was possible that Hashem chose to store His wisdom in such an ugly vessel. He responded with the following suggestion: Her father — the king — should store his wine in gold or silver vessels, as is fitting for a king, and not in ugly earthenware vessels, like everyone else does. She told the king to do so and the wine turned sour.

When questioned by the king why he gave such bad advice, he responded, "The way she spoke to me is how I replied to her." He wished to demonstrate that just as wine — even that belonging to the king — can be preserved only in ugly earthenware vessels, Torah wisdom is better preserved and longer retained by one lacking external beauty. One reason for this is that such a person will not be distracted by the frivolities of external beauty; this will keep him focused on spiritual endeavors, such as studying Torah.

But this goes even further. This concept is true not only when it comes to physical blemishes, but is true with regard to spiritual deficiencies as well; indeed, even someone not perfect spiritually can reach the highest levels of Torah. The Talmud (*Sotah* 4b) tells us that even a *mamzer* (a child born from an illicit marriage) who is a Torah scholar is greater than the Kohen Gadol, who enters the Holy of Holies on Yom Kippur, the holiest day of the year. Although the Kohen Gadol must reach an extremely high level of holiness to be allowed this unique privilege, one who studies Hashem's Torah can reach even greater heights, and be considered truly beautiful in the eyes of Hashem.

Indeed, Rambam (*Talmud Torah* 3:1) writes that the Jewish nation has three crowns. The "crown of priesthood" was given to Aharon and his descendants, and the "crown of royalty" was given to King David and his heirs. But the greatest crown of all — the "crown of Torah" — is available to all Jews, ready for the taking.

In short: A Kohen must be in perfect condition to uphold the prestige of the Temple service. But someone with a blemish or handicap can reach the highest levels of Torah.

Life and Death

89

Dying to Die

Q ***I have heard that the Next World is the "real thing," and this world is just the "antechamber." So why aren't people "dying to die"? And why is death a punishment? Shouldn't we rejoice when a person finally gets called into the Grand Ballroom from the waiting room?***

A Whether our focus should be on life in this world or the next is a paradox we find in *Avos* (4:22). The Mishnah first states that one "hour" of good deeds in this world is better than the entire World to Come. Then the Mishnah states that one "hour" of bliss in the World to Come is infinitely greater than any enjoyment one can get in this world. These two statements seem to give opposite messages. Which is the "place to be," this world or the next?

The answer is that both concepts are true. The *Mesillas Yesharim*, quoting our Sages, teaches that the very purpose of creation is for us to enjoy being close to Hashem, a goal that can be fully achieved only in the spiritual existence of the World to Come. That is why one should indeed look forward to the time when he will transcend this physical, mundane world and be able to enjoy a true closeness to Hashem. The *Chovos HaLevavos* adds another reason to look forward to leaving this world: because we will reconnect with the *tzaddikim* (righteous people) of past generations.

But this doesn't happen on its own. In order for a person to get a "good seat" in the Grand Ballroom, he must first come to this world to do mitzvos and deserve a good place there. And this is why we want to remain in this world as long as we can, because the longer we are here the more mitzvos we can do, earning us much greater reward for eternity.

There is another fundamental reason we want to remain in this world: because it is only here that we can serve Hashem. As wonderful as the Next World is, it is the place for receiving reward, not a place for mitzvah performance. If one truly appreciates the greatness of serving Hashem, his greatest wish will be to seek more opportunities to serve Him, without giving any thought to reward.

Just imagine if the Chofetz Chaim or Rav Moshe Feinstein walked into the room and needed a drink. Everyone would jump at the wonderful opportunity to serve the preeminent *tzaddik* of the generation! Serving the King of the entire universe should certainly be much more exhilarating, and no one wants to miss such opportunities.

So yes, the ultimate goal and the greatest pleasure is to come close to Hashem and understand the deep secrets of His Torah and of all creation in the Next World. At the same time, every moment of life is precious, as it provides us with another opportunity to serve Hashem. Indeed, the *Chovos HaLevavos* writes, the righteous look forward to the Next World, but also want to be here in this world as long as possible because they utilize, appreciate, and enjoy every moment here.

In short: We look forward to dying so we can be close to Hashem, but we also want to be in this world as long as possible, because it is here that we can serve Him and also earn even greater reward.

90

Cremation Questions

Q ***I know cremation is wrong, but if a parent asks to be cremated, should the child honor the request? And what about the souls of those who were cremated during the Holocaust, do they rest in peace? And if someone was cremated, should Kaddish be recited for that unfortunate soul?***

A Cremating a body is a grave sin. One reason for this is because while the body was alive, it housed a Divine soul and was its partner in mitzvah performance, so the body itself must be treated with respect.

Burying a dead body also demonstrates belief in one of the basic tenets of Judaism: *techiyas hameisim,* resurrection of the dead. Death is not the end of life, for if a person is deemed worthy, the soul and body will be reunited, and live for eternity.

These are reasons that Jewish law requires us to respect a body even after death, and why the body is washed and cleaned before burial. In fact, in earlier times, they would even bury the deceased in expensive garments (see *Kesubos* 8b). This all expresses our firm belief that the body is just resting peacefully, waiting for that great day when it will once again return to life.

Cremation, on the other hand, abuses and desecrates the body, and displays a lack of belief in the revival of the dead. It also makes the *techiyas hameisim* process much more complicated. As the Midrash (*Bereishis Rabbah* 28:3) teaches, the body will be reconstructed from the *luz* bone — one of the bones in the spine — and a cremated body will have a much more complicated time coming back to life.

Since cremation is a sin, there is no obligation to honor the request of a parent who wishes to be cremated. Although honoring parents is a great mitzvah, the mitzvah does not apply when their request contradicts the Torah, for they are also obligated to listen to Hashem. And in this case, even the person who made the request, now that his soul is in the World of Truth, certainly wishes it could be withdrawn.

This does not apply to the holy Jews who were sent to the crematoria during the Holocaust. Since this was done against their will, Hashem considers it as if they received a proper burial, and they will certainly merit coming back to life, with or without the *luz* bone.

Kaddish should certainly be recited for the soul of someone who was cremated. A person who makes such a request is obviously not very religious, and his soul certainly needs great spiritual elevation. While it is not our place to judge that person, who may not have known better, it is up to us to do whatever we can to elevate these unfortunate souls.

In short: Cremation demonstrates a lack of belief in techiyas hameisim and complicates the process. It also desecrates the body that housed the soul and was used to perform mitzvos. Since it is a sin, we do not obey a parent's request to cremate. This does not apply to the Jews cremated during the Holocaust who were not at fault. We should certainly recite Kaddish for the soul of someone cremated.

91

Yahrtzeit Candles and Stones on Graves

Q ***What is the point of lighting candles as a memorial for the deceased, either on a yahrtzeit or at the graveside? Do they do something for the soul? I have also seen people placing stones on graves. What is that all about?***

A In Judaism, there is a significant connection between a candle and the soul of the deceased. A person's soul is compared to a lamp, as the *pasuk* says (*Mishlei* 20:27), "The lamp of Hashem is a person's soul," because the soul is a spiritual entity, a "spark" from the light of Hashem.

Every person is comprised of a body and a soul. The physical body is rooted in the world of materialism, and draws a person toward worldly desires, such as envy, lust, honor, and the list goes on. The spiritual dimension of the person is his *neshamah*, his soul, which strives to connect to Hashem and achieve loftier goals.

Unfortunately, we live in a world full of people who are purely materialistic and often act like animals, committing the worst sins. But the Jewish people have the Torah as our guiding light, showing us the correct path to follow and teaching us how to live on a higher plane, enabling us to connect to Hashem. When a person follows the Torah, the Divine light of the soul becomes brighter, helping him tap into his spiritual essence.

Since the physical light of a candle represents the spiritual light of the soul, lighting a candle for a loved one demonstrates that even after a person dies, he or she is not gone. The body may be buried, but the "light" of the person — the soul — is still very much alive and shining just like this candle. When we see this candle and are reminded of the eternity of the soul, we are inspired to better ourselves and help our souls reach greater heights. This, in turn, will benefit the soul of the deceased, who was the catalyst for this inspiration. Thus, the lighting of a candle for a loved one will also help "light up" the soul of the deceased.

In addition to lighting a candle, a more effective way to elevate the deceased's soul is by doing mitzvos, such as giving extra charity in their merit and reciting *Kaddish*. This is particularly true when the one performing mitzvos is a child of the deceased. Being that the parent brought the child into the world and likely educated him to act properly, the parent gets credit for the child's good deeds and will earn reward in the World of Souls for the child's mitzvos. This is especially important on the *yahrtzeit*, because the soul faces judgment each year on this day, and good deeds performed by its offspring will elevate it to greater heights.

Placing stones on the grave reflects a similar concept. Although the dead person can no longer earn reward through performing mitzvos, if his influence is still having an effect, his soul will continue to rise to greater heights in the Next World. A person's children and students studying Torah because of him, or the money he donated — or inspired others to donate — to charity still being used to help the needy, are just some examples of this. Similarly, if the people visiting the grave accept upon themselves to improve themselves in the merit of the deceased, the soul will continue to grow even after death. Stones are like building blocks, and the custom of placing stones on the tombstone symbolizes that through our good deeds, the deceased will continue to grow.

In short: We light a candle to show that the soul is still alive and shining just like this candle. Stones are like building blocks, and demonstrate that the deceased will continue to grow through our good deeds.

Animal Life

92

Caring for Endangered Species

Q ***What is the Torah's view on endangered species? Should we be investing time, effort, and money into saving them, or is it the natural way of the world for certain animals to become extinct, and there is no need for us to get involved?***

A Hashem created a beautiful world, with a wide variety of creatures, each one with a distinct purpose, and it is our duty to take care not to ruin His world. When Hashem finished creating the world, the Torah (*Bereishis* 1:31) tells us that He took inventory of all that had been created, and declared, "Behold, it was very good." *Mesillas Yesharim* quotes a Midrash that after Hashem created Adam, He took him around and showed him the wonderful world He had created, and cautioned him not to ruin it.

Therefore, we must certainly be careful not to be involved in the extinction of these animals by hunting them or causing their destruction in any other way. Since Hashem created them for a reason, causing their disappearance would be going against His will.

Similarly, if you receive a request to help save the dolphins, it would be appropriate to send in a minimal donation. But bear in mind that there are many other more important charities — such as organizations that save lives, support Torah and Torah scholars, help the poor, and fund outreach programs, to name just a few.

And despite our obligation to maintain Hashem's world, don't spend time and effort on these causes. Our focus and efforts should be on fulfilling our primary mission in this world — studying Torah and performing mitzvos. Not only are those the reasons Hashem sent us to this world, they are the best way to help maintain the world as well. Every mitzvah a person performs, and every word of Torah he studies, brings untold blessing to the world, which can do a lot more to help save these endangered species than any funds and human efforts can.

The world exists only through Hashem's constant blessing, and every mitzvah we do provides the spiritual energy that makes the world worthy of receiving that blessing. And the greatest mitzvah of all is Torah study, which produces so much spiritual energy that it generates untold blessing to the entire universe. Therefore, the best way to save the world is not by spearheading organizations like "Save the Whales," but by redoubling our efforts in all our spiritual endeavors. Those are guaranteed to bring a greater quality of life and vitality to all of creation.

In short: Hashem expects us to preserve the world He created, and so we must not be involved in causing the extinction of these animals. But our focus should be on fulfilling our mission in this world — studying Torah and performing mitzvos — which also serves as the best way to help the world.

93

Dogs — Man's Best Friend?

Q ***We have owned a dog for a number of years, and our children are very attached to him. We recently moved to a more religious community, and I've noticed that other members of the community don't have pets. In fact, many of our neighbors won't even visit our home out of fear of our dog. I'm not sure what they have against our cute and very tame puppy, but this has been hindering our ability to integrate into the community. Is there something wrong with having a dog? And if there is, should we just let him go, even if our children will be very upset?***

A It is true that many religious families don't own dogs, and there are a number of reasons for this. Firstly, the Talmud (*Bava Kamma* 83a) frowns upon owning a dog, as many people are afraid of dogs and it is not right to frighten them. It notes that the fright caused by a barking dog can even cause a woman to miscarry. I myself am scared of dogs, having been bitten by one as a child.

Furthermore, pets in general, and especially dogs, require a lot of care and consume a lot of a person's time and energy. Time is precious, and we prefer to use it for more constructive activities, such as studying Torah, doing mitzvos, and spending time with our children. Caring for a dog can also be costly — buying the right foods, taking it to the vet, and all its other needs — and we feel that this money would be better spent on charity and other mitzvos.

There are also many halachos regarding pets that people are unaware of, some of which are not so easy to adhere to. For example, it is forbidden to eat before feeding your animals, which can at times be quite challenging. Imagine sitting down to breakfast and realizing that you are out of dog food. If your local grocery does not carry dog food, it can turn into a whole morning excursion.

A person must also be extremely careful not to transgress the laws of *tzaar baalei chaim,* causing an animal undue pain. In addition, according to many opinions a pet is *muktzeh*, making it complicated to handle on Shabbos and Yom Tov. And yet another item on your to-do list will be ensuring you have kosher for Pesach dog food, as it is forbidden to own or derive any benefit from chametz on Pesach.

These are some reasons why many religious people choose not to have pets. But while it is a good idea to let your dog go, at the same time, you must definitely take your children's feelings into consideration. I would suggest that you wean yourselves off the dog slowly. Find a kennel where you can leave your dog for a few days at a time, sending him away for longer intervals each time. Your family will become less and less attached to the dog, and eventually they will be able to move on.

If your children really want a pet, another option would be to replace your pet with a bird or fish, which are relatively easy and less time-consuming to care for.

In short: Many religious people don't have dogs, as people are afraid of dogs, and their care takes a lot of time and money, which would be better spent on more constructive purposes. There are also many difficult halachos that must be kept. Wean yourselves off the dog slowly, making it easier for your children to let go, or perhaps replace your pet with a bird or fish.

94

Parting With a Beloved Pet

Q ***Our beloved pet dog is starting to show signs of old age, and the vet told us that the time has come to "put him to sleep." But after being a part of the family for so many years, I am having trouble coping with this.***

A I just heard a wonderful story on this topic.

Rav Elchonon Wasserman was at the home of a woman who lived alone and owned a dog to help her feel more secure. After many years, she was no longer able to keep the dog in her home, and she was considering giving it away to the humane society. Since the great rabbi was there at the time, she asked him if this would be the appropriate thing to do.

Rabbi Wasserman inquired as to what the society would do to the dog, and she replied that they would "put it to sleep." To which he responded in disbelief, "You're going to send your dog to be put to death?! After it served you faithfully for so many years you must feel appreciation to it. As long as he is not suffering, you should let him die of old age, but don't have a part in killing him."

It is important to understand that *hakaras hatov* (appreciating the good one receives) applies even when the benefactor is an animal or even a lifeless object. This is why Hashem did not command Moshe to strike the water and the earth of Egypt to bring about the first three plagues. Since the Nile had helped save him when his mother hid him there, and the earth had concealed the body of the Egyptian he had killed, it would have been ungrateful of him to harm them.

Appreciating the good we receive from others brings us to appreciate the true benefactor and source of all good — Hashem. When you realize this, you will surely thank Hashem for the animal you benefitted from, along with everything He does for you.

In short: One must feel appreciation even to an animal who was his benefactor, and not put it to death unless it is suffering.

95

Perek Shirah — Singing the Song of Creation

Q ***I enjoy reciting Perek Shirah, the various verses sung by each element of creation — animals, birds, trees, oceans, mountains, etc. — in praise of G-d. Do inanimate objects or even animals actually sing these words? And will we be able to hear this singing when Mashiach comes?***

A Since animals and inanimate objects were not gifted with the power of speech, and are not capable of comprehending Hashem's greatness, they are not the ones that sing these verses. It is rather their spiritual source in the upper worlds who sing Hashem's praises. As *Tosafos* (*Chullin* 7a) explains, when our Sages speak of the conversations of animals or inanimate objects, they are referring to the angel or spiritual root of this creation.

The kabbalists expound on this concept as follows: Our physical world is actually the lowest of a chain of many worlds. Everything we see in our world is created by Hashem in an abstract spiritual form in higher echelons, which in turn empowers the form of these creations in the world beneath that, and the next, until reaching our physical world. As the creation goes down the chain, each world becomes increasingly physical, until our world, which is completely physical. As an example of this, I like to refer to H20, which can take on many forms: a solid form — ice; a liquid form — water; and a gas form — steam, depending on the temperature.

So no, it is not the lions or the oceans themselves singing Hashem's praises. Even so, some of the sounds we hear, such as the chirping of the birds, may be a ripple effect of the singing of their spiritual component in the higher spheres. In the World to Come, where we will be more spiritual and the world will be a more spiritual place, we will likely be able to hear these spiritual beings themselves singing Hashem's praises.

Although reciting *Perek Shirah* is not a priority, and the primary prayers certainly take precedence, it does have special significance. Everything in the universe was created for a specific purpose, and each creation sings the verse that reflects its purpose in the world. When all the creations sing their part, together they create a harmonious symphony, bringing out the true glory of Hashem.

But these strengths are not just found in the various creations featured in *Perek Shirah*. The Torah tells us that Adam was created last, after all the other creations. *Nefesh HaChaim* (1:6), based on *Zohar*, explains that this was done so that every creation would impart its unique characteristic into Adam, making him an "*olam katan*," a microcosm of the world, comprised of all these different strengths. This empowered man with the ability to accomplish all he needs to in this world.

For this reason, we are taught (*Avos* 5:23): "Be bold as a leopard, light as an eagle, swift as a deer, and strong as a lion." Although it may sound like a tall order, this can be expected from us because these strengths are all hidden within us, to be tapped into when needed in our service of Hashem. For example, there are times we must be swift, times we must be patient, and even times to show anger, each one in the proper time, place, and manner.

Reciting the song of creation helps a person understand the essence of each one, and then apply these strengths to oneself. This will help a person recognize his or her own potential and then use these strengths and abilities to serve Hashem.

In short: The spiritual root of each creation sings Hashem's praises, and we will likely hear them in the World to Come. Reciting the song of each creation helps us recognize our own hidden strengths, which we can use to serve Hashem.

Section 13

Shabbos

96

Waving Hands at Candle Lighting

Q ***Why are women the ones who usually light the Shabbos candles? And why do they wave their hands after lighting? Are they trying to catch angels?***

A The mitzvah of lighting candles before Shabbos was instituted to ensure that one's home is properly illuminated on Friday night. This helps maintain *shalom bayis* (tranquility in the home) because people won't stumble or have to sit in the dark. A well-lit home also enhances the Friday night meal, making it a more honorable and enjoyable experience. One reason this mitzvah was assigned specifically to women is because the home is the woman's domain, and she is the one with the ability to infuse it with a pleasant atmosphere. Nevertheless, the mitzvah is incumbent on all members of the household, and where the woman is not present, someone else should light.

The Shabbos candles also have a much deeper meaning. On Shabbos, Hashem comes close to us, and the physical light of the candles represents the spiritual light that descends to the world at the onset of this holy day. In addition, the light of the candles represents the light of the Torah, like the Menorah in the Holy Temple, whose light was the conduit to bring Torah and spirituality from Heaven and spread it throughout the world. Indeed, the Talmud (*Shabbos* 23b) tells us that one who fulfills the mitzvah of lighting Shabbos candles properly will merit children who are Torah scholars.

For this reason, candle lighting time is considered an auspicious moment to pray for children who will light up the world with Torah, as mentioned in the prayer recited by many after lighting the candles. And since the light of Torah brings with it all types of blessings, the floodgates of blessing are open and many women seize the opportunity to add other requests as well.

We can now understand the custom you mentioned, of women waving their hands next to the candles after lighting. Since Shabbos is the source of all blessing, this infusion of holiness that the Shabbos candles bring will spread out and illuminate the entire world. Waving hands is perhaps a way of demonstrating that through lighting these candles, and the proper intentions, she will bring down the light of the Torah and abundant blessing, which will fan out and light up the entire universe.

In short: The woman lights the candles because she is in charge of creating a peaceful and pleasant atmosphere in the home. Waving the hands demonstrates that the Shabbos candles bring illumination and blessing to the entire world.

97

Shabbos and Yom Tov Foods

Q ***Rabbi, I heard that the Shabbos and holiday foods have great significance. I find that hard to believe! They may be tasty, but what deep meaning can there possibly be in some simple challah, kugel, and gefilte fish?***

A There is nothing simple in Judaism, and even seemingly mundane and physical activities are laden with spirituality. The foods customarily eaten on Shabbos and on holidays contain significance and meaning, and have been on the Jewish menu for generations. Because we are physical beings, we get inspired by what we eat, and eating these foods helps us tap into the meanings and significance of the day. For example, the Shabbos meal begins with Kiddush, when we praise Hashem for choosing us with love and giving us this holy day. As the *Sefer HaChinuch* points out, Kiddush is recited over a cup of wine, a beverage that uplifts the spirit, to show our excitement as we usher in this wonderful day.

But the wine also has another important implication. There are certain prohibitions involved in drinking wine together with a non-Jew, and a cup of wine marks our separation from the other nations. By starting the meal with this cup of wine, we pronounce that we are not just eating a tasty meal for our personal enjoyment. Rather, the meal is *mei'ein Olam Haba*, a microcosm of the bliss awaiting our nation in the World to Come, where we will indeed be above all the other nations.

This is also why wine is used for the blessings at many Jewish ceremonies. At a *bris milah*, we welcome another child into our special covenant with Hashem, and recite the blessings holding a cup of wine, proclaiming that we alone are His devoted servants. Similarly, at a wedding ceremony, we use wine to express that a Jewish marriage is not a selfish pursuit, but a sacred endeavor to build a home for the sake of serving Hashem.

The two loaves of challah commemorate the double portion of manna that fell in the desert every Friday for forty years, where the Jews miraculously received their sustenance directly from Above. We also place a special cover over the challah to remember that the manna was covered with dew to keep it fresh. In fact, some say this is the reason behind the tradition of eating potato kugel, which has a crust on top and on bottom, just like the dew protected the manna above and below. These commemorations help us internalize the reality that Hashem cares for us each day, just as He personally took care of our every need in the desert.

Even the fact that the challah is braided has a special meaning. This represents the intertwining of the two dimensions of Shabbos: *zachor,* remember, a reference to the positive commandments of Shabbos; and *shamor,* safeguard, a reference to refraining from forbidden actions. Hashem expressed these simultaneously at Mount Sinai, teaching us that it is only with the full observance of Shabbos — both the positive commandments and the prohibitions — that we can transcend the mundane, materialistic world, sanctifying us and connecting us to Hashem.

Gefilte fish is ground and boneless, which helps ensure that we don't mistakenly separate the bones from the fish, an activity that is forbidden on Shabbos.

Cholent, hamin, or other hot foods are kept on a fire from before Shabbos and eaten at the Shabbos day meal. This is done to demonstrate that it is permissible to keep a fire burning on Shabbos, as long as it was lit before Shabbos.

Even the hot soup, I believe, contains an allusion to the spiritual dimension of Shabbos. The Hebrew word for soup is *marak*, which has the same root as *miruk,* cleansing. This teaches us the importance of not only cleaning our bodies and clothing for Shabbos, but also of cleansing our souls before Shabbos, to help us bask in the light of this holy day.

In short: All Jewish customs have deep spiritual meaning, and the special foods we eat on Shabbos and holidays represent the spirit and meaning of the days.

98

What's so Special About Fish?

Q ***I have noticed that fish is usually served at traditional Shabbos meals. Is there something special about fish? And what if I don't particularly enjoy fish, should I still make sure to have some?***

A On a simple level, fish is a delicacy, and just like any other tasty food, eating it is a fulfillment of the mitzvah of enhancing the enjoyment of Shabbos (*oneg Shabbos*). But it's not a requirement per se, and if someone does not like the taste of fish, he does not need to push himself to eat it; rather, he should fulfill this mitzvah with foods he enjoys.

However, on a deeper level, there is something very unique about fish. Since humans and animals are unable to live in water, life in the water is like life in a different world. For this reason, we find that although the animals all perished in the Great Flood (*Mabul*), the fish did not. The evil and immorality of the people at that time contaminated the world's very atmosphere, affecting even the animals and making them unfit to remain alive.

The fish, however, existing in their own world, remained pure and unaffected by the contamination of the world, and thus survived the Flood.

This is one reason why it is customary to eat fish on Shabbos. Shabbos is *mei'ein Olam Haba,* a semblance of the eternal life in the World to Come, and on this day we refrain from work, leaving behind the mundane and connecting to Hashem. Since fish live in the water and are "out of this world," it is an appropriate dish for the day we live on a higher sphere. We then strive to keep this lesson with us throughout the week, inspired to live a more spiritual existence.

As explained elsewhere ("The Mystical Power of a Mikveh"), the concept that life in the water is separate from life in this world can also help us understand the purifying power of immersing in a *mikveh* (ritual bath). By completely disconnecting oneself from this world, a person is essentially recreating himself, emerging from the water clean and pure. The physical immersion also helps a person reflect on his spiritual status, arousing him to be refreshed and rejuvenated, ready to serve Hashem with renewed vigor.

In short: Eating fish on Shabbos is a fulfillment of the mitzvah of oneg Shabbos, and since Shabbos is a day of spirituality, it is appropriate to eat fish that live in water, and are less connected to the human world. But if someone does not enjoy fish, he can fulfill this mitzvah with other foods.

99

Shabbos Table Talk

Q ***We often have guests — or even family members — at our Shabbos table who are not interested in hearing words of Torah, preferring other topics of conversation, such as politics, sports, or just the latest news in town. Should I allow this type of talk at the table so they will enjoy the Shabbos meal?***

A Of course, ideally, a Shabbos table should have only words of Torah and inspiration. But since you want everyone at the table to enjoy the Shabbos meal, being so restrictive may not be so advisable. Nevertheless, with some thought and creativity, almost any topic can be turned into something connected to the Torah.

For example, if someone begins discussing current events, you can point out that everything that happens in the world is orchestrated by Hashem, and discuss what message He may be sending. Similarly, if one of your guests starts talking about politics, you can steer the conversation toward one of the many political issues that have ramifications in halachah or *hashkafah* (worldview). A person who enjoys politics may welcome a debate on the pros and cons of voting for a candidate who pledges to help the Jewish community or is pro-Israel, but whose moral standards are not up to par. You can also share the Torah view on various contemporary issues, such as liberalism versus conservatism.

For someone who brings up sports, you can point out how every talent — whether it's the ability to hit a home run or the winning shot — is a gift from Heaven, and with hard work and perseverance, can be developed and used for good things.

You can also discuss how any position of prominence — political, athletic, or anything else — can be used to glorify Hashem's Name. One recent example is the Orthodox lawyer of a prominent politician who would not attend hearings on Shabbos, and was seen covering his head in order to recite a blessing before taking a drink. As these hearings were broadcast worldwide, this was certainly an international *kiddush Hashem* (sanctification of G-d's Name). And of course, you can point to the famous example of Sandy Koufax, who turned down the opportunity of a lifetime by refusing to pitch in a World Series game on Yom Kippur. By giving this up, he showed the world that he was willing to sacrifice fame and prestige for something of greater value. This can also be used as a springboard to discuss priorities in life.

But an even better idea would be to come to the meal prepared with a topic your audience will enjoy. In general, people are not against Torah discussions per se; it all depends on the presentation. The list of ideas is endless, but here are some examples:

Instead of a longwinded or "boring" Torah thought, you can share life-lessons found in the *parashah* of the week, making the Torah alive and relevant in today's world. Look for captivating stories that will pique their interest and bring out powerful lessons about serving Hashem, character development, or being kind to others. You can also ask trivia questions on a variety of engaging Torah topics, using this as a tool to teach interesting Torah laws and facts.

I've also heard another way to get the people at the table involved: Many families have someone pose an interesting *hashkafah* question, taken from the vast amount of Torah literature available. They then give everyone an opportunity to share their perspective, concluding with an authoritative Torah view.

So with a little bit of thought and planning, your Shabbos table can be enjoyable and spiritual, with food for both the body and the soul.

In short: Prepare things that your audience will enjoy, such as life-lessons from the parashah, trivia questions on Torah topics, captivating stories with lessons, or interesting hashkafah questions. But almost any topic can be connected to Torah.

100

Lengthy Shabbos Meals

Q ***How long should a Shabbos meal take? Should we have long meals, with lots of delicious food, along with engaging and inspiring family conversation? Or should we keep the meals short, allowing more time for other activities, such as Torah study, sleeping, and relaxing?***

A The Shabbos meal is a wonderful tool for enriching and uplifting your family's love of Judaism, and you should not squander this opportunity. In a society where everyone is "on the run" and families hardly spend time together, enjoyable and relaxing family time is more important than ever for everyone's emotional and spiritual growth. But like many other things, we need to find the right balance, and while you shouldn't rush the meal, it also shouldn't go on endlessly.

With a bit of foresight and preparation, much can be accomplished at the Shabbos table. A Shabbos meal is a time to share words of Torah that inspire and elevate everyone at the table. I often tell fathers and teachers that it is important to prepare enjoyable and age-appropriate Torah thoughts for the Shabbos table that also contain a message, such as examples of good deeds or character traits gleaned from the *parashah* of the week.

The Shabbos table is also a chance for children to shine. In a pleasant and unpressured setting, they can share some of what they learned in school. They can also discuss any exciting incidents or challenges they may have encountered at school or at home, and you can teach them how to deal with the situation in an appropriate way.

It is also a great opportunity to discuss the proper Torah outlook on current events and other topics of interest. Each person at the table can share their opinion, and then you can examine the Torah's perspective.

Singing the Shabbos *zemiros* — songs describing the beauty of Shabbos, the greatness of Hashem, and His love for His nation — should also be an enjoyable experience. Singing these songs with feeling and fervor can infuse everyone there with a joy and passion for being a Jew and inspire them to draw closer to Hashem.

The Shabbos table is a unique opportunity to convey these lessons. The relaxed atmosphere, along with the delectable foods served in honor of Shabbos, blended with the harmonious melodies and inspirational words, will help everyone walk away motivated and energized for the week to come.

Although you should certainly spend a nice amount of time at the Shabbos table, it is impossible to give an exact timeframe for how long the meal should take, since the dynamics and logistics of every family are different. The age and attention span of the family members, as well as many other variables, must be taken into account when achieving the specific formula that works for your family.

Another factor is the guests who may be at the table. Aside from the great mitzvah to host guests, they can also add much diversity and flavor. Guests often hail from different backgrounds or cities, and can share their unique customs as well as their observations and life experiences.

In short: Do not rush through a Shabbos meal. There is much to accomplish, including inspiring words of Torah, discussing the Torah perspective on relevant issues, and singing heartwarming zemiros, all in a relaxed and enjoyable atmosphere. The exact length of the meal depends on each family.

101

Singing Mizmor L'David at the Third Meal

Q ***Many people have the custom to sing Mizmor L'David (Psalm 23) three times at the third Shabbos meal. What is the reason for this, and if it's not done in my shul should I insist they start?***

A In this psalm, King David describes his feelings of inner peace and tranquility. He proclaims that he is not scared even when entering the "valley of death," comforted by the knowledge that Hashem is with him at all times, and he prays to be pursued only by Hashem's kindness. Since Shabbos is a day of rest and serenity and a day of great blessing, it is certainly most appropriate to sing these words as Shabbos ends, as we seek to internalize this feeling, and pray that these blessings accompany us throughout the week.

As we say Friday night in *Lechah Dodi*, Shabbos is the *mekor haberachah,* the source of all blessings. This means that all the good we receive throughout the week — spiritual or physical — is rooted in the blessings of Shabbos. On Shabbos, we step back from our work and focus on recognizing that Hashem created the world and continues to sustain it every second. This helps us realize that success and achievement are not our doing, but from Hashem, and this realization makes us more worthy of His blessing. The more we honor Shabbos, the more blessings we will enjoy during the workweek to come.

Indeed, when we encounter spiritual or physical challenges throughout the week, we sometimes wonder what we did wrong to deserve this difficulty. Yet the cause may actually be a deficiency at the source — our Shabbos observance. By improving the way we observe Shabbos, we can tap into this wellspring of blessing, enabling us to be more successful in all our endeavors throughout the week. This can be accomplished through increased Torah study, putting greater effort into the prayers, or with more words of Torah and inspiration, as well as Shabbos *zemiros* (songs) and serving special delicacies at the Shabbos table.

As we sit at the third and final meal of Shabbos, bidding farewell to this wonderful day, we try to internalize the lessons of Shabbos and take them along with us. Knowing that we are about to return to the dark and frightening world, we sing King David's message of calm and tranquility, reassuring ourselves that Hashem is our "Shepherd." He will lead us and shower us with His kindness, and provide us with all our needs.

Singing it three times emphasizes the importance of this message, like other prayers that are recited three times. Something done three times creates a *chazakah,* a halachic method of establishing the permanence of something. As King Shlomo teaches (*Koheles* 4:12), "A three-fold thread is not easily severed."

Although this is a wonderful custom, it is certainly not worth fighting over. Dispute and discord would have the opposite effect, as lack of unity weakens our connection to Hashem and can cause us to lose any blessings we wish to receive. If the people in your shul are opposed to it, just leave things as is. Singing it once with meaning is also beneficial, and if you want, you can sing it to yourself two more times.

In short: We internalize King David's message of calm and tranquility at the final meal of Shabbos, and try to carry it with us throughout the week. Three times emphasizes the message. Don't fight about it, as that can cause you to lose any blessings you wish to receive.

Section 14

Yamim Tovim — Jewish Holidays

Pesach

102

Pesach Cleaning — Is It Overdone?

Q ***Many women spend weeks or even months cleaning for Pesach, but much of it seems to be just "spring cleaning." Is it wrong for them to work extra for no reason, or, perhaps, is going beyond the letter of the law a hiddur mitzvah — a more beautiful way to perform the mitzvah? In addition, if they think they are doing a mitzvah, will they get rewarded for their good intentions?***

A It is important to know what is part of the mitzvah of cleaning for Pesach and what is not. Halachah clearly dictates that we are obligated only to clean places where there may be chametz, and scrubbing down areas in the house where no one ever brings food is clearly unnecessary. So if you never bring food into the bathroom, attic, or basement, or even a bedroom, there is no need to clean them at all.

And even if there are little children who may bring chametz into these rooms, you just need to take a quick look for chametz in the obvious places. That being the case, much of the work people tend to do while cleaning for Pesach is completely unnecessary.

But overdoing it is more than just unnecessary, it is actually problematic. By adding all this extra work, these women — and very often the rest of the family — feel anxious, stressed, and overwhelmed, turning what should be an enjoyable mitzvah experience into a burden and a nightmare.

Additionally, by the time Pesach arrives, these women are exhausted and are unable to properly experience and enjoy the Seder and the holiday. Even if someone feels that they are enhancing the mitzvah by working harder, they must realize that it would be a greater mitzvah to work less and arrive at the Seder attentive and energetic. Since the Seder is a time when we can reach elevated levels of *emunah* (belief), being rested and ready to be inspired can make a world of difference. Since both men and women are obligated to fulfill all the mitzvos of the Seder, this applies equally to all members of the family.

It is therefore advisable to speak to a halachic authority or study reliable halachic works to clarify what is required and what is not.

I once spoke to a group of women and told them that they should nap on Erev Pesach for at least a half hour or preferably an hour, so that they can come to the Seder more rested. A woman told me afterward that she just follows her mother's "custom" and falls asleep at the Seder!

So I strongly advise toning down the cleaning so that it is enjoyable and not a burden, and this will also help everyone come to the Seder excited and ready to take full advantage of the wonderful experience. When people are attentive at the Seder, they will be infused with *emunah* and excitement to serve Hashem, and that will remain long after the Seder is over.

In short: Only places where there may be chametz need to be cleaned. Spring cleaning should not be done while cleaning for Pesach, as it wears people out unnecessarily, causing them to not enjoy the mitzvah of cleaning, and to come to the Seder tired out.

103

What's so Bad About a Little Piece of Bread?

Q ***Before Pesach we go all out, cleaning all the nooks and crannies, wherever chametz is to be found! Yet, I don't see this done for any other forbidden foods. Why is chametz different?***

A As our rabbis tell us, chametz is more than just a forbidden food, it's a metaphor for the *yetzer hara* (evil inclination). The elements involved in producing chametz are similar to the bad *middos* (character traits) that cause a person to sin, and conversely, matzah represents purity from these bad *middos* and acquiring good ones in their stead. Each *middah* really deserves a lengthy explanation, but we will touch on each one briefly.

Chametz rises, representing haughtiness, whereas matzah is flat, depicting humility. Additionally, chametz can contain many ingredients, a symbol of filling one's desires, while matzah is plain flour and water, without any additives, devoid of luxury. Furthermore, the production of chametz is a slow, drawn-out process, whereas the baking of matzah requires alacrity (*zerizus*), with every step being done in a hurry and with extreme attention.

The Exodus from Egypt was the birth of our nation, and each year on Pesach, we relive this experience and begin to flourish anew. We must start off pure, by abstaining from worldly desires and working on perfecting our character. This is one reason that the Torah commands us to spend a week in a chametz-free environment, without eating — or even owning — a trace of chametz. It would be a wonderful idea to have this in mind as we search for the chametz, and then try to uncover and remove the bad *middos* from every nook and cranny of our souls. Similarly, while the chametz is burning is an auspicious time to pray that the evil in the world be similarly destroyed. And it would be even more powerful to find a way to eradicate some of the evil from within ourselves by committing to undertake some small change for the better.

Once we are infused with this weeklong dosage of purity, we can return to the mundane world empowered to deal with the evils of this world and our everyday challenges.

In addition, abstaining from the worldly desires and materialism represented by chametz makes us more prepared to receive the Torah on Shavuos. As *Tosafos* (*Kesubos* 104a) writes, before a person can pray for the Torah to enter his body, he should pray that [unnecessary] sweets not enter. We must therefore first abstain from the pleasures of this physical world and only then will we be able to receive the Torah.

This is a lesson we all need to learn, especially in the materialistic world we find ourselves. As I once heard from Rav Moshe Feinstein, every exile has its own unique *yetzer hara* and challenges. The *yetzer hara* of America, he observed, is to partake in all the pleasures and enjoyments the world has to offer, while ensuring that it is all perfectly kosher and kosher for Passover. Such a lifestyle prevents a person from reaching heights of spirituality. We must remember that the physical pleasures of this world are not an end unto themselves, but rather a means to help us live a healthy life, thereby connecting to Hashem and His Torah.

In short: Chametz symbolizes the evil inclination, as it embodies elements of the bad character traits that cause a person to sin. We start our rejuvenation by spending a week in a chametz-free environment, thereby making ourselves fit to receive the Torah.

104

Pesach Is Here, But I Don't Feel the Freedom!

Q ***We are supposed to act like royalty at the Seder, celebrating our freedom from slavery in Egypt. Yet as a housewife and mother, I work so hard cleaning the house for Pesach, cooking all that holiday food, and dealing with cranky kids, that I actually feel more like a slave than a queen! How do you expect me to feel like a free person?***

A This is a wonderful question, which really touches on the very essence of Pesach. But before we address your actual question, it is worth mentioning that you may be overworking unnecessarily, as discussed previously ("Pesach Cleaning — Is It Overdone?").

As far as feeling the freedom, let us elaborate on your question. Our liberation from Egypt was not to make us "free," but to make us servants of Hashem, requiring that our every action, word, and thought be totally subservient to His will. If that is so, why is Pesach called "the time of our freedom"? Similarly, the Mishnah tells us (*Avos* 6:2) that only one who is engrossed in Torah study is a free man. But this seems to be the exact opposite of reality. A happy-go-lucky person who has no obligations or restrictions is seemingly the free man, while someone toiling and sweating over difficult subjects for hours on end seems to be the slave!

To answer these questions, we must first understand the meaning of slavery. Slavery is forcing someone to do something against his will, whether or not he is performing backbreaking labor. However, someone who spends time doing something he wants to do — even if he is working hard — is not a slave.

But what do we truly want? While relaxation and satisfying our physical desires may offer temporary gratification, such fleeting pleasures are not real. Our genuine desire is to do what the soul wants, which is to connect to Hashem through the study of His holy Torah and serving Him, thereby achieving real and enduring pleasure in both this world and the next. Once a person appreciates the greatness of studying Torah and performing mitzvos, it all becomes a labor of love and is not slavery at all.

The same is true for a woman who works hard cleaning her house and getting rid of chametz, as well as cooking gourmet meals, all for the sake of keeping Hashem's mitzvos and honoring His holiday. Every crumb removed and every course prepared is a great mitzvah, elevating her soul to great heights. If you think about this as you clean and cook you won't feel like a slave, and when you sit down to the Seder you will be able to truly feel the freedom.

The same applies to a mother taking care of her children before and during Pesach — or, for that matter, any time of the year. There is no greater accomplishment for a Jewish woman than fulfilling her noble role of nurturing the next generation of G-d-fearing Jews. The Jewish nation owes its continuity and vibrancy to these unsung heroes, the selfless women involved in this demanding and often unappreciated work. Understanding the greatness of these actions will turn these seemingly mundane tasks into a pursuit of holiness.

As explained elsewhere ("Updating the Role of Women in Today's Society"), this is why Yocheved and Miriam are referred to as Shifra and Puah. Although they were great women and leaders of the nation, the Torah specifically chose to call them by the names that reflect their devotion to providing tender loving care to the Jewish babies.

In all of these situations, by doing what it really wants to do, the soul is actually enjoying life, which is anything but slavery. While at times we may feel overwhelmed and don't appreciate the significance of every mitzvah we perform, when we come to the Next World our souls will shine from all the hard work we put in.

In short: Doing what the soul wants to do — connecting to Hashem and doing His will — is our true desire and enjoyment, and is not slavery.

105

Remembering That We Left Egypt

Q ***On each one of the holidays, we recite in the prayers and Kiddush that the holiday is "zeicher litzias Mitzrayim — a memorial of the Exodus from Egypt." In what way are the other holidays a memorial for leaving Egypt? Why don't we focus on the point of each holiday? In addition, since the ultimate purpose of leaving Egypt was to receive the Torah, wouldn't it be more appropriate to focus on the focal point of the Exodus, which was the receiving of the Torah?***

A This is an excellent question, one I have been thinking about for a long time. In fact, the question is even more glaring on Shavuos — the very holiday that celebrates the receiving of the Torah. Instead of calling Shavuos "a memorial of receiving the Torah," we proclaim that the holiday is "a memorial of the Exodus from Egypt," seemingly shifting the focus to leaving Egypt, when the focal point of the festival is receiving the Torah!

On a basic level, this can be explained as follows: Our redemption from Egypt is the root of Judaism, and even receiving the Torah was an outcome of the Exodus. In fact, the very first words Hashem uttered on Har Sinai were, "I am Hashem Who took you out of Egypt." This proclamation was the preface to our accepting the Torah, because when Hashem redeemed us from bondage to Pharaoh, it was to become His servants, obligated to serve Him.

Thus, the Exodus is indeed the foundation of the Torah and all of Judaism, and when we mention it in our holiday prayers we are tracing the festival back to its root. Once we became Hashem's servants and subservient to Him, He gave us His Torah on Shavuos and took care of us in the desert (which we commemorate on Succos), making the other holidays rooted in Pesach.

But this concept goes even deeper. The Exodus from Egypt refers to more than the physical exodus from the land of Egypt and the freedom from our bondage there. Mitzrayim — the Biblical word for Egypt — is also an expression of "*meitzar,* boundaries." The Jews in Egypt were also slaves to the Egyptian culture, having been overcome by the impure ideals of the country that hosted them for more than two centuries, and they almost lost their identity as a nation. Even after they physically left Egypt, their souls were still tainted by Egypt's depravity and impurity. They then had to spend the next forty-nine days removing "Mitzrayim" from their psyche, step-by-step, growing spiritually until they were ready to accept Hashem's holy Torah.

In this context, the expression Exodus from "Mitzrayim" is in fact the focal point of all the festivals, since it refers to the entire process of leaving the impurities of Egypt to become Hashem's holy nation. This culminated with Hashem giving us His Torah, and His taking care of us in the desert, making all the holidays "*zeicher litzias Mitzrayim* — a memorial of the exodus from the impurities of Egypt and becoming Hashem's holy nation."

In short: Our Exodus from Egypt is the foundation of all the holidays, because once we became Hashem's servants, He gave us His Torah on Shavuos and took care of us in the desert, making the other holidays rooted in Pesach. It also includes the entire process of rising above the impurities of Egypt and becoming Hashem's holy nation.

106

What's the Rush?!

Q ***We say in the Haggadah that we must proclaim that we eat matzah because our ancestors were rushed out of Egypt with no time to let their dough rise. What is so significant about this rush, and why is this a focal point of the Haggadah?***

A This rush was indeed an integral part of the redemption. As long as we were under the jurisdiction of Pharaoh and the influence of the Egyptians, it was not possible to be true servants of Hashem. The moment we left Egypt, we became servants of Hashem and His Chosen Nation — the very purpose of creation. This is why Hashem took us out with great haste. Waiting even just for their dough to rise would have delayed their departure, causing them to become servants of Hashem that much later — a terrible tragedy. Eating matzah thus reminds us of the importance of every moment we have to serve Hashem, the very purpose of the redemption.

In fact, the magnitude of a delay of even seconds is manifested in the very matzah itself. The difference between dough rising and becoming chametz and not rising and remaining matzah is mere seconds. This is an important concept to think about while eating matzah on Pesach: the value of every second and the great importance of using the wonderful opportunity it affords us to serve Hashem. Although a second in this world seems so insignificant, we see the sanctity and power it has to make a spiritual explosion, which can create a special closeness to Hashem for eternity.

The rush also shows our great sacrifice, being ready to leave without any hesitation. Leaving Egypt and traveling into the desert without provisions was a great sacrifice made by the Jewish people, and we continue to reap the benefits of this great merit throughout the generations. Indeed, the prophet Yirmiyahu shared Hashem's message (*Yirmiyahu* 2:2): "כֹּה אָמַר ה׳ זָכַרְתִּי לָךְ חֶסֶד נְעוּרַיִךְ אַהֲבַת כְּלוּלֹתָיִךְ לֶכְתֵּךְ אַחֲרַי בַּמִּדְבָּר בְּאֶרֶץ לֹא זְרוּעָה — So says Hashem: I remember for you the kindness of your youth, the love of your marriage, your following me into the Wilderness, into a barren land."

Although, in the previous verses, Yirmiyahu had just chastised the Jewish people for their wrongdoings, he was making it clear that as much as they deserved reproof and punishment, Hashem still remembers their devotion and loyalty to Him. Millions of people — young and old alike — followed Hashem blindly into the desert, displaying total trust in Him. We were fully confident that if Hashem told us to go, He was going to take care of us and provide for all our needs. Hashem continues to remember this fondly, and appeals to us to live up to this greatness.

This is another important lesson to internalize on this special holiday: Some people mistakenly think that they must devote all their time and energy to making a living, and they therefore cannot keep Shabbos or devote enough time to pray and study Torah each day. However, since Hashem is the One Who provides us with our livelihood, we must trust that He can and will take care of us. We must put in the proper effort to make a living, but not at the expense of doing His will. Just as we put our trust in Hashem and He took care of all our needs when we left Egypt, we must continue to trust that He will provide for us in every situation.

In short: Hashem took us out in a rush because even a delay of seconds in being servants of Hashem would have been tragic. Leaving without provisions was also a source of great, lasting merit for the Jewish people, and reminds us to trust that Hashem will take care of us in every situation.

107

Thanking Hashem for Taking Us Out of Egypt

Q ***Why do we thank Hashem for taking us out of Egypt if He is the One Who sent us there? Wouldn't it have been better if we didn't have to go through the whole ordeal in the first place?***

A Why indeed did the Jewish people have to suffer so terribly as slaves in Egypt?

Rav Yaakov of Lisa (author of *Nesivos HaMishpat*), in his commentary on the Haggadah, *Maaseh Nissim*, shares the following perspective. The Talmud (*Berachos* 5a) tells us that Hashem gave us three special gifts, each of which can be acquired only through suffering: Torah, the Land of Israel, and the World to Come. These spiritual gifts help connect us to Hashem, and to receive them one must be pure and holy.

The Torah tells us that the suffering in Egypt refined and purified the Jewish nation. The pain and suffering subdued their physicality and helped make us a spiritual people, capable and worthy of being given these gifts. Our suffering in Egypt was part of the process that molded us into becoming the Chosen Nation, and that is why when we thank Hashem for taking us out of Egypt, we include our appreciation for Him sending us there.

This should be our perspective for every challenge and difficulty we encounter. Our very purpose on this world is to overcome the trials and tribulations Hashem sends our way, and each one is designed by Hashem for our benefit. By strengthening ourselves and serving Hashem through thick and thin we grow spiritually, and the adversity itself can serve as the catalyst to reach great spiritual heights. This is one reason the Talmud (*Berachos* 60b) tells us that we must thank Hashem for the bad just as we thank Him for the good, because every "bad" is really good, and every challenge helps us grow.

So whenever you express your gratitude to Hashem for taking us out of Egypt — whether during davening or at the Pesach Seder — don't forget to have in mind to thank Him for sending us there, too!

In the same vein, we thank Hashem for all our nation has endured, fortified with the knowledge that any pain and suffering helped us grow to great spiritual heights.

In short: Not only do we thank Hashem for taking us out of Egypt, we are also grateful for His bringing us there, because it helped purify our souls. Similarly, we thank Him for all our trials and tribulations, because they help our spiritual growth.

108

Chametz-Free Diet the Entire Year

Q ***As we bid farewell to Pesach and head back to the challah and pizza, it got me thinking about this whole process. Since chametz represents the evil inclination, shouldn't we always stay away from chametz, keeping ourselves pure and holy throughout the entire year?***

A What a question! Indeed, as we have discussed previously, our rabbis tell us that chametz represents the *yetzer hara* (evil inclination) because chametz reflects many of the bad character traits that cause a person to sin. Chametz rises — a symbol of haughtiness; chametz has many ingredients — a symbol of fulfilling desires; and the baking of chametz is a drawn-out process — a symbol of laziness. Matzah, on the other hand, is simply flour and water, not blown up, and must be baked in a hurry and with extreme alacrity. So while others can't wait to go back to the pizza shop, you have obviously internalized this message, and don't want to let go of the inspiration!

But while it is true that we want to keep away from evil, we were not put here in this world to live in a vacuum. We were sent down to Earth to earn reward by facing adversity and overcoming it, which is why Hashem gave us an evil inclination in the first place. Without an evil inclination enticing us to sin, we would naturally follow Hashem's will at all times. There would be no challenges, no struggles, and no way to grow from the struggles — and therefore no way to earn reward in the World to Come.

It is for that same reason that our calendar is not just filled with days of Shabbos and Yom Tov. As Ramchal writes in *Derech Hashem*, our mission in this world is to serve Hashem specifically amid the mundane, thereby infusing the physical world with spirituality.

While days of sanctity infuse us with holiness and bring us closer to Hashem, that is not the ultimate purpose of our mission on Earth. It is on the weekdays, when we grapple with earthly tasks and lack that extra dose of sanctity, that we can truly fulfill our mission in this world. The sanctified days help carry us through the "darkness" of the weekday, but our mission is to serve Hashem when it's dark, lighting up our souls with Torah and mitzvos.

So while Shabbos and Yom Tov enable us to soar to great heights, it is the Torah we study and the mitzvos we perform on plain, regular weekdays that truly light up the "darkness" of this world.

Similarly, we spend the days of Pesach on a chametz-free diet, abstaining from many of the worldly desires. This vacation from the appeals of the *yetzer hara* serves as our "charging station," empowering us to deal with the challenges we confront the rest of the year — the very purpose of our being sent to this world.

In short: Our mission in this world is to fight the evil inclination. This short chametz-free period empowers us to deal with our challenges throughout the year.

Chol HaMoed

109

Is Chol HaMoed Part of the Holiday?

Q ***I am confused about the status of Chol HaMoed — the intermediate days of Pesach and Succos — when some forms of work are forbidden but most are allowed. Are these days part of the holiday or not? Are they chol or moed — mundane or holy?***

A Indeed, the days of Chol HaMoed are both holy and mundane at the same time, and have a unique function in helping us accomplish our mission in this world.

On Shabbos and Yom Tov, we completely rise above the natural and physical world, refraining from work and concentrating on holiness and connecting to Hashem. We spend the day davening and studying Torah, as well as eating meals filled with words of Torah and songs of praise to Hashem, lifting ourselves to a lofty spiritual plane.

However, most of the days on our calendar are not Shabbos and Yom Tov. As discussed elsewhere ("Chametz-Free Diet the Entire Year"), Ramchal writes that our mission in this world is to serve Hashem specifically amidst the mundane, infusing the physical world with sanctity. These holy days of Shabbos and Yom Tov empower us to be able to illuminate the darkness of the weekdays.

But how do we transmit the lofty levels of spirituality we reach on the holy days into the physical and mundane world? To help achieve this, Hashem gave us the gift of Chol HaMoed — days that are part holy and part mundane — as an opportunity to carry the holiness of the holiday into everyday life. While on Yom Tov we are on a higher plane, completely disconnected from everyday life, on Chol HaMoed we bring this holiness and spirituality into the physical world, bridging the two, fusing holy and mundane.

Some people think that this world is an end unto itself, and spend their lives running after physical pleasures — gourmet food, fancy homes, the latest model cars, and extravagant vacations. However, a Torah Jew views the world as a means to achieve a connection to Hashem. Food is eaten to give us strength, a house is a place to live in, a car is to get you where you need to go, and a vacation is for resting up and rejuvenating. All of these are physical needs to help us serve Hashem, bringing holiness to the physical world.

Infusing spirituality into the mundane is a concept my rebbi, Rav Yaakov Yitzchak Ruderman, Rosh Yeshivah of Yeshivah Ner Yisroel, used to explain the unique status of Purim. The Talmud (*Megillah* 5b) tells us that although Mordechai proposed that Purim be a full-fledged holiday, with a prohibition against doing work, the Jewish nation did not accept his proposal.

This seems strange.

At the time, the Jews were overjoyed over their salvation and willingly reaccepted the Torah with renewed enthusiasm. Why then would they not agree to accept Purim as a full-fledged holiday?

Rav Ruderman explained that they were not seeking to relegate Purim to a second-class holiday. On the contrary, they wanted to make Purim in some ways even holier, by taking a "regular" day and infusing it with holiness.

Similarly, the Torah gave us the intermediate days of Pesach and Succos as an opportunity to bring holiness into a day on which we are engaged in worldly affairs. This will help ensure that even after the holiday is over, we don't leave the sanctity behind, but are equipped to take our newly-achieved levels of holiness and bring them with us into our unholy world.

In short: Chol HaMoed is both a holy day and a workday, preparing us to infuse holiness into the mundane and physical world.

Sefiras HaOmer

110

Why Do We Count the Days From the Omer?

Q ***I heard that counting Sefiras HaOmer is a way of showing our great anticipation for the holiday of Shavuos, when we received the Torah. If that is the case, why is the focus on the number of days from when we brought the Omer-offering on the second day of Pesach? Wouldn't it be more fitting to count down until we receive the Torah?***

A This is an excellent question, and I will share with you a beautiful insight I heard from my illustrious rebbi, Rav Dovid Kronglas. But before we can address your question, it is important to understand what the *Korban Omer* is all about: It was a communal barley offering brought from the new crop on the second day of Pesach. Until that point, it was forbidden to eat from the new crop of the five species of grain (wheat, barley, oats, spelt, and rye) — our main food staple. Only after we "give" the first harvest to Hashem, expressing our appreciation for the bounty He has given us, are we permitted to partake of the new crop.

Even today, when we have no Beis HaMikdash, new grain grown in Eretz Yisrael is forbidden until after the second day of Pesach, the day the *Omer* offering used to be brought. According to some opinions, this law applies even to grains grown outside Eretz Yisrael. That is why some bakeries advertise that their products are made from *yashan* (old) flour, meaning that the flour is from grain that had been planted and took root before the second day of the previous Pesach.

But what is the real reason to enjoy the new crop? In *Avos* (3:21) we are taught, "אִם אֵין קֶמַח אֵין תּוֹרָה, אִם אֵין תּוֹרָה אֵין קֶמַח — If there is no flour, there is no Torah; if there is no Torah, there is no flour." While one cannot study Torah or serve Hashem properly without eating nutritious food, the food we eat has true value only if it is used to aid us in our Torah study and service of Hashem, the ultimate purpose of creation.

Yes, we are counting toward receiving the Torah, but how does one prepare for receiving the Torah? By understanding that the food we eat, as well as all material bounty we receive from Hashem, is given to us for the sole purpose of keeping the Torah, and the purpose of eating and everything physical is to enable us to serve Hashem.

This is the message of the *Omer*. Before we begin preparing for the Torah, we may not eat from the new crop. We become worthy of eating from the new crop only after we establish that the purpose of the Exodus from Egypt was accepting the Torah, and we have begun climbing the spiritual ladder toward that goal. By counting from the *Omer*, we are proclaiming that we are one day closer to receiving the Torah, making us more worthy of enjoying the new crop.

This a great thing to think about when counting *Sefirah* each night: We are not people without a mission, who live with the view of "eat, drink and be merry, for tomorrow we die." We understand that our purpose in the world is to grow each day in Torah and mitzvos, and everything we have is to be used for the sake of Hashem and His Torah, thereby reaping our reward in the Next World.

In short: We count from when we offer the new crop to Hashem, because this shows that we understand the purpose of the crop — to serve Hashem — making us worthy of receiving the Torah.

111

Sefiras HaOmer — Days of Joy or Mourning

Q ***During the period of Sefirah, the days between Pesach and Shavuos, we mourn the 24,000 students of Rabbi Akiva, who died during this time of the year. But shouldn't they also be days of joy and excitement, as we count toward the day we received the Torah?***

A You are bringing up a very important point, as there is, indeed, a common misconception about the days of *Sefirah*.

The essence of this time period is one of spiritual elevation, as we prepare to receive the Torah on Shavuos, and it is certainly a time of joy and excitement. However, because of the laws of mourning observed during this time, many people treat *Sefirah* strictly as a period of mourning and overlook its true purpose, making it one of the most underutilized seasons on the Jewish calendar.

Each year on Shavuos we receive the Torah anew, and, as the *Sefer HaChinuch* writes, Hashem gave us the mitzvah of *Sefiras HaOmer* to prepare and make ourselves worthy of receiving the Torah. Each day of *Sefirah*, as we march closer to this monumental day, our excitement should continue to grow and increase each day.

To properly prepare to receive the Torah, one must make himself a worthy vessel. As discussed many times previously, possessing good *middos* (character traits) is the prerequisite to grasping the divine concepts of the Torah, because only one who is holy and pure can connect to the holy and pure wisdom of Hashem. This is a reason for the custom to study *Pirkei Avos* — which contains teachings of character refinement and proper conduct — every Shabbos afternoon during the weeks of *Sefirah*, helping us become more deserving of receiving the Torah.

In addition, as printed in many siddurim, each week of *Sefirah* corresponds to another *middah*, and it is commendable to focus on refining that particular *middah* during that week. Indeed, the *Zohar* teaches that the word *Sefirah* is similar to the word *sapir,* a sapphire. Every Jew's soul is like a gem, and during these days we polish our souls and make them shine like diamonds.

At the same time, however, there is an element of mourning during this period, but it has nothing to do with *Sefirah* per se.

The Talmud (*Yevamos* 62b) tells us that 24,000 students of Rabbi Akiva died during this period because they did not treat each other with proper respect. Although this tragedy took place nearly two thousand years ago, we cannot fathom the magnitude of the loss of such towering Torah scholars and its impact on all future generations, and we mourn this immense loss to this day.

Of course, it is no accident that their deaths took place during this auspicious time of the year. Since these are days of preparation to receive the Torah, it was incumbent on them to be exceedingly respectful of each other's Torah scholarship, and because, based on their exalted level, they were deemed lacking in this regard, they were punished severely.

So although we must mourn their deaths during this time, we must not allow it to overshadow our feelings of joy and excitement. These contradictory feelings are similar to the feelings a person has when a rich relative passes away, leaving him with a large inheritance. The Talmud (*Berachos* 59b) instructs such an heir to recite two blessings: one mourning the death of the relative, and one over the joy of his newfound wealth. Similarly, we must feel excited over the upcoming receiving of the Torah while at the same time mourn the deaths of these great Torah scholars.

But our primary focus during these days must be on tapping into the greatness of the season and refining our character in preparation for the great gift of the Torah.

In short: Sefirah is a joyous and exciting time, as we prepare ourselves and become more refined and worthy of receiving the Torah. Although we mourn the deaths of 24,000 students of Rabbi Akiva, our primary focus must be on the auspiciousness of these days and our preparation for receiving the Torah.

Shavuos

112

Shavuos — Celebration of the Torah or of the Harvest?

Q ***We say in the prayers that Shavuos is "Zman Mattan Toraseinu — the time of the Giving of the Torah." I therefore find it strange that the Torah describes Shavuos merely as a festival celebrating the wheat harvest. While that may be noteworthy for farmers, it doesn't seem to be nearly as significant as receiving the Torah!***

A As I heard from Rav Moshe Feinstein, one of the reasons the Torah does not call Shavuos "the time of the Giving of the Torah" is because receiving the Torah is not limited to one specific day on the calendar. Our Rabbis tell us that the words of Torah should be fresh in our eyes every day of the year, as if they were just given. This is similar to why we don't subscribe to the concept of Mother's Day or Father's Day, since the Torah commands us to honor our parents every day of the year, not just one Sunday a year.

As far as why the Torah bases the holiday of Shavuos on the harvest, I would note that the Torah actually associates each of the three Festivals — Pesach, Shavuos, and Succos — with stages of the agricultural cycle. Pesach is in Chodesh HaAviv — the beginning of the spring, when the harvest season begins; Shavuos is "Chag HaKatzir — Festival of the Harvest," when the grain is reaped; and Succos is the final stage, "Chag HaAsif — Festival of the Ingathering," when the crops are gathered in from the fields.

There is an important message in this association. The Jewish nation is called "His first grain" (*Yirmiyahu* 2:3), and the three stages of the harvest correspond to the three phases of the creation of the Jewish nation, commemorated by these festivals. The birth of the Jewish nation took place when we left Egypt on Pesach, just as the new vegetation begins to sprout in the spring. On Shavuos we received the Torah — the purpose of our becoming a nation and the very purpose of creation, which corresponds to reaping the harvest, which is the purpose of planting the grain.

Succos commemorates the climax of our development. This is when Hashem showed His great love for us, taking us under His wings and enveloping us in His Clouds of Glory — just as the harvest culminates with the ingathering of the grain. Succos is also the climax of the Yamim Nora'im, the High Holy Days. After having merited atonement for our sins on Yom Kippur, the barriers are removed and our souls are in a pure and lofty state, making us worthy of dwelling together with Hashem in His home, the succah.

Each year, as we celebrate these festivals, we strive to relive these experiences, gathering the fruits of our spiritual harvest and cultivating an even greater level of connection to Hashem, keeping us inspired until the next holiday.

In short: Shavuos is not described as the day we received the Torah because receiving the Torah is not limited to one specific calendar day. The agricultural stages correspond to the stages of the creation of the Jewish people, and the gathering of the fruits of our spiritual harvest.

113

Is Shavuos Celebrated on the Wrong Day?

Q ***Shavuos is called "Zman Mattan Toraseinu — the time of the Giving of the Torah," and is celebrated on the sixth of Sivan. But I heard that when the Jews left Egypt, the Torah was not given until the seventh of Sivan. So why do we celebrate on the wrong day?***

A There is actually a dispute in the Talmud (*Shabbos* 87b) whether the Torah was given on the sixth or the seventh of Sivan. But, as I heard from my rebbi, Rav Dovid Kronglas, even if it wasn't given until the seventh, there is an important reason that the holiday was established on the sixth.

The purpose of the Exodus from Egypt was for the Jews to become Hashem's nation and receive the Torah, yet the Torah was not given to them right away. This was because Hashem is holy and His Torah is holy, and in order for the Jews to receive the Torah, they had to become holy as well. After living in Egypt for so many years, they had been influenced and contaminated by the Egyptian culture, and the nation as a whole was not at the exalted spiritual level that was required. Although they had physically left Egypt, they still had to ensure that Egypt and its impurities had left them.

They were therefore given forty-nine days to prepare and make themselves spiritually fit to be given the Torah. They spent the days and weeks leading up to the awaited day perfecting their character and removing any residue of the Egyptian impurities. After seven weeks of intense refinement, they were finally deemed worthy of receiving the Torah, which Hashem then gave to them as a gift on the following day.

Rav Kronglas compared this to what Rav Itzele Peterberger responded when he was asked if his rebbi, Rav Yisrael Salanter, had *ruach hakodesh* (Divine Inspiration): *Ruach hakodesh* is a Heavenly gift, given to a person who climbed the spiritual ladder of refinement, as spelled out in the classic *sefer, Mesillas Yesharim*. Since Rav Salanter reached the top of this spiritual ladder, he was certainly worthy of this gift, and whether Hashem actually gifted him with *ruach hakodesh* doesn't matter.

Similarly, Shavuos is celebrated on the sixth of Sivan — the day we became worthy of receiving the Torah — to show that we must also celebrate the efforts we expended to make ourselves worthy of the Torah. This great achievement brought tremendous satisfaction to Hashem, and is also worthy of celebrating. If we would celebrate on the seventh, the actual day we received the Torah, this aspect of the celebration would be lost.

This is a lesson we should remember each year. As mentioned previously, each week of *Sefirah* corresponds to another *middah* (character trait), and we work on refining that particular *middah* during that week, thereby making us worthy of once again receiving the Torah on Shavuos. At the end of the seven-week period, along with celebrating the great gift of the Torah, we also celebrate the achievements that made us worthy of receiving the Torah.

Even the name of the holiday, "Shavuos — weeks," a reference to the seven weeks of *Sefirah*, brings out this point. Hashem gave it this name to teach us that we are not merely celebrating our having received the Torah, but also our part in becoming fit to receive this special gift. This is why, in *Parashas Pinchas*, the Torah refers to Shavuos as "*Shavuoseichem* — your Shavuos." The Torah is emphasizing that this holiday is "yours," because you worked hard during these weeks to make yourselves worthy of receiving the Torah.

In short: We celebrate Shavuos on the sixth of Sivan, even if the Torah was actually given on the seventh, because we are also celebrating the spiritual heights we reached that made us worthy of receiving Hashem's Torah.

Rosh Hashanah

114

The Death of Queen Elizabeth

Q ***We know that everything that happens in this world is for us Jews to learn from it. What message can we take from the death of the Queen of England, which took place right before Rosh Hashanah?***

A This is an excellent question, something I was hoping would be asked.

There is no question that this event occurred at this time of year to teach us an important lesson. As we prepare for Rosh Hashanah, we ready ourselves to once again accept Hashem as our King. When a new king is proclaimed, a grand parade is held in honor of his coronation, with trumpets blowing, accompanied by other musical instruments. Similarly, on Rosh Hashanah, we "crown" Hashem as our King with great fanfare and the blowing of the shofar.

In the days when kings actually ruled their countries, a king wielded tremendous power, and everyone was required to obey his laws. If the king sensed that a subject was disloyal, he could immediately sentence him to death. This struck awe and fear of the king into the hearts of his subjects. If the king was kind-hearted and caring, the people would appreciate his benevolence and adore him, and they would become dedicated and devoted subjects, while looking for ways to reciprocate.

This real-life example of royalty was a model of the kingdom of Hashem, and the awe and love we must have for Him. People were able to build on these feelings of awe and love and apply them to the King of all kings.

But the connection between human sovereignty and Divine sovereignty runs even deeper. A human king's power is given to him by

Hashem Himself, and his rule is considered an extension of Hashem's kingship. This is true, on some level, even for non-Jewish kings, which is why Hashem told Moshe to respect Pharaoh even though he was wicked. This is referred to in the blessing recited upon seeing a non-Jewish king, "שֶׁנָּתַן מִכְּבוֹדוֹ לְבָשָׂר וָדָם — Who gave of His Glory to flesh and blood."

This is all the more so for a Jewish king, who is invested with spiritual power and greatness, which is why the blessing recited upon seeing a Jewish king is "שֶׁחָלַק מִכְּבוֹדוֹ לִירֵאָיו — Who apportioned of His Glory to those who fear Him." Hence, the awe and love for a king is an extension of the awe and love we must have for the King of all kings.

However, in today's society, the concept of kings and royalty is almost forgotten. Because we lack this real-life illustration, it is harder for us to relate to what it truly means that Hashem is our King. With the respect and honor being shown to the deceased queen and the newly appointed king, Hashem is giving us a glimpse of this concept. So let us utilize this opportunity to learn valuable lessons that we can then apply to the act of crowning Hashem as our King, feeling awe in His presence, and completely subordinating ourselves to Him.

In short: In today's society, the concept of kings and royalty is almost forgotten. When we observe the honor shown to the deceased queen and the newly anointed king, we are able to apply these feelings to the crowning of Hashem as our King, and subordinate ourselves to Him.

115

Substitute Simanim on the Night of Rosh Hashanah

Q ***On the night of Rosh Hashanah, we dip the apple in honey and eat the head of a fish as omens for a good year. How important is this? If I skip them, am I at risk for the year? And if my kids don't like the head of the fish, should I push them to eat some anyway? And what about using the head of "jellyfish" candy instead?***

A Your question reminds me of the story of the man who complained to his rabbi, "Rabbi, if you would only know how much honey cake I ate this past Rosh Hashanah, and yet I had the worst year ever!" This unfortunate man thought that eating honey is what brings a person their good year. But no, it is neither the honey nor any of the *simanim* (symbolic foods) themselves that are a source of blessing. Rather, the purpose of these foods is to get a person to think about what needs to be done to merit a sweet year.

As the *Mishnah Berurah* writes in the name of the Shelah HaKadosh, when a person partakes of these *simanim*, he should be aroused to repentance (*teshuvah*) and recite the associated prayer with great fervor. It is by improving our actions, words, and thoughts that we become more worthy of a good year.

This may be why we specifically dip the apple in honey rather than something else that is sweet. Although a bee produces sweet honey, it also stings. This should remind us to think about what needs to be done to merit a sweet year and not a year that "stings."

For children who squirm at having to eat the head of a fish — or adults for that matter — a simple solution would be to serve tongue, which is part of the head and considered a delicacy by many. If that's not an option, you can encourage them to taste a tiny piece of the head of the fish, but there's no need to make an issue and force them to eat it. And as far as using the head of a jellyfish candy, even though it technically qualifies, I would not recommend it, since it is not traditionally used, and maintaining tradition is very important. Even so, eating the head of a jellyfish is certainly better than nothing, as it can bring the same inspiration; but I would advise you to, at the very least, have the head of a fish on the table in order to keep the tradition.

As explained elsewhere ("Shabbos and Yom Tov Foods"), the foods customarily eaten on Shabbos — such as kugel, cholent, and gefilte fish — and on holidays, like kreplach and stuffed cabbage, have great significance and meaning, and have been on the Jewish menu for generations. Because we are physical beings, we get inspired by what we eat, and eating these foods helps us tap into the meanings and significance of these days.

The uniqueness of the Jewish nation is that we find holiness not only in the spiritual realm. Our greatness lies in transforming the mundane and physical aspects of this world into a way of connecting to Hashem, so that even choosing the menu becomes a spiritual act. As we eat these unique *simanim* at the festive meal on Rosh Hashanah, we are reminded to better our ways on this auspicious day — and that serves as a vehicle for us to deserve a good year.

In short: The symbolic foods do not generate blessings, but remind a person to become better, making him more worthy of a good year. A little piece of the fish head will suffice, or you can serve tongue instead, but don't force those who refuse. Jellyfish is better than nothing, but is not recommended since it's not traditional.

116

No Shofar This Year?!

Q ***This year, the first day of Rosh Hashanah will be on Shabbos and we won't blow shofar. But I am frightened, as I've heard that a year without blowing shofar can be very bad! Is there anything we can do to replicate the shofar? I also find it strange that the entire Jewish nation for all generations should forfeit the much-needed shofar because of a far-fetched concern that someone may carry the shofar.***

A You have nothing to fear! It is true that the shofar blowing plays an essential part on this Day of Judgment in awakening us to better our ways and to "confuse" Satan. Indeed, our Rabbis (*Rosh Hashanah* 16b) tell us that a year without the blowing of the shofar on Rosh Hashanah can have dire results, as Satan was not flustered. But as *Tosafos* points out, this rule does not apply when we do not blow shofar because it is Shabbos. Although we are seemingly lacking the power of the shofar, since we are following the dictate of Chazal who told us not to blow shofar, nothing bad will come out of it.

One reason for this is as follows. The *pasuk* (*Shir HaShirim* 1:2) states, "Your love [for the Jewish nation] is better than wine," which the Talmud (*Avodah Zarah* 35a) explains is a reference to the words of the Rabbis, which are more beloved than the "wine" of the Torah itself. But how can a Rabbinic mitzvah be more beloved than a mitzvah commanded by Hashem Himself?

Rabbeinu Yonah (*Shaarei Teshuvah* 3:7) explains that because the purpose of Rabbinic decrees is to safeguard the mitzvos of the Torah, they are an expression of *yiras Hashem* (fear of Hashem), one of the Torah's mitzvos. But fear of Hashem is more than just one mitzvah; it is a foundation of the Torah that leads us to perform many other mitzvos, and is therefore equivalent to the performance of multiple mitzvos. This is why the words of the Rabbis are more beloved than mitzvos of the Torah.

The same is true when we abstain from blowing shofar on Shabbos. As the *pasuk* (*Amos* 3:6) states, "אִם יִתָּקַע שׁוֹפָר בְּעִיר וְעָם לֹא יֶחֱרָדוּ — If a shofar is blown in the city, will the nation not tremble?" The essence of Rosh Hashanah and the shofar is fear of Hashem and accepting Him as our King, which helps us merit a good year. As you mentioned, the decree not to blow shofar was enacted out of concern that someone may carry the shofar in a public domain to learn how to blow, thereby desecrating Shabbos. Since following this decree helps ensure that no Jew ever mistakenly desecrates Shabbos, it is a tremendous display of fear of Heaven, and that itself will help earn us a good year.

In addition, blowing the shofar is so crucial on this Day of Judgement because we need its sound to pierce the Heavens. But the way it does this is by piercing our hearts and arousing us to become better people, thereby making us more worthy of being inscribed for a year of health and happiness. Refraining from performing this special mitzvah in order to ensure that no Jew sins can have the same effect.

The very fact that the Sages deemed it worthwhile to cancel the shofar on Shabbos for all generations, just to ensure that Shabbos never be violated, should help us realize the magnitude of even one sin and the effect it has on this world and on the upper spheres. When we recognize how terrible sin is, we are instilled with a great fear of sin that helps us become better people, and worthy of receiving a good year.

So while we are lacking the actual blowing of the shofar, the lesson of our not blowing it captures its message, making us worthy of meriting another year of good life.

In short: There is nothing to fear when we fulfill the Rabbinic decree not to blow shofar on Shabbos. We are showing a tremendous display of fear of Heaven and capturing the essence of the shofar. This also instills in us a fear of sin, taking the place of the wake-up call of the shofar.

Succos

117

Happy in a Flimsy Hut

Q ***Succos is called "Zman Simchaseinu — the Time of our Joy." But how can I rejoice when I have to leave the conveniences and comforts of my home and move into a hut, where I am exposed to the elements and have to run into the house every time it rains?***

A Your question is based on a misunderstanding of the true meaning of joy. In fact, dwelling in the succah should not diminish your happiness, but actually fill you with great joy. As you spend a week in the flimsy succah and internalize its message, you will hopefully rethink your values and become filled with joy.

Many people walk around with the mistaken belief that happiness is attained through physical comfort and pleasure. But in truth, material pleasures are fleeting, and can never provide a person with true happiness. As the *Mesillas Yesharim* writes, only connecting to Hashem brings true and lasting happiness, the greatest pleasure attainable, because Hashem is the Source and the highest degree of goodness and pleasure.

The flimsy structure of the succah is a declaration that our dwelling places in this world are only temporary, and our focus is on spirituality and connecting to Hashem, not on material comfort. This is why we read the Book of *Koheles*, which describes the futility of this world, on Succos: because only one who rises above the frivolities of this world can be truly joyful.

Indeed, this is why Succos is celebrated right after Yom Kippur. Our Rabbis (*Taanis* 30b) tell us that Yom Kippur is one of the happiest days of the year, the day we receive the greatest gift possible

— atonement for our sins and purification of our soul. Sin prevents us from connecting to Hashem, and through *teshuvah* (repentance) we remove these barriers, enabling us to renew our connection. In this newfound state of purity, Hashem invites us to join Him in the succah, His home, free of all physical distractions, making Succos the ultimate "time of our joy."

This brings us to another aspect of the joy of succah. The succah is a reminder of the "succos" with which Hashem sheltered us in the Wilderness. The Talmud (*Succah* 11b) tells us that these "succos" refer to either the *Ananei HaKavod* (Clouds of Glory) or the physical huts Hashem provided for us to protect us. Every year we commemorate this special protection from Hashem, and are reminded that He continues to protect us at all times. Living with the realization that we are always under the personal care of Hashem should infuse a person with great joy.

Even if the huts in the Wilderness were not an open miracle like the Clouds of Glory, commemorating them hammers home a very important lesson: As the commentators explain, building these huts and surviving in them for forty years in the desert was a clear manifestation of Hashem's guiding hand. By sitting in the succah we are reminded that even our basic possessions come from Hashem and must not be taken for granted. Just as Hashem provided for us then, He continues to provide all of our needs, and without Him, we would have nothing.

So, as we sit in the succah, we must take a moment to appreciate the roof over our heads, and remember that Hashem continues to provide for us. There is nothing more comforting and reassuring than living with this realization, and this brings great feelings of joy. After internalizing this message during the week of Succos, we are ready to return to our homes with a greater sense of gratitude to Hashem for providing us with a home to live in and enjoy.

In short: The flimsy structure reminds us that true joy is attained only by connecting to Hashem, not through material comfort. The succah also reminds us that Hashem watches over us and provides us with our needs at all times, infusing us with great joy.

118

Welcoming and Thanking the Ushpizin

Q ***I had a few questions regarding the ushpizin, the seven exalted "guests" — Avraham, Yitzchak, Yaakov, Yosef, Moshe, Aharon, and David — whom we customarily invite into our succah. Firstly, I was wondering why this is only done on Succos. Also, is it appropriate to thank the ushpizin for their great contributions to the Jewish nation? And finally, I heard that the Matriarchs also come. Is there a source for that, and if so, why don't we greet them as well?***

A We invite the *ushpizin* specifically on Succos, because the succah is imbued with a special sanctity and is like Hashem's home. After having merited atonement for our sins on Yom Kippur, our souls are in a pure and lofty state, and we are deemed worthy of dwelling together with Hashem in His home. It is to this lofty spiritual environment that we invite these illustrious guests.

For this reason, your focus should not be on thanking the *ushpizin*. It would be much more meaningful to think about their lofty ways and connect to them by following in their footsteps, making you truly worthy of hosting them. (You can thank them if you want, but we generally don't have lengthy conversations with spiritual beings, as they are not our colleagues or friends.)

Imagine the Chofetz Chaim sitting at your table. You would certainly take extreme care to ensure that absolutely no *lashon hara* (gossip) is spoken. Similarly, if we want these spiritual guests to feel welcome in our succah, we must try to emulate their greatness. For example, before inviting Avraham, who was the paragon of hospitality, we should be sure that the needy are taken care of, perhaps by inviting them to our succah. But if we don't show compassion to others, how can we have the audacity to invite Avraham to our home?

The same goes for Yitzchak, who was ready to willingly give up his life to fulfill the will of Hashem. Before we invite him to our succah, we have to think whether or not we are ready to give up our lives — or at least go out of our comfort zone — for the sake of Heaven. And the same is true for each one of these spiritual giants, each of whom exemplified another great attribute. It is beyond the scope of these few lines to go into the details of each one, but we can mention some pointers.

Yaakov was dedicated to Torah study, even in the most trying circumstances. Yosef is the classic example of someone who overcame the most difficult trials and tribulations. Moshe was the devoted shepherd of the Jewish nation, taking care of them through thick and thin. Aharon was the peace-seeker in all interpersonal relationships. And David used his kingdom to publicize Hashem's sovereignty over the world.

With regard to the Matriarchs, I would say that since a husband and wife are considered one unit, and the Matriarchs shared in the holy work of our forefathers, we can assume that they come as well. The same is true when we invoke the merits of the Avos in our prayers; the merits of their wives are included. They are not mentioned explicitly because they are a single unit. Similarly, there is no need to specifically greet the Matriarchs, since greeting the Avos includes them as well. In addition, great Jewish women are modest and stay out of the limelight, so we don't mention them by name.

In short: Only after the atonement of Yom Kippur, when we are in Hashem's home, can we invite these spiritual giants. The best way to connect to them is by following in their footsteps. As one unit with their husbands, we can assume that the Matriarchs also come, and greeting the Avos includes them as well.

Chanukah

119

Small Flames of the Menorah

Q ***Every year, as we light our menorah, my children express their disappointment that our little flames seem so insignificant next to all the elaborate decorations and lights of our non-Jewish neighbors. How can I help them appreciate the greatness of our small flames amidst all the glamor?***

A This is a perfect opportunity to teach your children a vital lesson about Torah and about life in general: the importance of internal quality. Many things may seem glorious on the outside, but what's inside is what really counts, and we must never lose focus of this. Indeed, our Rabbis tell us (*Avos* 4:27), "Don't look at the bottle but at what is inside," or as the saying goes, "Don't judge a book by its cover."

There is much more to the flames shining in our windows than meets the eye. The light of the menorah commemorates the miracle of the small jug of oil, which contained enough oil for only one night, yet miraculously lasted for eight nights. This miracle was the culmination of the Jewish nation's victory over the Greeks. For many years, the Greeks tried mightily to get the Jews to embrace their Hellenistic culture, torturing them and enacting decrees against Torah study and mitzvah observance. With the fire of the Torah burning in their hearts, the Jews defied their decrees, even endangering their lives to study Torah and keep all the mitzvos.

Their perseverance and self-sacrifice made them worthy of a great miracle, and Hashem empowered the small and weak group of Jewish warriors to triumph over the mighty Greek army. The light of the menorah represents the eternal light of the Torah, and the miracle of the oil symbolizes the triumph of Torah over foreign Greek culture.

This everlasting light of the Torah is what lights up the darkness of our long exile and has warmed our hearts throughout the ages, helping us survive the horrors of the inquisitions and holocausts. As the *Chovos HaLevavos* writes, just as a little bit of light has the ability to dispel the vast darkness, a small amount of truth can chase away much falsehood. So far from being insignificant, the tiny flames of the Chanukah candles shine brighter than all the flashy lights and ornaments, symbolizing the victory of Torah-true life over anti-Torah influences, the very essence of a Jew and the eternity of our religion.

In a society caught up in the glamor and glitz of external beauty, this is an important lesson to internalize. One example of this is when seeking a potential spouse. While a person should certainly choose a marriage partner who appeals to them, the primary focus should not be on outward appearance. Torah outlook, personality, and good character traits are so much more important in any relationship, and certainly when establishing a Torah-true home and raising children.

So look at your menorah burning bright and internalize the lesson of Chanukah. What makes someone a Jew is not bagels and lox, and not even Israel. While it's a holy land and we're always looking to live there, it's not what makes us Jews. What makes a person a Jew is the Torah. Only the study of Torah and observing its laws has sustained us throughout the ages and their many challenges, and Torah is what will bring the ultimate redemption.

In short: The small flame of the menorah shines brighter than all the bright lights. It represents the light of the Torah, which lights up the darkness of our exile and warms our hearts, keeping us connected to Hashem for eternity.

120

Praying and Sitting at the Chanukah Candles

Q ***I know that women have special prayers they recite after they light Shabbos candles. Should we also be praying after we light Chanukah candles? And is there any point in sitting and watching the Chanukah candles?***

A You certainly should pray after lighting the Chanukah candles! The Talmud (*Shabbos* 23b) tells us that someone who is meticulous in the mitzvah of kindling Shabbos and Chanukah candles will merit children who are Torah scholars. The reason for this is that light in general, and the light of the Chanukah candles in particular, represents the light of the Torah. As the *pasuk* (*Mishlei* 6:23) states, "כִּי נֵר מִצְוָה וְתוֹרָה אוֹר — For the commandment is a lamp, and the Torah is light."

In addition, as Ramban writes, the lighting of the Chanukah menorah is considered an extension of the lighting of the Menorah in the Beis HaMikdash (Holy Temple). Every service in the Beis HaMikdash had the spiritual power to bring a specific flow of blessing down to this world. For example, the *Lechem HaPanim* (Showbread) placed on the *Shulchan* (Table) brought sustenance down to the world, and the lighting of the Menorah brought the light of Torah down from Heaven.

Just as physical fire creates light and warmth, the lighting of the Menorah in the Beis HaMikdash brought the light and spiritual warmth of the Torah to the world. This illumination helped people understand Torah on a deeper level, and to better connect to Hashem through their Torah study. Similarly, when we kindle the Chanukah menorah, we help bring the spiritual light and warmth of the Torah to the world, helping us connect to Hashem. The purer and more sanctified a person is, and the more lofty his intentions, the greater power his mitzvah will have, and the more he will be able to bring this light and warmth into the world. So it is certainly an auspicious time to pray for children who will light up the world with Torah, as well as other requests that come along with the light of Torah, such as health, livelihood, and *nachas*.

Sitting and looking at the candles is a nice thing to do, if that helps you internalize their message by focusing on the great miracles Hashem performed for us and the abundant love He has for us. But there is no requirement to do so. So if you have the time, great, but as is true with many things, you have to balance it with your other responsibilities.

In short: Chanukah candle lighting is an auspicious time for prayer. Sitting at the candles and internalizing the message of the lights is a nice thing to do if you are able.

121

Hairstyling of Yosef vs. Greek Culture

Q ***Does external appearance have any place in Judaism? On the one hand, it is well known that we reject the philosophy of the Greeks, which greatly emphasized the body and physical appearance. Yet we find that Yosef was occupied with styling his hair and enhancing his facial beauty. Does that mean that there is some value to externalities?***

A Putting excessive emphasis on physical appearance for its own sake is undoubtedly rooted in Greek philosophy. However, outward appearance does have value if used as a tool to advance the glory of Heaven in the world.

If we take a closer look at the life of Yosef, we see that he was blessed with tremendous leadership qualities along with the ability to influence others. Sforno (*Bereishis* 37:3) explains that the special multicolored garment Yaakov made for Yosef was a symbol of royalty, as he was being groomed by his father to become the next leader. Noble attire gives its wearer the appearance of prestige and authority, enabling him to maximize his influence on others.

This concept is expressed in the prayer recited during *Bircas Kohanim* (the Priestly Blessing). We pray that our words be accepted to influence people to serve Hashem, just as Yosef found favor in the eyes of all who saw him when he was dressed in his special tunic. Clearly, his special clothing made a profound impression on his surroundings as he preached the existence and will of Hashem.

This is why a person as great as Yosef paid attention to his outward appearance. Since the reality is that people are attracted to external beauty, it is imperative for a leader to ensure that his attire befits his position, so that he will be able to exert his full influence. Indeed, after being placed in charge of Potiphar's house, Yosef again began to pay attention to his appearance. Now that he was in a position of leadership, he felt the need to improve how he looked to maximize his ability to impact others. Yosef then used his position to publicize the name of Hashem in the land of Egypt, and even in front of the mighty Pharaoh, he gave Hashem the credit for his ability to interpret the dreams.

Indeed, many of the great sages throughout the ages would be sure to dress neatly and immaculately when in public, in order to maximize their influence on their surroundings. On a similar note, they would utilize their talents or strengths — such as praying aloud and with emotion — to inspire and influence others. I vividly recall, at 2 a.m. on Simchas Torah, hearing Rav Yitzchok Hutner, Rosh Yeshivah of Yeshivah Rabbi Chaim Berlin, recite the verse, "אַתָּה הָרְאֵתָ לָדַעַת... אֵין עוֹד מִלְּבַדּוֹ — You have been shown to know... there is no power beside Him." His thunderous and emotional recital of the words left everyone present with no doubt that there is no power other than Hashem.

This is true not just for leaders, but for everyone. Every person can influence others, either directly or indirectly, in every place and in every situation, helping them come closer to Hashem and His Torah. Rav Moshe Feinstein would say that this is why, in the blessing before *Shema*, every person — whether or not he is a teacher — prays, "Instill in our hearts [the ability] to learn and to teach." Even if a person is not formally an educator, he is still a teacher, on some level, through his behavior. It therefore behooves us to act and dress appropriately, so we can maximize the effect we have on others.

Another reason to dress nicely is to show respect to our bodies, which Hashem created to serve Him — the very purpose of creation and the key to eternal life. Maintaining a proper and dignified appearance constantly reminds us of why Hashem created us, and that we should act accordingly.

In short: External appearance is not an end unto itself, as was the Greek philosophy. But if used to help promote service of Hashem, it can take on a lofty role in a person's mission of spreading the glory of Hashem in the world.

122

Chanukah — the Culmination of the Yamim Nora'im

Q ***I heard that Chanukah is the culmination of the Yamim Nora'im (the High Holy Days of Tishrei), and the final verdict for the year comes at the end of Chanukah. I always thought that the verdict is given at Ne'ilah on Yom Kippur, or perhaps on Hoshana Rabbah! Is there any source for this extension?***

A According to kabbalistic sources, Chanukah is considered the culmination of the Yamim Nora'im. This can be understood as follows: On Rosh Hashanah and Yom Kippur we are judged as to how much blessing we will receive that year. But the verdict isn't handed down until after all the mitzvos are performed, and the bull offerings were brought, on Succos, giving us the opportunity to merit a more favorable verdict.

While the Greeks were in power they did not allow the service to be performed in the Holy Temple. After the Jews' victory, they instituted the holiday of Chanukah for eight days. One of the reasons they made a holiday of eight days was to compensate for the tremendous spiritual loss of the eight days of offerings on Succos. Lighting the menorah is an especially powerful tool to bring down great blessings from Above, and helps make up for the loss of these sacrifices.

The great power of the menorah can be explained based on the words of the Shelah HaKadosh on the *pasuk* in the beginning of *Parashas Beha'aloscha*, which we read on the last day of Chanukah. "*El mul pnei hamenorah ya'iru shivas haneiros* — Toward the center of the Menorah the seven lamps shall give light" (*Bamidbar* 8:2). However, the Menorah in the Beis HaMikdash had seven lights, one of which was in the center, so there were actually only six lights casting light toward the center. Why, then, did the Torah not write, "Toward the center of the Menorah, six lamps shall give light"?

The Shelah answers that the Torah is telling us that the seven lamps of the physical Menorah burn toward the spiritual Menorah in Heaven, thereby invoking its light and its shower of blessings.

Since our lighting of the Chanukah menorah is a continuation of the lighting of the Menorah in the Holy Temple, our lighting also generates great blessing from Above, and helps make up for the loss of the eight days of offerings on Succos, even today.

We can now understand Beis Shammai's opinion regarding how the lights of our Chanukah menorah should be lit. According to his opinion, we start by lighting eight candles on the first night, and decrease the number of candles each night. He explains that this parallels the bull offerings brought on Succos, which decreased in number each day.

What connection would there be between the Chanukah candles and the bull offerings of Succos? Since we now know that our lighting helps make up for the loss of these offerings, it would make sense that we light them following the same pattern.

We can now understand how Chanukah is the culmination of the Yamim Nora'im. On Rosh Hashanah and Yom Kippur we are judged as to how much blessing we will receive that year, with the final verdict handed out after the *korbanos* are offered on Succos. When we lack these offerings, the lighting of the menorah on Chanukah takes their place, and helps bring down the full shine of those blessings into this world, making Chanukah the culmination of the Yamim Nora'im and the eight days of Succos.

In short: The light of the menorah compensates for the eight lost days of offerings on Succos, and helps bring down the full flow of blessings from the Yamim Nora'im and the eight days of Succos into this world.

123

Holding Onto the Inspiration of Chanukah

Q ***We just celebrated a wonderful and uplifting Chanukah. As we bid farewell to the holiday and head into the long winter ahead of us, are there any ideas you can share with us as to how we can try to hold onto the inspiration?***

A You are bringing out a very fundamental point! A Yom Tov is not just a time for passing moments of elevation; each Yom Tov is actually meant to give a dose of inspiration, infusing us with intense feelings of closeness to Hashem that carry us along until the next Yom Tov. Indeed, every person should look for something to take along with him, and accept upon himself a new commitment, appropriate for his level, that will take this connection to Hashem to a higher level.

There's much we can discuss, but let's focus on one of the basic themes of Chanukah and see what we can take with us. Two great miracles took place in the Chanukah story: The first was that the small band of Chashmonaim was victorious over the mighty Greek army. The second was that one day's supply of oil burned supernaturally in the Menorah in the Holy Temple for eight days.

Why did Hashem perform these miracles? It was all because of the tremendous love He has for us, His chosen nation. This love never wavers, and this is the feeling that we must keep with us throughout the dark nights of our exile. No matter how dark things may appear, we must remember that Hashem is with us at all times, lighting up the way and taking care of all our needs — when things are pleasant and when they're tough. Our rabbis have stated that the very fact that our nation is still in existence after two thousand years in exile — having survived inquisitions, crusades, and holocausts, and outlasting one mighty nation after another — is the greatest miracle of all. This is the strongest testament to Hashem's eternal love and connection to His people.

If you internalize these ideas, you will become deeply inspired to reciprocate some of that love, and be aroused to thank Hashem constantly for all that He does for us. And the least we can do is pray to Him properly and follow the rules and regulations He set down for us in the Torah and *Shulchan Aruch*.

The *Kuzari* writes that just as each Yom Tov infuses us spiritually and keeps us connected to Hashem until the next Yom Tov, our prayers keep us constantly connected to Him. Each of the three daily prayers is meant to keep us connected to Hashem and spiritually elevated until the next one. Just as a person cannot expect to stay healthy if he skips meals and just tries to get by with quick snacks instead of nutritious meals, one cannot expect to have the spiritual vigor he needs if he does not make use of the three daily prayers, spread out throughout the day. So one great thing to accept would be to concentrate more on the meaning of the words of prayer.

There is a fascinating incident involving Rav Shlomo Wolbe *zt"l* that underscores this point. The venerated Mashgiach was asked to join a daily *minyan* for Minchah that took place in the late afternoon, but he declined. After being pressed to disclose his reasoning, he explained that he always davened Minchah at the first opportunity, and didn't want to wait until later in the afternoon. After so much time had already passed since Shacharis, he was looking forward to the next dose of spiritual energy and wanted to pray as soon as the opportunity arose.

In short: A basic lesson of Chanukah is Hashem's eternal love and connection to His people, taking care of us at all times. This should leave us inspired to thank Him constantly for all that He does for us and to follow His Torah. Accept a new commitment according to your level.

Purim

124

Getting Drunk on Purim

Q ***I find the mitzvah of getting drunk on Purim very strange, as I see grown men and boys acting inappropriately and unbecomingly. Perhaps they have it all wrong, and letting loose is really meant just for kids!***

A The intense celebration of Purim is meant for all — children and adults, men and women, scholar and layman — and getting drunk is one of the special mitzvos of Purim, as spelled out in the Talmud (*Megillah* 7b) and *Shulchan Aruch* (*Orach Chaim* 695:2). Drinking sensibly on Purim can actually help a person reach great spiritual elevation. But in order to appreciate and properly fulfill this unique mitzvah, we must first understand what the celebration of Purim is all about.

Megillas Esther begins with Achashverosh throwing a grand party, celebrating the solidification of his rule. As the Talmud (*Megillah* 11b) explains, Achashverosh mistakenly thought that the seventy-year deadline for the liberation of the Jews had passed, and it was clear to him that they had been deemed unworthy of redemption and were doomed to remain in exile. The wicked Haman then took this to the next level, convincing Achashverosh that they were free to kill the Jews because their G-d was already "old," and no longer cared for them. As our Rabbis (*Megillah* 12a) tell us, the Jews were indeed deserving of annihilation, because they had enjoyed themselves at Achashverosh's grand party. With Hashem seemingly forsaking us, there was never a bleaker moment in our history.

But the message of the Purim story is that Hashem loves us unconditionally and will never forsake us. Immediately after the evil decree was passed, Mordechai asked some children what they had learned that day. One responded with the *pasuk* (*Yeshayahu* 8:10), "*Ki imanu Keil* — For G-d is with us," while another quoted the *pasuk* (ibid. 46:4), "*Ve'ad ziknah Ani hu* — [Hashem declares:] Even when I [seem] old, I remain the same." The message rang loud and clear: Hashem's love for His beloved nation never gets old, and He is there to help them no matter how far they may have fallen.

Every year on Purim, we relive this feeling and refresh this deep-rooted connection with Hashem. The realization that Hashem is with us in *every* situation — no matter how hopeless it may seem — should make a person so euphoric that he should literally be dancing for joy.

Getting high on Purim is merely an offshoot of this expression of true elation and a means to help express this joy. Every Jew has an innate spiritual connection to Hashem, but since we are typically a more contained and subdued people, we are often inhibited by our nature. Drinking helps a person transcend these inhibitions and bring this inner spiritual yearning to the fore. Seeing people in a state of such true and unadulterated joy and love of Hashem, singing His praises without constraint, is truly uplifting and inspiring.

It is also worth mentioning that although it is a mitzvah to get drunk on Purim, it is not an obligation, and if one cannot drink responsibly he is not allowed to get drunk. One can also follow the advice of the Rema, and fulfill the mitzvah by drinking a little more than usual and then falling asleep. It is unfortunate that some people who can't handle the alcohol just act silly. They may mean well, but they are squandering the great levels of spirituality that can be attained on this amazing day, and are sadly creating a misconception of this great holiday. Indeed, they should not get drunk.

In short: On Purim we celebrate Hashem's closeness to us, and drinking can help express this deep feeling of elation. But if someone cannot drink responsibly he should not get drunk.

125

Is Purim Greater Than Other Holidays?

Q ***I heard that Purim is considered the greatest of all holidays, even greater than Pesach, Shavuos, and Succos. Is it possible that Purim, which is merely a Rabbinic festival, can be greater than all these Biblical holidays?***

A Purim has an element of greatness that no other holiday has! As the Midrash states, the other holidays will no longer be observed after Mashiach comes, but the holiday of Purim will remain forever.

What makes Purim so extraordinary? Purim and the other holidays can be compared to a wedding and a fiftieth anniversary celebration. While weddings are celebrated with great pomp and fanfare, no one can be sure that the union will last. But fifty years later, as the couple sits back and basks in the *nachas* of their children and grandchildren, we can all truly rejoice over the success of their marriage. Looking back at how the couple stayed together through thick and thin, navigating the many bumps along the way, we can now say with certainty that the bond was a lasting one, and that the festive wedding celebration was truly in order.

Similarly, the Biblical holidays commemorate our redemption from Egypt and the supernatural miracles Hashem performed for us in the Wilderness, when we became His nation. The Jewish nation at that time was on an extremely high spiritual level. They had followed Hashem into the desert unquestioningly, risked their lives to enter the sea, and accepted the Torah unequivocally. All of this made them worthy of these great miracles — the Splitting of the Sea, the skies opening up as the Torah was given, the Clouds of Glory, and many more.

But what happens when the Jewish people don't do what they are supposed to do, and instead of serving Hashem, commit terrible sins such as idol worship? One may think that if we are unfaithful in our relationship with Hashem, He will sever His bond with us.

This is where Purim comes in. As we mentioned, *Megillas Esther* begins with Achashverosh throwing a grand party, celebrating the fact that the Jews were doomed to remain in exile. And then, because of their sins, Hashem sends Haman and Achashverosh to decree that they be annihilated. It surely appeared that Hashem was no longer interested in us.

But the Purim miracle teaches us that nothing can be further from the truth! Hashem may punish us and send us wake-up calls, but He will never forsake us. As soon as the Jewish people repented, Hashem welcomed them back with "open arms."

So whereas the Biblical holidays commemorate our "wedding" with Hashem, as we became His nation, Purim is like the fiftieth anniversary. It brings to light that our bond with Hashem is everlasting, something worthy of celebrating even after Mashiach comes.

Even the name of the month, Adar, demonstrates this lesson. Adar is an acronym for "*Alef Dar* — the One [Above] is dwelling [amongst us]," the essence of the Purim message: Hashem is always with us, even in exile, making the entire month a joyful one.

In short: In some ways, Purim is greater than the other holidays because it teaches us that Hashem is eternally connected to us. Although He punishes us and sends us wake-up calls when we sin, He will never forsake us, and as soon as we repent, we are welcomed back with "open arms."

126

Dressing Up as Hitler

Q ***Is there anything wrong with my child dressing up on Purim like Hitler, may his name be eradicated? I know we want his memory to be obliterated, but is it any different from the common practice of dressing up like the evil Haman, whose name we also want obliterated?***

A Although children have always dressed up like Haman, I believe that dressing up as Hitler is very wrong. But let us first understand the reason for dressing up.

The custom of masquerading on Purim serves as a reminder that things are not always the way they seem on the surface. Even when it seems as if Hashem is out of the picture, He is merely "hiding behind the scenes," orchestrating all the events. My rebbi, Rav Dovid Kronglas, Mashgiach in Yeshivah Ner Yisroel, used to compare this to a mother walking with her child when the child suddenly refuses to continue, so the mother walks away without him. Even if she turns the corner and is out of the child's sight, she is still peeking back to ensure his safety.

Similarly, even when things look bleak, we must realize that Hashem is always there looking out for us, and even if we may not realize it, our lives are full of hidden miracles. For this reason, there is an obligation to read the entire *Megillah* — including the portions where it seemed like Hashem was abandoning us — because that, too, was really just another link in the miraculous chain of events.

Every year, as we relive the Purim story, we refresh this powerful feeling of connection with Hashem. This is symbolized by the custom of dressing up in costumes on Purim, signifying that Hashem was "wearing a mask," orchestrating the entire sequence of events from behind the scenes. Even when the present and future seem gloomy, we know that Hashem is merely disguising Himself, just as He did in the days of Purim, and everything happening is for our ultimate good.

This is why dressing up like Haman is fine, because Haman's decree aroused the entire Jewish nation to complete and genuine repentance, making him responsible for the greatest collective *teshuvah* (repentance) movement in our history. As the Talmud (*Megillah* 14a) attests, the inspiration generated by this decree was more powerful than all of the prophets' calls to repentance throughout the ages. Furthermore, after the Jewish people witnessed their miraculous salvation and the intense love Hashem has for His nation, they were inspired to reciprocate that love, and accepted the Torah once again with renewed excitement (see *Shabbos* 88a).

For this reason, our Rabbis teach that a person should get intoxicated on Purim until the point that he even blesses Haman, as he was the catalyst for the Jewish nation's collective repentance. His role in causing the greatest revival of Torah in Jewish history might also be why he merited descendants who converted and became great Torah scholars.

Children throughout the ages have been dressing up like Haman, because we realize that even when we are confronted with adversaries it is really all Hashem, hiding behind the face of the enemy, which indeed aroused us to reach the greatest spiritual levels.

But as I heard from Rav Ruderman, Rosh Yeshivah of Yeshivah Ner Yisroel, the plot of Hitler — may his name be eradicated — had a very different and catastrophic outcome. No massive repentance took place, and the results were, therefore, tragically different. Thus, any reference to this terrible and wicked man should be downright repulsive, and we shouldn't want to remember him in any way, making it very wrong to dress up like him.

In short: Haman was a catalyst for a great spiritual renaissance with a happy ending, so one can dress up like him. Hitler's plot, however, had a tragic outcome and one should not recall him in any way.

127

Celebrating Purim in Challenging Times

Q ***After all the challenges we have gone through this past year with so much lost due to the coronavirus pandemic, are we really expected to rejoice on Purim?***

A Your very question actually gives us the answer! Although we must tone down the celebrations at a time when our nation is suffering, the eternal message of Purim — more than any other holiday on the Jewish calendar — speaks to us specifically during challenging times.

As we mentioned, the Purim miracle took place when the Jewish nation was at an all-time low. The Holy Temple lay in ruins, the Jews had been sent into a bitter exile, and it appeared that Hashem had forsaken them. Indeed, Haman used this claim to convince Achashverosh that the fate of the Jews was sealed, because Hashem was already "old" and no longer cared for them. Thus, the timeless message of Purim is that even in the darkest of moments, when it seems as if Hashem no longer cares about His children, He is really there for them, ready to help through thick and thin.

But our joy runs even deeper.

Not only is there a light at the end of the tunnel, the dark tunnel itself is what leads us to this great spiritual light. The trials and tribulations we experience are tailor-made for our growth, and we trust Hashem implicitly that they are for our benefit. Yes, it has been a tough year, but we Jews have been through much tougher times, and the fact that we are still around affirms the eternal bond we have with Hashem.

Our challenges are similar to a patient whose doctor informed him that he needs several operations and must follow a very strict regimen, after which his health will be restored. The patient readily accepts and follows these instructions, knowing that it is well worth the effort. However, when a doctor gives his patient no guidance and lets him do as he pleases, it may mean that the doctor has given up hope.

Similarly, if the Great Doctor would leave us be, we would have reason to be concerned that we have done irreparable damage and He has forsaken us. It is precisely because of the challenges He sends our way that we are able to recognize that we are under His loving care. We are comforted by the knowledge that every "surgery" brings us closer to Hashem, and that following His directions enables us to reach the greatest spiritual heights. This gives us reason to celebrate.

In short: The message of Purim is as relevant as ever. We celebrate Hashem's closeness to us even in the darkest of times, and recognize that He is guiding us to reach the greatest spiritual heights.

128

Killing the Little Children of Amalek

Q ***We read in Parashas Zachor about the mitzvah to eradicate the nation of Amalek from the world. I was wondering: As Jews, aren't we supposed to be nice, pleasant people? Why is there a mitzvah to go on a rampage, murdering every member of an entire nation — even little children?***

A To answer this question, we must first understand what Amalek is. Amalek is the antithesis of anything and everything connecting us and the world to Hashem, which is the very purpose of creation. Our mission in this world is to publicize Hashem's Divine Presence and His intimate involvement in our world, and Amalek is diametrically opposed to this worldview. They claim that after Hashem created the world He left it to run on its own, and everyone has the right to do as they please, without any restrictions. This evil philosophy stands to destroy everything we strive to accomplish in this world.

As we read in the Torah, after hearing about the supernatural miracles the Jewish nation had experienced on their way out of Egypt, the nations of the world were in awe of them. Then, as the Jews were marching through the Wilderness on their way to the land of Israel, Amalek came and waged war with them for no personal gain, purely out of hatred for what we represent. By doing so, they cooled everyone down, announcing to the world that the Jewish nation is also vulnerable, and Hashem does not care for them.

But (as discussed at length in the previous pieces on Purim) nothing could be further from the truth!

As we learn from the Purim story, Hashem is there for us in every situation. Even after the Jews committed a terrible sin and deserved to be annihilated, Hashem turned everything around and saved them. That is why we read about the mitzvah to destroy Amalek on the Shabbos before Purim, preparing for this great holiday when we celebrate our intimate connection with Hashem and His unconditional love for us.

The purpose of this mitzvah is not just to kill the people of Amalek, but to destroy their worldview. We must destroy them before they destroy us — and all that we stand for — by spreading their poisonous views and influencing the world with their false philosophy. Even little children must be killed, before they are indoctrinated in this philosophy and continue to spread its evil.

Indeed, we are commanded to destroy even the possessions of Amalek, like a home infested with termites, where the only way to really get rid of them is to destroy anything they may have gotten into. Similarly, anything that has any hint of Amalek and their falsehoods must be eradicated.

Since the purpose of destroying Amalek is to destroy their evil, if an Amalekite accepts upon himself to keep the Seven Noahide Laws, we are no longer commanded to kill him. Once he has changed his ways and left their corrupt culture behind, he is no longer a danger and does not need to be killed.

In short: Wiping out Amalek means destroying their evil and poisonous outlook, which preaches against Hashem's intimate connection to the world, and must therefore be eradicated.

Asarah B'Teves

129

Fasting on Asarah B'Teves as We Enter Shabbos

Q ***In general, we do not fast on Friday, as we want to welcome Shabbos joyfully, something difficult to do when fasting. Yet Asarah B'Teves (The Fast of the Tenth of Teves) is occasionally on Friday, which means that we enter Shabbos fasting! Why is that?***

A It is indeed interesting that Asarah B'Teves is the only fast on our calendar that can fall on a Friday. But let me add to your question: According to some opinions, although not possible on our calendar, if Asarah B'Teves were to actually fall on Shabbos we would have to fast on Shabbos, just like when Yom Kippur is on Shabbos! Even if Tishah B'Av — the fast marking the anniversary of the actual destruction of the Beis HaMikdash — falls on Shabbos, it is postponed until Sunday! Why, then, would we fast on Asarah B'Teves, which merely commemorates the beginning of the siege of Jerusalem, a far less tragic event?

I once heard Rav Moshe Feinstein explain this with the following powerful thought: Although Asarah B'Teves commemorates only the beginning of the siege, with the actual destruction of the Beis HaMikdash taking place nearly three years later, this date marks the beginning of the end. The Jewish people at that time were not conducting themselves the way they should, and the prophets had repeatedly warned them that they must repent or they would lose the merit of having the Beis HaMikdash in their midst. But, sadly, they failed to heed these warnings, so Hashem sent Nevuchadnetzar to lay siege on Yerushalayim.

This siege was the final warning, intended to wake them up from their slumber. With the enemy at their doorstep, they should have realized that it was now or never, and they could no longer ignore the threat of the impending tragedy. But the Jews still didn't get the message, thinking they could change their ways at some later time. Tragically, that was not the case and the Beis HaMikdash was destroyed.

Fast days are not just for remembering tragic events of days gone by; they are also meant to be a part of our own *teshuvah* process, to rectify the sins that caused these terrible tragedies in the first place. When we fast on Asarah B'Teves, we must look to correct the sins that brought about the siege that ultimately led to the destruction of the Beis HaMikdash. Since the root of their sin was procrastination and a lack of urgency to repent, it is our duty to fast and repent immediately — on the very day we received this severe warning — and not to even postpone the fast until after Shabbos.

Although our calendar does not allow Asarah B'Teves to actually fall on Shabbos, when it falls on Friday we experience fasting and hunger pangs as Shabbos begins. This is a powerful lesson to think about as we fast on Asarah B'Teves, as well as a message to take with us throughout the year. When a person sins, he must not wait for Yom Kippur to repent, but do his best to repent immediately.

In short: We enter Shabbos fasting, and we would even fast if Asarah B'Teves were to fall on Shabbos. Since the fast is to teach us not to delay repentance, we must fast immediately, and not wait until after Shabbos.

Section 15
Jewish Heritage and History

130

Understanding Yitzchak Avinu

Q ***The Book of Bereishis discusses at great length the many trials and challenges our forefathers Avraham and Yaakov faced. Yet, we don't see much about the challenges Yitzchak experienced. In fact, he seemed to have been oblivious to the world around him, not even aware of how wicked his own son Eisav was! Was he as great as the other forefathers?***

A As one of our forefathers, Yitzchak was exceedingly great, far beyond our comprehension, and in some ways, even greater than the other forefathers! And although the Torah tells us very little about his life, if we look more carefully at the few incidents it does mention, we can gain insight into some of his greatness.

One of the greatest tests Avraham faced was *Akeidas Yitzchak,* the binding of Yitzchak on the altar, when he demonstrated his willingness to sacrifice even his beloved son for the sake of Hashem. Yet in some ways, Yitzchak's sacrifice was even greater. Avraham was following a command he had received directly from Hashem, and was not giving up his own life. But Yitzchak was ready to give up his very life based on a message he heard from his father, not directly from Hashem, teaching us to follow the words of our sages for all generations.

Furthermore, his was not merely a one-time test. Rashi tells us that for the rest of his life, Yitzchak was considered an *olah temimah* (an offering completely devoted to Hashem), and he was even forbidden to leave the Holy Land.

Through his total subservience to Hashem, Yitzchak reached the highest levels of sanctity, until he was no longer under the influence of the evil inclination. Because of this subservience, Yitzchak represents the attribute of *gevurah,* spiritual strength, and was completely devoted to the service of Hashem with every fiber of his being, every moment of his life.

Recognizing the lofty level of her husband, Rivkah undertook the mission to facilitate his holy occupation, fiercely shielding Yitzchak from even the slightest distraction in his service of Hashem. This is why she withheld from Yitzchak any information about the wickedness of their son Eisav, as such knowledge may have disturbed his sacred work.

And when we do find Yitzchak interacting with others, we see that he excelled in interpersonal relationships as well. In *Parashas Toldos,* Avimelech, king of Gerar, tells Yitzchak to leave the country after the Philistines began to envy his immense wealth. Later, after seeing that Hashem was with Yitzchak, Avimelech had a change of heart and approached Yitzchak with a request for a treaty. Although Avimelech and his people had treated him terribly, Yitzchak accepted their proposal and treated them to a feast, even calling them brothers.

This character trait is discussed by Rav Moshe Cordovero in his classic *sefer Tomer Devorah*. He describes at length the thirteen attributes of Hashem, and explains how every Jew is commanded to follow these lofty ways and conduct himself according to these attributes. He writes that just as Hashem pushes aside His anger even when we sin, we must do the same, and not bear a grudge against those who harm us, even though we may be right. He adds that just as Hashem accepts our repentance, we must also be willing to "forgive and forget," and refresh our friendship with those who may have harmed us. Thus, we see that Yitzchak was exceedingly great, serving Hashem every moment, and excelled in interpersonal relationships as well.

In short: As one of our Patriarchs, Yitzchak was exceedingly great. He was completely devoted to serving Hashem and also excelled in interpersonal relationships, and we have much to learn from his example.

131

King Shlomo Marrying 1,000 Wives

Q ***Why did King Shlomo marry a thousand wives from all different nations? This type of behavior sounds more appropriate for a person steeped in the pursuit of physical desires, not for the wisest of all men!***

A King Shlomo was one of the greatest men who ever lived. He was also known as Yedidya, the beloved of Hashem, so he was obviously not occupied with physical desires. Since these women converted to Judaism he was permitted to marry them, and he was surely involved in a lofty mission.

The simple understanding is that by marrying daughters of kings and noblemen from various nations, he hoped to bring these leaders closer to him and thereby establish peaceful relations with them. When people live in constant fear of their enemies, their minds are preoccupied and they are unable to focus on properly serving Hashem. Shlomo created a peaceful and serene society so that the people were able to channel their time and energy toward doing good things and serving Hashem to the best of their abilities. Indeed, this created an era of tranquility for the Jewish people that did not exist before his time or after.

On a deeper level, the kabbalists explain that King Shlomo had lofty intentions and wished to accomplish great things with his actions. By marrying these women and bringing them closer to Hashem, he was seeking to take all the nations of the world "under His wings," thereby subduing and purifying the various impure powers of the world.

Although from the simple reading of the story it would appear that Shlomo was a sinner, the Talmud tells us (*Shabbos* 56b) that this is incorrect, and anyone who claims that Shlomo sinned is mistaken.

The *pasuk* (*I Melachim* 11:4) states, "The heart of Shlomo was not perfect with Hashem ***as was the heart of David,*** his father." This teaches that Shlomo's failing was only that he did not live up to the lofty level of his father in his service of Hashem, but he did not actually sin.

The Gemara continues that even when the *pasuk* (ibid. v. 6) states, "Shlomo did evil in the eyes of Hashem," it means merely that he was at fault for not properly protesting the idol worship of his wives. One who has the power to prevent others from sinning and does not do so is considered to have sinned. Because Hashem expects more from the righteous, Shlomo's slightest wrongdoing is discussed in magnified terms, but Shlomo remained Yedidya — the beloved of Hashem.

In short: King Shlomo was a great man and certainly had lofty intentions. By marrying these women, he sought to create an era of tranquility in the world and to subdue the powers of evil.

132

Sins of the Earlier Generations

Q ***Throughout the Torah and Tanach, we read about terrible sins committed by the Jewish nation, and especially kings who led the nation to worship idols. Does that mean they were not so righteous?***

A The people mentioned in the Torah were on a very high spiritual level, way beyond our comprehension. For example, the generation that left Egypt is known as the *Dor Dei'ah* (Generation of Knowledge) and was one of the greatest in our nation's history. At the splitting of the Reed Sea, a simple maidservant saw visions that the prophet Yechezkel never merited to see. They subsisted on manna, a spiritual food designated for angels. At Mount Sinai, the Heavens opened up, and they saw with clarity that Hashem is the only G-d and the Source of all existence. Similarly, many of the kings you mentioned were heirs to King David's throne, and on an extremely exalted level of spirituality.

Because Hashem expects more from such great people, even their minor misdeeds are considered great sins, and the Torah describes their slightest sins in magnified terms — not despite their greatness, but because of it. As the Talmud (*Bava Kamma* 50a) tells us, the righteous are judged with extreme severity, and are punished even for the smallest of infractions. The Vilna Gaon compared this to a woman who examines her face for blemishes under a magnifying glass, searching to fix even the tiniest speck in order to look her best.

For example, the Torah writes that Yosef's brothers were jealous of him. But as my rebbi, Rav Dovid Kronglas, pointed out, they certainly didn't realize they were jealous; had they realized that, they would have fled from it like from a fire. Only Hashem, Who knew their subconscious motivation, attested to this small hidden speck of jealousy hidden deep within their hearts.

There are also times when the Torah attributes sins to great people because they should have objected or prevented others from sinning, and the Torah considered it as if he himself sinned. For example, when the Jews were defeated by the people of Ai shortly after entering the Land of Israel, Hashem told Yehoshua that this happened because (*Yehoshua* 7:11) "the Jewish nation sinned, went against the treaty with Hashem, took from the booty, stole, and lied." Although only Achan was guilty of taking from the booty of Yericho, the sin was ascribed to the entire nation, since they were all responsible for each other and were expected to guard the booty.

When it comes to idolatry, there is another fundamental point that must be mentioned. To us worshiping idols sounds silly, because the desire for idolatry was destroyed by the Men of the Great Assembly. Before that, however, the temptation to worship idols was stronger than any temptation we have today, and they were expected to overcome this overwhelming desire only because they were so great.

The Talmud (*Sanhedrin* 102b) relates a fascinating story that illustrates this point. Rav Ashi once announced that the following day's lecture would be about "our colleagues — kings who lost their portion in the Next World," such as Menashe, who had led the people to worship idols. That night, Menashe appeared to Rav Ashi in a dream and proved that he was a much greater Torah scholar than Rav Ashi, and told Rav Ashi that he had no business considering himself an equal. Rav Ashi then asked Menashe, "Since you are so learned, why did you worship idols?" Menashe responded, "You cannot fathom the great temptation there was for idol worship. Had you been living at that time, you would have lifted the hem of your garment to pursue it even faster than we did!"

In short: Actions of great people are magnified in the Torah, as they are judged more severely for minor infractions and for not objecting to others who sin. There was a powerful desire for idol worship, and great people were expected to overcome these strong temptations.

133

Democracy or Monarchy — Which Is Better?

Q ***With the war in Ukraine, we have once again witnessed tremendous cruelty inflicted by someone with unchecked power. Unfortunately, this has been a common phenomenon throughout history, which seems to be a clear indication that democracy is the correct method of government. How, then, do we understand the mitzvah in the Torah to appoint a king?***

A Every mitzvah in the Torah is from Hashem, and we must follow Hashem's will whether we appreciate the reasoning behind it or not. But in this case, it's not difficult to explain the advantages of a monarchy over a democracy.

In a democracy, leaders are elected, which causes them to spend a lot of time and energy trying to find favor in the eyes of the people, instead of focusing on doing what is right and being devoted to the welfare of their country. We have seen the great havoc caused to our country when politicians base decisions solely on popular opinion.

In addition, having a country run by the people is not necessarily a good thing, because the general population very often doesn't really know the best approach that should be taken on issues. And even when they try to choose the candidate they think will represent them correctly, their votes are often based on the candidate's charisma or positions on a specific issue, rather than on his integrity or real leadership abilities.

A king, on the other hand, never has to base his decisions on the next election. His role is to remain objective and use his power to implement laws solely for the good of the nation. In fact, this is the very reason that justices of the Supreme Court of the U.S. are given lifelong positions. This ensures that their decisions are not swayed by outside influences, and reflect what they sincerely believe to be the whole truth and nothing but the truth.

However, as you mentioned, authority has the power to corrupt people, and, unfortunately, a king can abuse this power for things such as personal power or financial gain, hurting others along the way, which is why monarchies have been rejected. Even Winston Churchill famously called democracy a necessary evil, meaning that although it is not the ideal form of government, it was necessary for lack of a better alternative.

A true king is a servant of the people, and as Rambam writes, he is humble and soft-spoken, totally devoted to the good of the nation, caring for everyone — great or small. As discussed elsewhere ("Death of Queen Elizabeth"), a Jewish king is also guided by Hashem and invested with spiritual power and greatness, which is why we recite the blessing, "שֶׁחָלַק מִכְּבוֹדוֹ לִירֵאָיו — Who apportioned of His Glory to those who fear Him," upon seeing a Jewish king. King David and his righteous heirs were certainly worthy of sitting on the throne.

For this reason, a king was required to have a Torah Scroll at his side at all times. Constant Torah study would serve to remind him that all his actions must be rooted in the ways of the Torah, and they must be performed to uplift the honor of Hashem and His Torah. A king was also required to ask the High Court before making major decisions.

This concept of true devotion is true for every level of leadership. For example, every parent or teacher must realize that a true leader will use his authority to do his or her utmost to help others, and be dedicated to help their charges reach their greatest potential. When a child sees that his parent or teacher has his best interest in mind, as a Jewish leader should, not only will the child not resent being told what to do, they will want to follow the instructions, knowing that it is for their benefit.

In short: In a democracy, leaders try to find favor in the eyes of the people instead of leading the country properly. A king has the ability to implement rules solely for the good of the nation.

134

Death Penalty

Q ***I am a strong opponent of capital punishment, as I feel that it is a waste of life and an inhumane way of dealing with criminals. Yet I see that the Torah imposes the death penalty for many sins! Wouldn't it be better just to lock the person up or give him some other severe punishment, and then give him a second chance after he learns his lesson?***

A Human life is the very purpose of creation, and the Torah considers each and every life very precious. In fact, the Talmud (*Sanhedrin* 37a) tells us that saving one life is like saving the entire world, and we must do whatever possible to save a life, even at the cost of committing most sins. Not only is it permitted to desecrate Shabbos or eat on Yom Kippur when a life is in danger, it is actually a requirement and a great mitzvah.

However, there are certain sins that are so severe that the Torah deems this person evil and commands us to eradicate such evil from our midst, and even a life sentence will not suffice. Having such an evil person around harms everyone, as it prevents the Divine Presence from dwelling in our midst, which can bring terrible tragedies. In addition, the mere fact that the sinner is around weakens our disgust for sin, and he therefore must be killed.

Additionally, some crimes make the one who commits them a threat to society, and he too must be executed. Any civilized nation must have a system to maintain law and order, and there are situations that necessitate these dire consequences. Locking someone up for years or even for life is not a solution, as these criminals are often released and promptly terrorize the community once again. In addition, the death penalty also serves as a warning to others not to follow the ways of this evildoer, and if the punishment is not severe enough, people may not be deterred.

It is also worth noting that although the Torah does impose the death penalty for various sins, it was highly uncommon for the Jewish courts to actually implement it. The Torah requires many conditions to be met before one can actually be sentenced to death, and the courts are actually required to look for ways to exonerate the offender. In fact, the Mishnah (*Makkos* 7a) declares that a court that carried out the death penalty even once in seventy years was considered a murderous court, for not having tried hard enough to find a defense for the accused.

We must also realize that death is not the greatest calamity for this person. For those who do not believe in the World to Come, death is the end of one's existence, and the greatest tragedy possible. But as we know, this world is not a person's final destination, and we are here only to earn a place in the World to Come. This sinner has committed such grave sins that even after repenting, he will achieve atonement only through death, and this will enable him to receive his portion in the World to Come. So although loss of life is indeed tragic, in the overall picture it is not the "end of the world." On the contrary, it is very worthwhile for his soul, as it allows him entry into a world of eternal bliss.

In short: Some sinners are so evil that they prevent the Divine Presence from dwelling in our midst and weaken our disgust for sin. Some are also a threat to society. Additionally, his death is the atonement he needs to allow him entry into the World to Come.

135

Favoritism for Descendants of the Patriarchs

Q ***In our prayers, we constantly invoke the merits of our forefathers — Avraham, Yitzchak, and Yaakov. Why do we deserve special treatment just because we had great ancestors? And what about the other descendants of Avraham and Yitzchak — can they also invoke their merit?***

A First of all, the favoritism that Hashem shows is a reward to these spiritual giants for their great deeds. Since they went all out for Hashem, putting their lives on the line to spread His Name in the world, Hashem chose them and their descendants as His beloved nation, and promised to help them. So it is they who were promised special treatment for their descendants, and even if we are undeserving, we ask Hashem to fulfill the promise He made to them.

In addition, invoking the merit of the Avos in our prayers does not mean that we expect our requests to be granted simply because of our ancestry. Rather, our main intention is to recall their great deeds, and thereby awaken in ourselves the aspiration to act as befits their children, following in their exalted footsteps. Showing our desire to connect to this greatness, at least on some level, makes us even more deserving of Heavenly blessing, and helps us merit that our prayers are answered.

The other offspring of Avraham and Yitzchak are not included in their special merit. The Torah states clearly that Hashem made this promise only to Avraham and Yitzchak — and those of their descendants who were continuing their legacy, making us the sole spiritual heirs to our great Patriarchs and Matriarchs. As the holy books explain, after the sin of Adam, humanity and the entire universe became contaminated. In order to return the world to its original state and establish a nation close to Hashem, a purification process was needed, and that was begun by our forefathers. Most of the impurities that still remained after they purified themselves were transmitted to their other offspring, leaving Yaakov and his descendants much more refined.

But even after all these impurities were removed, we were still not pure enough to be worthy of becoming the Chosen Nation and receiving Hashem's Torah, and a more intense purification was needed. For this reason, we had to endure tremendous suffering in Egypt, which completed the process necessary for us to become the nation eternally connected to Hashem. Because we are the true continuation of these great forefathers, we are the ones who have this distinct privilege of invoking their merits.

In short: This special treatment is a reward for our forefathers. We are their sole spiritual heirs, which is why we have the unique privilege of invoking their merits, and by emulating them we become even more deserving of Heavenly blessing.

Section 16

Kiruv Questions

136

Making Changes Later in Life

Q ***Although I grew up religious, I have strayed far from the path of Torah, and have even committed many serious sins. I recently met someone who is trying to convince me to turn my life around. Do you really think G-d still wants me after all these years? I even remember hearing that there can be no repentance for some of the sins I committed! So is there any point?***

A Yes, He certainly wants you back!

Let me share a story that I happen to know first-hand. A child got angry at his parents and severed all ties with them, causing them much heartache. After not being in touch with them for some thirty years, the child finally came to his senses and sent a message to his parents that he would like to restore the relationship. Although they had every right to be upset with him, the parents were elated at the opportunity to reunite with their long-lost child.

The same is true for us, Hashem's children. No matter how many years have gone by, and no matter how severe our sins might be, Hashem eagerly awaits the return of every one of His beloved children. This is true whether one grew up religious and strayed from the true path, or if one grew up irreligious and never kept anything in the first place. As soon as we take the first steps to try to return, He will embrace us and take us under His wings. He will accept us with open arms, and proclaim, "Welcome home!"

No sin is beyond repentance; even Nevuzaradan, who killed millions of Jews, was able to repent (*Gittin* 57b)! As Rambam writes, nothing stands in the way of *teshuvah* (repentance) and sincere remorse. It is also never too late to change, as the Talmud (*Kiddushin*

40b) tells us, "Even if one was wicked his entire life but repents sincerely at the last moment, he will be accepted!"

The Talmud (*Avodah Zarah* 17a) relates the dramatic story of Elazar Ben Durdia, who committed grave sins throughout his lifetime, but when he finally realized how low he had fallen, he repented, and wept with great remorse until his soul departed. A Heavenly voice then cried out, "Rabbi Elazar Ben Durdia is now worthy of entering the World to Come!" When Rabbi Yehudah HaNassi heard this story, he cried and said, "Some take many years to earn their place in the World to Come, while others earn it in a single moment!"

While it is true that certain sins are so severe that they require the sinner to endure suffering to cleanse its impurities, this doesn't have to be through terrible pain or sickness. Exerting oneself for a mitzvah or Torah study, such as staying up late at night studying, or traveling in inclement weather to help others, can take the place of suffering and help a person achieve atonement.

Thus, even someone who has sunk to the lowest levels of sin can still repent, and will be welcomed back by our loving Father.

In short: We are all Hashem's children, and no matter how low one has fallen, Hashem will accept His child back with open arms. Nothing stands in the way of teshuvah, even the gravest sins.

137

Should I Get Other Jews to Keep Shabbos?

Q ***I have some relatives who unfortunately don't keep Shabbos. Is it my responsibility to make sure that they do, or should I just mind my own business and leave them alone?***

A Yes, it is your responsibility! The Jewish nation is one big unit, and we are all responsible for each other's spiritual and physical well-being. At the same time, when bringing others closer to mitzvah observance, we must be careful to use the right tools and methods. Generally speaking, being aggressive and speaking harshly is wrong and even counterproductive, as this will just aggravate them and give them a bad taste for Judaism. Even if doing so may temporarily keep them from desecrating Shabbos, it may also cause them to drift even further away, and you will lose more than you gain.

The key to successfully inspiring others to come closer to Hashem is to become a student of Aharon (*Avos* 1:12), "Love people and bring them closer to Torah." This must be the guiding light for anyone involved in outreach. The way to bring people closer to Hashem and the Torah is with love and genuine concern for their welfare. When people see that you truly care for them, they will understand that you are not just trying to push an agenda, but seeking to help them enjoy the wonderful life of Torah and mitzvos and merit a portion in the World to Come.

So be friendly, speak nicely, and describe the beauty of Shabbos and the benefits and enjoyment a person will have when keeping Shabbos. Indeed, I remember taking part in peaceful Shabbos parades, in which we would sing Shabbos songs and talk to store owners about the beauty of Shabbos.

You can also try to invite your relatives to join you for a Shabbos meal, or send them presents or nice foods for Shabbos, like Avraham Avinu did. The unique Shabbos atmosphere and the delicious Shabbos foods — such as potato kugel, chicken soup, or cholent — will help them enjoy the beauty of Shabbos first-hand, and can go a long way in inspiring them toward observing Shabbos. Many not-yet-religious Jews who have never seen a Shabbos meal in their lives are blown away by the experience. We once had a young boy who joined us for a Shabbos meal and, in the middle of the meal, my wife found him crying. She asked him what was wrong, and he answered that everything was fine, he was simply overcome by the beauty of the experience. He had never seen a family actually sit down together for a meal every week, singing and enjoying each other's company.

With this in mind, we can understand a ruling I received from Rav Moshe Feinstein. We wanted to invite non-religious guests to our home to experience an authentic Shabbos, but they were unwilling to stay for the entire twenty-five hours. What should I do? Rav Moshe responded that it is permitted to invite them for just a meal, even if they will desecrate the Shabbos in the process, provided I feel that this can eventually help them become more religious. He did add one very important caveat: You cannot invite them if you know that they will desecrate the Shabbos publicly — such as driving up to a house in a Jewish neighborhood — as it would be a desecration of Hashem's Name. As mentioned, seeing the beauty of a Shabbos meal can be very powerful, and inspire them to become more connected to Judaism.

In short: Every Jew is responsible for all his fellow Jews. The way to bring others close to Hashem and the Torah is by showing love and concern, not by being aggressive. Invite them for a Shabbos meal, and provide them the opportunity to taste the beauty of Shabbos.

138

Just One Shabbos

Q ***A number of years ago, an initiative was started to get as many people throughout the world as possible to keep one specific Shabbos. Is there any point in someone keeping only one Shabbos, and is there any benefit in many people keeping specifically the same Shabbos?***

A Yes, many people keeping one Shabbos is a great accomplishment!

Some people make a big mistake and think that keeping the Torah is either all-or-nothing, and if someone is not religious there is no point in keeping any mitzvos. When it comes to money, people appreciate every dollar; no one says, "If I can't be a millionaire I won't bother trying to make money at all." Similarly, every mitzvah a person performs is priceless. And performing just one mitzvah, even one time, is a tremendous accomplishment. Indeed, we find (*Chagigah* 14a) that there are angels who are created just to sing to Hashem one time.

This is especially true when it comes to Shabbos. We cannot begin to comprehend the greatness of keeping even one Shabbos — or even one moment of this holy day. As our Rabbis tell us (*Yerushalmi Taanis* 1:1), if all Jews would keep "just one Shabbos" the Final Redemption would come. So getting people to observe one full Shabbos is certainly a worthwhile endeavor.

Additionally, the experience of keeping "just one Shabbos" can have a tremendous impact on a person. By tasting the beauty of Judaism in general — and Shabbos in particular — a person will hopefully connect to Hashem and develop a life-long bond to Torah, leading him to observe many more Shabbosos in the future.

As far as having many Jews keep one specific Shabbos, there are several benefits to this. First, there is the psychological aspect. Even after people hear about the greatness of Shabbos they may not be ready to take the plunge on their own. But when they hear that they are part of a group of so many like-minded others, they will hopefully be inspired to "jump on the bandwagon" and join all the others keeping Shabbos.

Furthermore, there is a concept of "בְּרָב עָם הַדְרַת מֶלֶךְ — With a multitude of people [performing a mitzvah] there is [more] glory to the King." It is a great glory and prestige for the king when a large cheering crowd greets him. But when there are only a few people there to greet the king, it is a lack of appropriate honor. Similarly, the more people there are joining forces to perform a mitzvah, the greater the honor it is for the King, and the glory of Hashem is increased. This is why halachah dictates that a person should try to perform a mitzvah together with others, as doing so will be according Hashem more honor.

Additionally, the spiritual effect produced by a few people performing a mitzvah cannot compare to the effect of masses of people performing a mitzvah. The Torah (*Vayikra* 26:8) tells us that whereas five righteous Jews will be able to pursue 100 of the enemy — a ratio of 1:20, 100 righteous Jews will be able to pursue 10,000 — proportionately five times the amount! As Rashi explains, the spiritual energy generated by the greater number of people serving Hashem makes even their physical powers exponentially greater.

In short: Even keeping one Shabbos is in itself a great accomplishment, and it may also be the catalyst for keeping many more. Being part of a group can inspire a person to join others keeping Shabbos. The more people performing the mitzvah, the greater the honor it is to Hashem, and the greater the spiritual energy generated.

139

How the Newly Religious Can Enjoy Shabbos

Q *We have been keeping Shabbos for almost four years, and everyone keeps telling me how great I am, but I find it really difficult. While my husband goes to shul and has a social life, I am stuck at home with the little ones. Being from a non-religious background, my friends and relatives hold many of their social events and get-togethers on Saturdays, making me feel like I am missing out on so much of life. What advice can you give me to help make keeping Shabbos a little easier?*

A You are true heroes! And the fact that it is hard for you makes you even more remarkable, as our Rabbis tell us (*Avos* 5:26), "לְפוּם צַעֲרָא אַגְרָא — The reward [for a mitzvah] is in proportion to the difficulty." You should also realize that you are by no means alone. Many newly religious people find it difficult to spend time with their old friends and relatives, but at the same time, they have trouble finding new ones, leaving them with the feeling of being stranded on a desert island.

The way to combat this issue is to compensate for what you are missing by using your new surroundings to make life meaningful and enjoyable. I suggest you find a way to get out of the house every Shabbos, and attend a class given by the rabbi or rebbetzin. If there is no such class in your community, take the initiative and arrange one. This will certainly provide you with a much-needed weekly dose of spiritual inspiration. More importantly, it's a wonderful opportunity to mingle with others in the community and even make new friends, turning a boring day into an enjoyable one.

You should also find other ways of getting together with others on a regular basis, such as by sharing Shabbos meals with other families in the community. Make sure to invite others to your home, and get yourselves invited out, too. Aside from making your Shabbos more enjoyable and entertaining, it will help offset your feelings of missing out by giving you a sense of belonging to the community.

Get something good to read. There is a wealth of educational and inspirational reading material available — Jewish books, magazines, and newspapers — with essays and articles on a wide variety of topics that can keep you engaged for hours. Your children should also invite friends over, and treat everyone to a nice Shabbos party with special Shabbos nosh, turning the day into one of pleasure that you will look forward to all week long.

Being part of a religious community will also provide you with an abundance of social events and gatherings to attend. Religious people keep themselves very busy attending weddings, *bris* and bar mitzvah celebrations, and many other happy occasions. Don't be shy and make it your business to go to these events. By participating in these enjoyable and uplifting celebrations, you won't feel like you are missing out by not attending the parties of your old friends and relatives.

So with a bit of creativity and ingenuity, you can find many ways to compensate for the things you are missing out on. Doing this will turn a long, boring weekend into a wonderful and exciting time, one that you will actually look forward to every week.

In short: There are many ways to make Shabbos enjoyable. For example: Go to a class, which provides both inspiration and an opportunity to mingle with others; have Shabbos meals together with others; get good reading material; and make a nice Shabbos party for your children's friends. Additionally, sharing in other's celebrations will help compensate for whatever you may miss out with your previous circle of friends.

140

What's so Bad About Public School?

Q ***I currently attend public school, but my friend has been trying to convince me to enroll in yeshivah. Since I study Torah with him for many hours each afternoon, I don't see the need. In addition, I am a star player on the school basketball team, and I really love the thrill of the cheering spectators. It's something I don't want to give up!***

A You have obviously never been to a yeshivah, and have no idea what true Torah study is all about. Let me try to give you a better appreciation for a yeshivah way of life and true Torah study, and you will hopefully see things differently.

First and foremost, the influences of one's surroundings are very powerful. As statistics confirm, most Jews who attend public school become completely assimilated in the "melting pot" of American society, and many of them intermarry, disappearing from the Jewish people forever. For this reason, today more than ever, a yeshivah is more than just a Jewish school; it's a safe haven from the immoral world and deteriorating society we live in.

Furthermore, the crowning achievement of every Jewish male is to become a true Torah scholar, and if you don't devote your formative years to Torah study, it is almost guaranteed that it will never happen. Studying every day for a few hours is simply not enough to become fluent in the vast amount of Torah literature that is required. Just as no one becomes a doctor by picking up some medical knowledge on the side, you cannot expect to become proficient in Torah without making it the focus of your studies during your school years. In addition, Torah is Hashem's infinite wisdom, and without the proper diligence and devotion, it will be impossible to grasp its profound nuances.

You must also realize that there is a fundamental difference between Torah study and other forms of knowledge. Torah study is not just acquiring information, but acquiring a way of life, which you will never be able to attain from just a study partner or textbook. Being around people who live and breathe Torah will help you absorb the Torah way of thinking, helping you slowly but surely transform, until you will start to think, talk, and act like a Torah-true Jew.

As far as losing the thrill of the cheering spectators, I would like to share a true story of someone who has been there and done that. A former basketball star who became Torah observant once spoke to a group of young newly observant boys. He vividly described for them a game at Madison Square Garden, where he had been the star player and the entire arena was chanting his name, making him feel on top of the world. The young group of boys excitedly relived the thrilling moment with him.

But then he dropped the bomb, and exclaimed, "But all this delight is nothing compared to the thrill and excitement I have when I study a deep topic of Torah and understand it!" This powerful declaration, coming from the former basketball star, made a deep impact on his impressionable audience, teaching them the true meaning of pleasure.

So if you are looking for true gratification and not just a fleeting cheer, you should enroll in yeshivah, where you can taste the sweet waters of Torah, and get the real enjoyment this world has to offer. And perhaps one day your colleagues will cheer you on as you become a true Torah scholar!

In short: Yeshivah is the place where one can stay spiritually safe and become a true Torah scholar. Being around people who live and breathe Torah transforms a person. True thrill in life can be attained only by tasting the sweetness of Torah.

141

Getting Involved in Kiruv

Q ***I have been thinking about getting involved in Jewish outreach. Should I be concerned that it will take away too much of my learning time? And should I be nervous that interacting with people who do not believe in Hashem or keep Torah and mitzvos might have a negative influence on me?***

A Getting involved in helping others come closer to Hashem is very praiseworthy. The Chofetz Chaim, in his books, implores us to go out and teach Torah and Judaism, and do our utmost to bring Hashem's children closer to Him. He praises those who dedicate themselves to teach Torah to the unlearned, calling them extremely beloved in the eyes of Hashem.

As far as taking up too much of your time, Rav Moshe Feinstein ruled that just as a person should give *maaser* (tithe) from his income, he should also give a tenth of his time to help others. In fact, Rav Moshe told his close confidant, Rav Elimelech Bluth, that although he ruled to give ten percent, he himself devoted half of his time to the Jewish community. Rav Bluth then added that Rav Moshe really gave even more than half.

As far as negative influences are concerned, we can refer to the famous words of the Ohr HaChaim in *Parashas Re'eh*. After the Torah commands us to destroy the *ir hanidachas*, city of idol worshipers, the *pasuk* declares (*Devarim* 13:18), "[Hashem] will give you mercy." What is the need for this infusion of mercy? The Ohr HaChaim explains that because a person is affected by his actions, it is natural for those involved in the mass murder of an entire city to become heartless and cruel. In fact, he quotes executioners who told him that they actually lost their natural feelings of compassion and came to actually enjoy killing people. The Torah therefore promises that since they are fulfilling the will of Hashem, instead of turning into cruel people, they will be infused with renewed feelings of compassion.

The same Heavenly assurance applies to any adverse spiritual effect that can potentially result from mitzvah observance. The Chofetz Chaim writes that anyone who dedicates himself to teach Torah to others will be granted increased wisdom in Torah, and will merit children who are Torah scholars. And Rav Aharon Kotler would send students to far-flung communities to inspire other Jews, and is known to have given his word that they and their families would not suffer any spiritual harm. At the same time, it is a good idea to study some extra *mussar*, to counteract any negative influences.

Thus, for those who make the commitment to get involved in outreach, there is a general assurance to protect them. However, this is only true for people who are strong in their religious commitment, not for those who themselves are shaky. If you have doubt, you should consult your mentor.

But this goes even further. Not only will you not be adversely affected, you yourself will grow from the experience! I have heard many people attest that through their involvement in *kiruv* (outreach), their Judaism was actually strengthened. For example, in our camp, The-Zone, many staff members relate how much they grow in their appreciation and understanding of Torah when challenged by their not-yet-religious campers to explain Torah concepts they always took for granted. Additionally, as role models, they must demonstrate the beauty and excitement of being a religious Jew.

And even more than you inspire them, they may inspire you. When someone not yet religious commits to keep Shabbos or kosher, and especially if he becomes a complete *baal teshuvah*, he is literally turning his life upside down. Watching such self-sacrifice will make you stop and think about how much you are willing to sacrifice for Hashem and His Torah, and inspire you to strive for greater heights in your mitzvah observance.

In short: Rav Moshe Feinstein ruled that a person should give a tenth of his time to help others. When performing Hashem's mitzvos, we merit a special

Heavenly blessing and should not be concerned about negative influences. And most people even become stronger in their Judaism.

Index of Personalities

Index of Personalities